BIBLIOGRAPHIC GUIDE TO

# GABRIEL GARCÍA MÁRQUEZ, 1979–1985

**Recent Titles in**
**Bibliographies and Indexes in World Literature**

Psychocriticism: An Annotated Bibliography
*Joseph P. Natoli and Frederik L. Rusch, compilers*

Olaf Stapledon: A Bibliography
*Harvey J. Satty and Curtis C. Smith, compilers*

Spanish Literature, 1500–1700: A Bibliography of Golden Age
Studies in Spanish and English, 1925–1980
*William W. Moseley, Glenroy Emmons, and Marilyn C. Emmons, compilers*

Monthly Terrors: An Index to the Weird Fantasy Magazines
Published in the United States and Great Britain
*Frank H. Parnell, compiler, with the assistance of Mike Ashley*

The Independent Monologue in Latin American Theatre: A Primary
Bibliography with Selective Secondary Sources
*Duane Rhoades, compiler*

J.R.R. Tolkien: Six Decades of Criticism
*Judith A. Johnson*

BIBLIOGRAPHIC GUIDE TO
# GABRIEL GARCÍA MÁRQUEZ, 1979–1985

*COMPILED BY MARGARET EUSTELLA FAU
AND NELLY SFEIR DE GONZALEZ*

BIBLIOGRAPHIES AND INDEXES IN WORLD LITERATURE, NUMBER 7

GREENWOOD PRESS
NEW YORK • WESTPORT, CONNECTICUT • LONDON

**Library of Congress Cataloging-in-Publication Data**

Fau, Margaret Eustella, 1923-
  Bibliographic guide to Gabriel García Márquez,
1979-1985.

  (Bibliographies and indexes in world literature,
ISSN 0742-6801 ; no. 7)
  Bibliography: p.
  Includes index.
  1. García Márquez, Gabriel, 1928-      —Bibliography.
I. Gonzalez, Nelly S.  II. Title.  III. Series.
Z8323.63.F378   1986      016.863      86-371
[PQ8180.17.A73]
ISBN 0-313-25248-3 (lib. bdg. : alk. paper)

Library of Congress Catalog Card Number: 86-371
ISBN: 0-313-25248-3
ISSN: 0742-6801

First published in 1986

Greenwood Press, Inc.
88 Post Road West, Westport, Connecticut 06881

Printed in the United States of America

The paper used in this book complies with the
Permanent Paper Standard issued by the National
Information Standards Organization (Z39.48-1984).

10 9 8 7 6 5 4 3 2 1

*To the suffering people of Latin America,*
*that they may find the way of freedom,*
*the truth of justice, and the life of peace.*

# Contents

viii    Contents

# Preface

With the publication of Cien años de soledad in 1967, and its subsequent translation into English in 1970 by Gregory Rabassa as One Hundred Years of Solitude, the Colombian author, Gabriel García Márquez was skyrocketed into prominence in the literary world.  The resultant avid interest in the man and his works brought before the reading public his other novels, stories, and writings which before the phenomenal success of One Hundred Years of Solitude had been little known or recognized outside of Latin America.

Following upon translations of Cien años de soledad into more than twenty-five languages, together with demands for his other stories and novels, there appeared a flood of critical articles, reviews, theses, and dissertations from all over the world.  Since there was a need for a guide to the sources of all these materials to be collected into one reference book, Greenwood Press, published in 1980, the first book-length annotated bibliography devoted exclusively to the Latin American author, under the title, Gabriel García Márquez:  An Annotated Bibliography, 1947-1979 by Margaret Eustella Fau.

After producing his novel of power and dictatorship, El otoño del patriarca, Autumn of the Patriarch, in 1975, García Márquez maintained that he would never write another novel until certain political problems in Latin America had been resolved.  Some critics, however, attributed his disappearance from the narrative scene as annoyance with adverse criticism of his El otoño del patriarca.  Nevertheless, in 1981, García Márquez announced his return to the literary world with the appearance of what some critics consider his best work to date, Crónica de una muerte anunciada, Chronicle of a Death Foretold.

The following year, came the ultimate reward, the announcement that Gabriel García Márquez had won the Nobel Prize for Literature.  The consequent proliferation of publications by and about García Márquez created the need for an additional bibliography which would supplement and up-date the former and which would include all available items from 1979 through 1985.

Therefore, with the intention of presenting the most comprehensive and current bibliography, we have consulted more than four
hundred journals, newspapers, and books, more than eighty-five percent
of which are available from the excellent research resources of the
Library of the University of Illinois at Urbana-Champaign, together with
additional verification from inter-library loans and a variety of other
sources.  Any omissions can be attributed to a lack of response to
correspondence, or to the loss of materials through various means.

If this book provides scholars, professors, librarians, and
students with a reference tool to aid in further study and research,
then the time and effort expended in its production have been well
worthwhile.

# Acknowledgments

In the process of completing a work of this scope a debt is always incurred. To the members of the faculty, the research committees, and the staff of the Library of the University of Illinois for their many kindnesses and encouragement; to our research assistants and typists for their patience in meeting the demands of producing this manuscript; and to all those who aided in any way in the culmination of this work, the authors extend their sincere gratitude.

# Introduction

The purpose of this book is to present a comprehensive, annotated bibliography of books and articles on the career and works of the Colombian novelist, journalist, and winner of the Nobel Prize for Literature, Gabriel García Márquez.

Included in this text, divided into two sections, i.e. Part One: Primary Sources and Part Two: Secondary Sources are annotated lists of, in Part One, narrative works of Gabriel García Márquez, preferably latest editions; non-fiction articles and books; audio-visual materials, including voice recordings by García Márquez, and movies by and about him; various stories of his found in anthologies; and translations of his works in addition to those listed in the previous bibliography. Part Two consists of bibliographies; books, theses, and doctoral dissertations on García Márquez and his works; critical articles from scholarly journals and periodicals; interviews; biographical articles; a section referred to as Miscellanea, into which we have placed all the materials which do not fit into the categories listed above but are included here because they briefly refer to García Márquez or his literary influence and may be of some use to scholars doing research; and finally we have included reviews of his works.

In order that this book may be of the greatest use to those for whom it was intended, we have made every effort to copy titles as accurately and completely as possible, and have given place of publication, publisher, dates of publication, and pages. In addition we have briefly annotated each citation. These annotations are not meant to be scholarly criticisms, or criticism of the critics, but rather summaries of the contents of each article, book, or review, in order to enable the user to discriminate among the items listed. A task such as this is a challenge, proves to be quite time consuming, and tends to lend itself to repetition, especially in the annotation of book reviews.

Since a short biographical account of García Márquez had been included in the previous volume, we did not think it necessary to repeat it in this one. Besides there are some excellent biographies in English of Gabriel García Márquez already available, such as those written by Raymond L. Williams, George R. McMurray, and Peter G. Earle, among others.

With the exception of several items, unavailable to us before, but which we have since acquired and cited in this volume, all of the materials annotated in this text have been published between 1979 and 1986.

# Chronology

1928   Gabriel García Márquez is born on March 6 in Aracataca, Colombia to Gabriel Eligio García and María Márquez Iguarán.

1928   Lives with Nicolás Márquez Iguarán and Tranquilina Iguarán Cotes, his maternal grandparents.

1936   Studies in Barranquilla.

1946   Completes his "bachillerato" at the National College in Zipaquirá to which he has won a scholarship.

1947   Enters the National University of Colombia at Bogotá.
Publishes "La tercera resignacion" in El Espectador.

1947   Publishes within the next five years, fifteen short stories in El Espectador and several in Crónica and El Heraldo.

1948   Moves to Cartagena, enters the University there and continues his law studies.
Works as journalist at El Universal.

1950   Discontinues law studies, resigns from El Universal to join El Heraldo in Barranquilla to which city he has recently moved.
Publishes several stories in Crónica and El Heraldo.
La casa, first "novel" is rejected by the publisher.

1954   Returns to Bogotá to work for El Espectador as a movie critic and reporter.

1955   Wins the prize for a competition sponsored by the Association of Artists and Writers of Bogotá for his story, "Un día después del sábado."

Writes "Monólogo de Isabel viendo llover en Macondo" and also the account of Velasco's survival at sea after a shipwreck. Travels to Geneva as reporter for El Espectador, and then to Italy and Paris. El Espectador is closed down by the Colombian government.

1956    Lives in Paris, unemployed, and works on manuscripts, La mala hora and El coronel no tiene quien le escriba.

1957    Travels to eastern Europe, lives about two months in London and returns to Caracas at the end of the year as an editor for the newspaper Momento.

1958    Marries Mercedes Barcha.
        Publishes El coronel no tiene quien le escriba.
        Resigns from Momento to work for Venezuela Gráfica.

1959    Works for Prensa Latina in Bogotá, Cuba and New York.

1961    Goes to México after resigning from Prensa Latina to become a movie script writer.
        Writes "El mar del tiempo perdido."
        Wins the Esso Literary Prize for La mala hora.
        Works as editor for two magazines La Familia and Sucesos.

1962    La mala hora, published in Spain is denounced by Márquez.
        Los funerales de la Mamá Grande is published in México.

1963    Leaves La Familia and Sucesos to work for Thompson Publicity Agency and begins writing film scripts.

1964    Writes film scripts Tiempo de Morir and H. O.

1965    Goes into seclusion to begin writing Cien años de soledad.

1966    Publishes second edition of La mala hora.

1967    Cien años de soledad is published by Editorial Sudamericana in Buenos Aires.

1968    In collaboration with Marlo Vargas Llosa publishes La novela en América Latina: diálogo.
        Also publishes the stories: "El ahogado más hermoso del mundo," "Blacamán el bueno vendedor de los milagros," "Un señor muy viejo con unas alas enormes," and "El último viaje del buque fantasma."

1969    Wins the Chianchiano Prize for Cien años de soledad in Italy.
        Cien años de soledad is proclaimed Best Foreign Book in France.

1970    Harper and Row of New York publishes an English translation of Cien años de soledad, which American critics choose as one of the twelve best books of the year.

1971    Mario Vargas Llosa publishes the first book length study of García Márquez's works entitled García Márquez: historia de un deicidio.

1972    Wins the Romulo Gallegos Prize in Venezuela.
        Is awarded the Neustadt International Prize by Books Abroad.
        Publishes La increíble y triste historia de la cándida Eréndira
        y de su abuela desalmada.
        Without Marquez's approval Los ojos de perro azul is published in
        Argentina and Nabo, el negro que hizo esperar a los ángeles is
        published in Uruguay.

1973    Travels to France, Spain and México.
        Publishes Cuando era feliz e indocumentado: un reportaje.
        Arrives in the United States in Oklahoma to receive the Neustadt
        Prize.

1974    Founds Alternativa, a news magazine, in Bogotá.

1975    El otoño del patriarca and Todos los cuentos de Gabriel García
        Márquez are published in Barcelona.
        Returns to Latin America.
        Continues as editor and editorial consultant for Alternativa.
        Takes up residence in Cuernavaca, México and Bogotá.

1977    Publishes Operación Carlota about Cuba's participation in the
        Angolan revolution.

1978    Periodismo militante, a book of García Márquez's opinions and
        political writings is published.

1979    In the process of writing a book about Cuba.

1981    Crónica de una muerte anunciada is published in Spain.

1982    Is awarded the Nobel Prize for Literature.
        Publishes El olor de la guayaba.

1983    Returns to live in Colombia after a self-imposed exile in México.

1985    In the process of writing a novel about love and old age.

BIBLIOGRAPHIC GUIDE TO

# GABRIEL GARCÍA MÁRQUEZ, 1979–1985

# PRIMARY SOURCES

# The Narrative Works of
# Gabriel García Márquez

1.  "El ahogado más hermoso del mundo." México: Caballero, (November, 1970), pp. 112, 114, 138 y 139.

    In Todos los cuentos de Gabriel García Márquez. Barcelona: Plaza and Janes, 1975, pp. 239-245.

2.  "El ahogado más hermoso del mundo." In Selección del cuento colombiano. Calí, Colombia: Taller Gráfico, 1981, pp. 83-98.

3.  "Alguién desordenava estas rosas." Barranquilla: Crónica, (December 2, 1950).

    In Todos los cuentos de Gabriel García Márquez. Barcelona: Plaza and Janes, 1975, pp. 85-89.

4.  "Amargura para tres sonámbulos." Bogotá: El Espectador. Suplemento Dominical, (November 13, 1949), p. 11.

    In Todos los cuentos de Gabriel García Márquez. Barcelona: Plaza and Janes, 1975, pp. 41-44.

5.  "Blacamán el bueno, vendedor de los milagros." México: Revista de la Universidad de México, v. 23, nos. 2 y 3, (October-November, 1968), pp. 16-20.

    In Todos los cuentos de Gabriel García Márquez. Barcelona: Plaza and Janes, 1975, pp. 263-272.

6.  Cien años de soledad. Edición de Jacques Joset. Madrid: Cátedra, 1984, 493 p.

7.  Cien años de soledad. 59th edition. Buenos Aires: Editorial Sudamericana, 1983, 359 p.

8.  _Cien años de soledad_. Barcelona:  Editorial Vosgos, 1977, 101 p.

9.  _Cien años de soledad_. Barcelona:  Círculo de Lectores, 1973, c1967, 357 pp.  Critical essay by Carlos Ayala González-Nieto on pp. 351-357.

10. _Collected Stories_. Gregory Rabassa and J. S. Bernstein, trans. New York:  Harper and Row, 1984, 311 p.

11. _El coronel no tiene quien le escriba_. Bogotá:  _Mito_, año 4, no. 19, (May-June, 1958), pp. 1-38.

    17th edition.  Buenos Aires:  Editorial Sudamericana, 1975, 91 p.

12. _El coronel no tiene quien le escriba_. Edited by Giovanni Pontiero. Manchester, England:  Manchester University Press, 1981, 90 p.

13. _Crónica de una muerte anunciada_. 1st. edition.  Barcelona: Bruguera, 1981, 192 p.

14. _Crónica de una muerte anunciada_. 1st. edition.  Bogotá:  La Oveja Negra, 1981, 156 p.

15. _Crónica de una muerte anunciada_. 1st. edition.  Buenos Aires: Edotiral Sudamericana, 1981, 192 p.

16. _Crónica de una muerte anunciada_. Nicaragua:  Nicaragua Libre, 1981, 156 p.

17. _Cuatro cuentos_. México:  Comunidad Latinoamérica de Escritores, 1974, 124 p.

    Contents:  "Monólogo de Isabel viendo llover en Macondo;" "En este pueblo no hay ladrones;" _Los funerales de la Mamá Grande_; "Un hombre muy viejo con unas alas enormes."

18. "El cuento de los generales que se creyeron su propio cuento." Madrid:  _El País_, (December 9, 1980).

19. "De como Natanael hace una visita." Barranquilla, Colombia: _Crónica_, no. 2, (May 6, 1950), pp. 5-12.

20. "De como Natanael hace una visita." Toulouse:  _Caravelle_, no. 29, (1977), pp. 171-178.

21. "Un día de estos." In _Los funerales de la Mamá Grande_. Xalapa, México:  Universidad Veracruzana, 1962, 151 p.

22. "Un día después del sábado." Bogotá:  _El Espectador_, (August 8, 1954), pp. 17 y 27.

    In _Los funerales de la Mamá Grande_. Xalapa, México:  Universidad Veracruzana, 1962, 151 p.

23. "Un día después del sábado." In _Los monstruos cuentan_, v. 1. Montevideo, Uruguay:  Comentarios Bibliográficos Americanos, 1972, pp. 5-38.

24.  "Diálogo del espejo." Bogotá:  El Espectador, Suplemento Dominical, (January 23, 1949), p. 11.

     In Todos los cuentos de Gabriel García Márquez. Barcelona: Plaza and Janes, 1975, pp. 45-51.

25.  "En este pueblo no hay ladrones." Bogotá:  Mito, año 6, (July-October, 1960), nos. 31-32, pp. 5-26.

     In Los funerales de la Mamá Grande. Xalapa, México: Universidad Veracruzana, 1962, 151 p.

26.  "Eva está dentro de su gato." Bogotá:  El Espectador, sección Fin de semana, año 60, no. 86 (October 25, 1947), p. 8.

     In Todos los cuentos de Gabriel García Márquez. Barcelona: Plaza and Janes, 1975, pp. 29-40.

27.  "La extraña idolatría de la Sierpe." Bogotá:  El Espectador, no. 311, (March 28, 1954), pp. 17 y 30.

28.  "Final de Natanael." Barranquilla, Colombia:  El Heraldo, (October 13, 1950), p. 3.  Under the pseudonym, Septimus en the column, "La Jirafa".

29.  Los funerales de la Mamá Grande. Xalapa, México: Universidad Veracruzana, 1962, 151 p.

30.  "La herencia sobrenatural de la Marquesita." Bogotá:  El Espectador, Suplemento Dominical, no. 310 (March 21, 1954), pp. 17 y 27.

31.  La hojarasca. Bogotá:  Ediciones S. L. B., 1955, 137 p.

     10th edition.  Buenos Aires:  Editorial Sudamericana, 1974, 133 p.

32.  "Un hombre muy viejo con unas alas enormes." La Habana, Cuba: Casa de las Américas, año 8, no. 48, (May-June, 1968), pp. 62-67.

     In Madrid:  Cuadernos Hispanoamericanos, no. 245, (1970), pp. 273-278.

     In Todos los cuentos de Gabriel García Márquez. Barcelona: Plaza and Janes, 1975, pp. 213-220. (Entitled: "Un señor muy viejo con unas alas enormes").

33.  "Un hombre viene bajo la lluvia." Bogotá:  El Espectador, Suplemento Dominical, no. 317, (May 9, 1954), pp. 16 and 31.

34.  La increíble y triste historia de la cándida Eréndira y de su abuela desalmada. Mexico: Ediciones Era, 1983, 43 p.

35.  La increíble y triste historia de la cándida Eréndira y de su abuela desalmada. 4th edition. Buenos Aires: Editorial Sudamericana, 1974, 163 p.

36.  Isabel viendo llover en Macondo. Buenos Aires:  Editorial Estuario,
     1967, 43 p.

37.  La mala hora. Premio Literario ESSO 1961.  Madrid:  Talleres de
     Gráfica, "Luis Pérez," 1962, 224 p.  (This edition has been dis-
     claimed by Gabriel García Márquez).

     Bogotá:  Espiral, no. 37, (1963), pp. 90-91.

     10th edition.  Buenos Aires:  Editorial Sudamericana, 1974, 203 p.

38.  "El mar del tiempo perdido."  México:  Revista Mexicana de Litera-
     tura, nueva época, nos. 5-6, (May-June, 1962), pp. 3-21.

     In Todos los cuentos de Gabriel García Márquez.  Barcelona:  Plaza
     and Janes, 1975, pp. 221-238.

39.  La maravillosa obra de Gabriel García Márquez con cassette de viva
     voz.  Bogotá:  Editorial La Oveja Negra, 1983?  (13 volumes in
     paperback and a cassette in a box).

     Contents:  Cien años de soledad, El coronel no tiene quien le
     escriba, El otoño del patriarca, Crónicas y reportajes, Los
     funerales de la Mamá Grande, De viaje por los países socialistas,
     Cuando era feliz e indocumentado, La mala hora, Relato de un
     náufrago, La hojarasca, Ojos de perro azul, Crónica de una muerte
     anunciada.  (One cassette with fragments taken from his books,
     read by the author.)

40.  "La marquesita de la Sierpe."  Bogotá:  Lámpara, v. 1, no. 5
     (November-December, 1952), pp. 15-18.

     Bogotá:  El Espectador, Suplemento Dominical, no. 308 (March, 1954),
     p. 11.

41.  "El mono."  Cartagena, Colombia:  El Universal, (June 8, 1948),
     p. 4.

42.  "Monológo de Isabel viendo llover en Macondo."  Bogotá:  Mito, año
     1, no. 4 (October-November, 1955), pp. 221-225.

     In Todos los cuentos de Gabriel García Márquez.  Barcelona:  Plaza
     and Janes, 1975, pp. 97-104.

43.  "El muerto alegre."  Bogotá:  El Espectador, no. 312, (April 4,
     1954).

44.  "Muerte constante más alla del amor."  In Todos los cuentos de
     Gabriel García Márquez.  Barcelona:  Plaza and Janes, 1975, pp.
     247-255.

45.  "La mujer que llegaba a las seis."  Barranquilla:  Crónica, no. 8,
     (June 24, 1950).

     Bogotá:  El Espectador, Suplemento Dominical, no. 210 (March 30,
     1952), pp. 16, 23 and 25.

In <u>Ojos de perro azul</u>. Buenos Aires:  Editorial Sudamericana, 1974, pp. 85-101.

46. "Nabo, el negro que hizo esperar a los ángeles." Bogotá: <u>El</u> <u>Espectador</u>, Suplemento Dominical, no. 157 (March 18, 1951), pp. 17-23.

(Entitled: "El negro que hizo esperar a los ángeles"). Buenos Aires: Ediciones Alfil, 1973, 119 p.

47. "La noche de los alcaravanes." Bogotá: <u>Crítica</u>, (1952).

Barranquilla: <u>Crónica</u>, no. 2, (July 29, 1950).

48. "Ojos de perro azul." Bogotá: <u>El Espectador</u>, Suplemento Dominical, (June 16, 1950), p. 16.

5th edition. Buenos Aires: Editorial Sudamericana, 1975, 133 p.

49. <u>El otoño del patriarca</u>. 6th edition. Barcelona: Bruguera, 1984, 243 p.

50. <u>El otoño del patriarca</u>. Barcelona: Plaza and Janes, 1975, 271 p.

<u>El otoño del patriarca</u>. 3rd edition. Buenos Aires: Editorial Sudamericana, 1975, 271 p.

51. "La otra costilla de la muerte." Bogotá: <u>El Espectador</u>, no. 23, (July 25, 1948), pp. 6 and 12.

In <u>Todos los cuentos de Gabriel García Márquez</u>. Barcelona: Plaza and Janes, 1975, pp. 19-27.

52. "La pesadilla." Barranquilla, Colombia: <u>El Heraldo</u>, (June 16, 1950), p. 3. Under the pseudonym, Septimus in the column, "La Jirafa."

53. "La prodigiosa tarde de Baltazar." En <u>Los funerales de la Mamá Grande</u>. Xalapa, México: Universidad Veracruzana, 1962, 151 p.

En <u>Todos los cuentos de Gabriel García Márquez</u>. Barcelona: Plaza and Janes, 1975, pp. 147-154.

54. "El rastro de tu sangre en la nieve." Bogotá, Colombia: <u>El Espectador</u>, no. 26446, (September, 1981).

55. <u>El rastro de tu sangre en la nieve. El verano feliz de la Señora Forbes</u>. Bogotá: William Dampier Editores, 1982, 74 p.

56. "Rosas artificiales." In <u>Los funerales de la Mamá Grande</u>. Xalapa, México: Universidad Veracruzana, 1962.

In <u>Todos los cuentos de Gabriel García Márquez</u>. Barcelona: Plaza and Janes, 1975, pp. 187-192.

57.  "La siesta del martes." In Los funerales de la Mamá Grande.
     Xalapa, México: Universidad Veracruzana, 1962, 151 p.

58.  "Los signos oscuros." México: Revista de la Universidad de México.
     v. 16, (September, 1961), pp. 6-7.

     In Montevideo: Marcha, año 25, no. 1193 (February 7, 1964), p. 29.

59.  "La tercera resignación." Bogotá: El Espectador, Sección Fin de
     semana, año 60, no. 80, (September 13, 1947), p. 8.

     In Ojos de perro azul. Buenos Aires: Editorial Sudamericana,
     1974, pp. 7-20.

60.  Todos los cuentos de Gabriel García Márquez, 1947-1972. Barcelona:
     Plaza and Janes, 1975, 320 p.

     Contains all the stories included in Ojos de perro azul; Los
     funerales de la Mamá Grande; and La increíble y triste historia de
     la cándida Eréndira y de su abuela desalmada.

61.  "Tubal-Caín forja una estrella." Bogotá: El Espectador, sección
     Fin de semana, no. 97, (January 17, 1948), p. 8.

62.  "El último viaje del buque fantasma." Paraguay: Alcor, v. 47
     (primer trimestre, 1969), pp. 34-39.

63.  "El verano feliz de la señora Forbes." Bogotá, Colombia: El
     Espectador, no. 27704, (September, 1981).

64.  "El verano feliz de la señora Forbes." Tegucigalpa, Honduras:
     Alcaraván, no. 16, (October, 1982), pp. 29-33.

65.  "La viuda de Montiel." In Los funerales de la Mamá Grande. Xalapa,
     México: Universidad Veracruzana, 1962, 151 p.

# Nonfiction Articles and Books

1.  "A todos los hombres democráticos y progresistas de América Latina
    y el Caribe." Los Angeles, CA: Literatura Chilena en el Exilio,
    v. 3, no. 2, (April, 1979), pp. 18-20.

    Defense of human rights in Latin American and the Caribbean.

2.  "Actuellement. . ." Paris: Silex, no. 11, (March, 1979), pp. 139-
    141.

    García Márquez explains why he ceased writing at this time and
    discusses the political situation in Latin America.

    This same material was published in Madrid: Cuadernos para el
    Diálogo, no. 272, 2a época, (July 15-21, 1978).

3.  "Algo más sobre literatura y realidad, crónicas de García Márquez."
    Lima: Marka, año 7, no. 212, (July 9, 1981), pp. 42-43.

    In describing reality and literature in Latin America, García
    Márquez offers insights of his thoughts about the wonders of the
    land, its reality, folklore, people, and tradition.

4.  Alternativa. Bogotá, Colombia, 1974-1980.

    A periodical published bi-weekly from 1974- and edited by Gabriel
    García Márquez, O. Fals Borda and J. Villegas Arango.

5.  "The Argentinian Who Made Everyone Love Him: Julio Cortázar, In
    Memoriam." Potsdam, East Germany: Sinn und Form: Beitrage sur
    Literature, v. 36, no. 5, (September-October, 1984), p. 1109.

    In tribute to Julio Cortázar, Gabriel García Márquez recounts from
    memory a train trip from Paris to Prague which he experienced with

Julio Cortázar and Carlos Fuentes when the three authors discussed
Julio Cortázar's La noche de mantequilla and his views on death.

6.   El asalto. Managua:  Editorial Nueva Nicaragua, 1982, 143 p.

This was originally published under the title Viva Sandino in
Nicaragua in 1982.  Written in cinematographic form, the publisher's
note states that it was intended for French cinema, but never was
filmed.

7.   "Autocrítica."  Bogotá, Colombia:  Eco, v. 34, no. 209, (March,
1979), pp. 485-490.

A personal letter to a friend, Gonzalo, in which García Márquez
terms his story, "La mujer que llegaba a las seis" a disaster,
written only to please Alfonso Fuenmayor and not intended for
publication.

8.   "Bexigas de tuburão com molho de menta."  Cláudia Schilling, tr.
Porto Alegre, Brazil:  Oitenta, v. 3, (1980), pp. 1-16.

An exclusive report by Gabriel García Márquez upon his return from
a visit to Vietnam.

9.   "Bogotá:  la calle."  Bogotá, Colombia:  Eco, v. 34, no. 209, (March,
1979), pp. 491-492.

Gabriel García Márquez characterizes street life in Bogotá from a
retrospective point of view.

10.   "Ceremonia inicial."  Bogotá:  Eco, v. 38/3, no. 231, (January, 1981),
pp. 328-331.

In a prologue to a novel by George Lee Biswell Cotes, García Márquez
discusses the vocation of a writer.

11.   "Chronicle of a Film Foretold:  How I Found the Seed for Eréndira in
a Chance Encounter in the Tropics."  Lisa Wyant, tr.  Washington,
D.C.:  American Film, v. 9, no. 10, (September, 1984), pp. 12-13.

García Márquez relates the incident which inspired the novel, La
increíble y triste historia de la cándida Eréndira y de su abuela
desalmada and admits that originally he had written it as a screen-
play since he could not envision it as a novel.

12.   "Crónica de una muerte anunciada est mon meilleur roman."  Madrid:
El País, (January 5, 1981), p. 36.

The author criticizes his latest work and maintains that despite the
critics, he considers it one of his best works.

13.   "Crónica del asalto a la 'Casa de los Chanco'," and "García Márquez
entrevista a los sandinistas."  In Los Sandinistas:  Documentos,
reportajes de Gabriel García Márquez y otros.  Bogotá:  Editorial
La Oveja Negra, 1979, pp. 29-48 and 135-167.

Two chapters in this book were authored by García Márquez. The
first deals with an incident during the rule of Somoza and the
second consists of interviews with members of the sandinista
movement.

14. Crónicas y reportajes. 9th edition. Bogotá: Editorial La Oveja
   Negra, 1982, 398 p.

   A collection of García Márquez's writings which appeared in El
   Espectador of Bogotá, Colombia, between the years, 1954 and 1958.

15. Cuando era feliz e indocumentado. 5th edition. Bogotá: Editorial
   La Oveja Negra, 1982, 141 p.

   This collection of journalistic writings was taken from Momento, a
   Venezuelan newspaper, for which García Márquez was a reporter in
   1958.

16. "Cuba in Angola: Operation Carlotta." In Fidel Castro Speeches:
   Cuba's International Foreign Policy, 1975-1980. Edited by Michael
   Taber. New York: Pathfinder Press, 1981, pp. 339-357.

   García Márquez presents a complete picture of Cuba's intervention
   in Angola and its implications for the Cuban Revolution.

17. "El cuento de los generales que se creyeron su proprio cuento."
   Madrid: El País, (December 9, 1980).

   An editorial comparing the electoral stance of the military regime
   in Uruguay to that of two European generals - Franco and de Gaulle.

18. De Europa y América (1955-1960): Obra Periodística, v. 4.
   Recopilación y prólogo de Jacques Gilard. Barcelona: Bruguera,
   1983, 861 p.

   This volume contains all of García Márquez's articles published in
   newspapers in Colombia, the U.S., and abroad, from 1955 through
   1960, arranged in chronological order. Appendix I contains pieces
   published in the newspaper Momento, January through May 1958, which
   have been signed "Gastón Galdós," but which have been tentatively
   attributed to García Márquez. Appendix II contains articles,
   published in Momento in January of 1958, written by García Márquez
   and Plinio Apuleyo Mendoza. Appendix III contains work attributed
   to García Márquez, but published anonymously.

19. "Desventuras de un escritor de libros." Bogotá: Eco, v. 35, no.
   212, (June, 1979), pp. 113-115.

   The difficulties encountered and differences between American
   authors and those of developing countries or socialist states
   because of their respective political and economic conditions.

20. De viaje por los países socialistas: 90 días en la "Cortina de
   hierro". 5th edition. Bogotá: Editorial La Oveja Negra, 1980,
   208 p.

   Impressions while traveling behind the Iron Curtain.

21.  "Dos o tres cosas sobre 'La novela de la violenia'." Bogotá,
     Colombia: Eco, no. 205, (November, 1978), pp. 103-108.

     A writer's personal experiences become the foundation of his
     writings.

22.  "El drama de las dos Cubas." New York: Círculo de Cultura Cubana,
     Areito, v. 9, no. 36, (1984), pp. 64-66.

     Written while he was a reporter for La Prensa Latina, stationed in
     New York during the years 1959-1961, García Márquez presents the
     position of Cubans living in both New York and Miami in 1961. This
     article signed by García Márquez, New York, 1961 is a reprint of
     that published in Areito, v. 6, no. 21, (1979).

23.  "En Chile como en Chicago." Madrid: Araucaria de Chile, no. 15,
     (1981), pp. 183-184.

     Gabriel García Márquez details the series of murders of various
     political prisoners, and political figures in Chile in an article
     originally printed in the daily newspaper El País.

24.  "El éxodo vietnamita, entre la realidad y la mitificación." Madrid:
     El País, (December 16, 1979), pp. 8-10.

     The condition of minorities and racial persecution in post-war
     Vietnam.

25.  "Fantasía y creación artística en América Latina y el Caribe."
     Xalapa, México: Texto Crítico, v. 5, no. 14, (July-September,
     1979), pp. 3-8.

     García Márquez explains and defines fantasy versus reality in
     literature.

26.  "France's Man of Letters." E. Brunet and L. Wyant, trs. New York:
     Nation, v. 233, no. 6, (September 5, 1981), pp. 184-185.

     Portrays Francois Mitterand, not as a politician describing a
     writer, García Márquez, but as a writer describing a writer.

27.  "La función comienza cuando se llega al cuento." Los Angeles, CA:
     Literatura Chilena en el Exilio, v. 3, no. 3, (July, 1979), pp. 21-
     22.

     A defense of the many exiled Latin American writers.

28.  García Márquez habla de García Márquez, 33 reportajes. Rentería
     Mantilla, Alfonso, ed. Bogotá: Rentería Editores, 1979, 218 p.

     A series of essays, articles and interviews, taken from various
     periodicals, and written during the years 1967-1979. Each of these
     appears in this present bibliography.

29.  "Hemingway--Our Own." Introduction to Hemingway in Cuba by Norberto
     Fuentes. Secaucus, NJ: Lyle Stuart, 1984, pp. 7-16.

García Márquez provides valuable insight into what Cuba meant to
Hemingway as well as what Hemingway meant to Cuba.

30. "Hemingway's Life in the Enticing Swirl of Cuba." Chicago: The
    Chicago Tribune, (August 12, 1984), Section 13, p. 11.

    An abridged version of the introduction to the book, Hemingway in
    Cuba, by Norberto Fuentes.

31. "La importancia de la letra X." Bogotá: Correo de los Andes, v. 1,
    no. 1, (November, 1979), p. 94.

    Written under García Márquez's pseudonym, Septimus, this whimsical
    essay appeared originally in the column "La Jirafa" in the
    periodical El Heraldo, (May 5, 1950).

32. "Kil'ka zapytan' hazety. Habrieliu Harsia Markesu." Kyïv, Ukraine:
    Vsesvit, no. 11, (November, 1981), pp. 54-55.

    García Márquez discusses what he considers his best work, El
    coronel no tiene quien le escriba and the process in writing
    Crónica de una muerte anunciada.

33. "Latin America's Impossible Reality." Elena Brunet, tr.  New York:
    Harper's, v. 270, no. 1616, (January, 1985), pp. 13-15.

    In this essay on reality in his fiction, García Márquez remarks,
    "perhaps the source of my frustration is this: nothing has ever
    occurred to me, nor have I been able to do anything that is more
    awesome than reality itself."

    This essay, under the title, "Fantasy and Artistic Creation in
    Latin America and the Caribbean" appeared in translation by Elena
    Brunet in the August 4, 1984, issue of Sábado, from the Mexican
    newspaper, Unomasuno.

34. "La literatura colombiana, un fraude a la nación." Bogotá: Eco,
    v. 33, no. 203, (September, 1978), pp. 1200-1206.

    Gabriel García Márquez regrets the dearth of what he considers
    quality literature in Colombia and concludes that its authors have
    defrauded the nation.

35. "La littérature explore le réel." J. Sarret, co-author.  Paris:
    Cahiers Confrontation Paris, no. 5, (1981?), America Latina, pp.
    113-122.

    García Márquez speaks about his methods of writing, the relation-
    ship between readers and writers, his symbolism, the differences
    between fantasy and reality, and several other subjects.

36. "Lost Tales." Marcela Loiseau de Rossman, tr.  Pittsburgh, PA:
    Latin American Literary Review, Special Issue Gabriel García
    Márquez, v. 13, no. 25, (January-June, 1985), pp. 158-160.

    A succession of tales related by García Márquez and an appeal to
    readers to help him find the sources.

37.  "Márquez on the Fear of Flying." New York: Harper's, v. 269, no.
     1610, (July, 1984), p. 29.

     Translated by Lisa Wyant, this article taken from El Espectador of
     Bogotá is a column written by García Márquez on his fear of air
     travel.

38.  "'Me doy cuenta de lo que significa que el Rey de España tenga un
     pensamiento democrático.'" Madrid: El País, (January 31, 1979),
     p. 40.

     Gabriel García Márquez relates his impressions during his audience
     with the king and queen of Spain.

39.  "Memoria feliz de Caracas." In Así es Caracas, edited by Soledad
     Mendoza. Caracas: Editorial Ateneo de Caracas, 1980, pp. 4-8.

     García Márquez's nostalgic description of a "happy Caracas."
     Spanish article is followed by an English translation.

40.  "Moj Hemingvej." Gabriela Arc., tr. Belgrade, Yogoslavia: Knji-
     Knjizevnost, v. 72, no. 11, (November, 1981), pp. 2117-2120.

     This version of Gabriel García Márquez's first encounter with
     Ernest Hemingway in 1957, gives brief critical comments on
     Hemingway's major works, and on Hemingway's continued popularity
     in contemporary Cuba.

41.  La novela en América Latina: Diálogo. García Márquez, Gabriel
     and Mario Vargas Llosa. Lima: Carlos Milla Batres, 1969, 58 p.

     This dialogue between two Latin American writers is an exposition
     of the present state of Latin American literature, the past and its
     direction for the future.

42.  "Nueva York, 1961: el drama de las dos Cubas." New York: Areito,
     v. 6, no. 21, (1979), pp. 31-33.

     Gabriel García Márquez investigates the soaring number of Cuban
     refugees into the U.S. in the 1960s.

43.  "Obregón o la vocación desaforada." Asturias, Spain: Los Cuadernos
     del Norte, v. 5, no. 26, (July-August, 1984), p. 78.

     While commenting on the art of Alejandro Obregón, García Márquez
     intimates that some of his paintings inspired the characters in the
     stories about drownings.

44.  "Obregón, o la vocación desaforada." Bogotá: Eco, v. 41/6, no. 252,
     252, (October, 1982), pp. 561-564.

     Some personal observations about the artist Alejandro Obregón and
     his works.

45.    El olor de la guayaba:  Conversaciones con Plinio Apuleyo Mendoza.
       Barcelona:  Bruguera, 1982, 186 p.  Published also by Bogotá:
       Editorial La Oveja Negra, 1982.

       An insight into the character of García Márquez as he expresses his
       thoughts on politics, women, literature, human rights, and life in
       general.

46.    "El origen de mis historias en el cine."  Edited by Humberto Ríos
       and Adolfo García Videla.  México:  Plural, segunda época, v. 12-
       10, no. 142, (July, 1983), pp. 7-10.

       García Márquez speaks about his other vocation, film-making, the
       movie of Eréndira, and the difficulties encountered in script-
       writing.

47.    Periodismo militante.  Bogotá:  Son de Máquina, 1978, 250 p.

       García Márquez's views on politics and government together with
       interviews and journalistic reports.

48.    Persecución y muerte de minorías:  dos perspectivas polémicas.
       Buenos Aires:  Juárez Editor, 1984, 61 p.

       In the first of the articles in this book, which appeared earlier
       in El País, Madrid, December 16, 1979, under the title, "El éxodo
       vietnamita, entre la realidad y la mitificación" García Márquez
       presents a vivid picture of the post-war social conditions and
       racial persecution in Vietnam.  Guillermo Nolasco-Juárez responds
       to García Márquez in the second of two articles in this book.

49.    "La poésie à la portée de tous."  Paris:  Magazine Littéraire, no.
       178, (November, 1981), p. 31.

       Gabriel García Márquez critizes the fact that many professors of
       literature force their interpretations of poetry on their students.
       He claims that the best way to teach literature is to give the
       students the freedom to explore the contents of literature without
       any researched interpretations fed to them by their instructors.

50.    "Préface."  In Le maitre de la Gabriela, roman, by Alvaro Cepeda
       Samudio.  Jacques Gilard, tr.  Paris:  Pierre Belfond, 1984, 138 p.

       In this two-page preface, Gabriel García Márquez comments on the
       content of this Colombian novel about the banana laborers, written
       under the title, La casa grande.

51.    "Prologo."  In La hora cero by Frank Pérez Palacio.  Santo Domingo:
       Colección Nacional, 1980, p. 7.

       In the prologue to this work by Frank Pérez Palacio, García Márquez
       praises this author's innovation, and his skill as a story teller.

52.    "¿Qué pasó al fin en Grenada?"  Buenos Aires, Argentina:  Revista
       Cordobesa de Literatura y Política, año 1, no. 1 (January, 1985),
       pp. 60-66.

García Márquez comments on the invasion of Grenada by the United States.

53.    "Le récit du récit."  Paris:  Magazine Littéraire, no. 178, (November, 1981), pp. 33-35.

Gabriel García Márquez writes of the murder of one of his very close friends, and states that this event, and other politically related tragedies have led him to decide to cease his career as a novelist.

54.    Relato de un náufrago.  La Habana:  Editorial Arte y Literatura, 1981, 213 p.

Contains also, Ojos de perro azul.

55.    Relato de un náufrago que estuvo diez días a la deriva en una balsa sin comer ni beber, que fué proclamado héroe de la patria, besado por las reinas de belleza y hecho rico por la publicidad y luego aborrecido por el gobierno y olvidado para siempre. (Reportaje escrito en 1955).  3rd Edition.  Barcelona:  Tusquets Editor, 1970, 88 p.

56.    "Los Sandinistas se toman el Palacio Nacional de Managua," in La Batalla de Nicaragua.  Mexico, D.F.:  Bruguera Mexicana de Ediciones, 1979, pp. 7-21.

This introductory essay in the book containing others by Ernesto Cardenal, Gregorio Selser, and Daniel Waksman Schinca deals with the politics and government of Nicaragua and the position of the Sandinistas and their cause.

57.    García Márquez, Gabriel.  El secuestro:  Relato cinematográfico. Salamanca, Spain:  Lóguez Ediciones, 1983, 143 p.

A motion picture script based on the attack by the guerrillero Juan José Quezada on the home of José Martía Castillo the 27th of December of 1974, in order to free several Sandinistas from prison.

58.    "La soledad de América Latina."  Caracas, Venezuela:  Nueva Sociedad, no. 64, (January-February, 1983), pp. 126-128.

Acceptance speech on receiving the Nobel Prize for Literature.

59.    "La soledad de América Latina."  Los Angeles, CA:  Literatura Chilena, creación y crítica, v. 7, no. 1, año 7, no. 23, (1983), pp. 2-3.

García Márquez's acceptance speech for the Nobel Prize.

60.    "La soledad de América Latina."  Santiago, Chile:  Araucaria de Chile, no. 21, (1983), pp. 97-100.

García Márquez's speech on accepting the Nobel Prize for Literature.

61.  "La solitude de l'Amerique latine." Annie Morvan, tr.  In Fiction
     et réalité:  la littérature latino-américaine.  Bruxelles,
     Belgique:  Université Libre de Bruxelles, Institut de Sociologie.
     Centre d'Etude de l'Amerique latine, Editions de l'Université,
     1983, pp. 11-16.

     Acceptance speech on receiving the Nobel Prize for Literature.

62.  "The Solitude of Latin America:  A Nobel Prize Winner Reflects on
     His Homeland."  Chicago Tribune, (March 6, 1983), Section 2, p. 4.

     In his speech to the Swedish Academy after receiving the Nobel
     Prize in 1982, Gabriel García Márquez talks about the conflicts
     in Latin America, and how they cause the people of Latin American
     to question their own reality.

63.  "To the People of the United States."  New York:  New York Times,
     (April 17, 1983), p. 25.

     Gabriel García Márquez and six other authors speak out against the
     U.S. invasion of Nicaragua in 1983, and ask the American people
     for their support against the movement.

64.  "The Vietnam Wars."  Gregory Rabassa, tr.  New York:  Rolling Stone,
     no. 318, (May 29, 1980), pp. 43-46.

     A look at Vietnam four years after the American pull-out, describ-
     ing the effect of a past war and the threat of future war on this
     recently united country.

# Audio-visual Materials

1. El asalto: un relato cinematográfico. Managua, Nicaragua: Nueva Edición, 1984, 143 p.

   The second edition of García Márquez's Viva Sandino, retitled El asalto, written in cinematographic form.

2. Beaumont, José F. "Una obra de García Márquez, llevada al cine por Miguel Littin." Madrid: El País, (February 23, 1980), p. 23.

   "La viuda de Montiel," García Márquez's short story, is made into a movie coproduced by México, Colombia, Venezuela, and Cuba.

3. Calle, Angel Luis de la. "García Márquez, guionista de una película sobre el Canal de Panamá." Madrid: El País, (October 14, 1977), p. 31.

   García Márquez will be the consultant for a film on the Panama Canal.

4. Camacho, Eduardo. "El coronel no tiene quien le escriba." Adapted for television by Eduardo Camacho. Bogotá: Teatro Estudio, Universidad de Los Andes, 197-, 33 leaves.

   A theatrical adaptation of El coronel no tiene quien le escriba, prepared for television broadcasting.

5. Castro Caycedo, Germán. "Gabo cuenta la novela de su vida." Bogotá: El Espectador, v. 6, (March 21, 1977), p. 5-A; (March 22, 1977), p. 5-A.

   This is part six of a continuing series of interviews with García Márquez published in El Espectador. The occasion was the production of La mala hora for television viewing.

6. Cien años de soledad (fragmento). Sound recording read by author,
1 disc, 33-1/3 rpm, mono, 12 in. México: Universidad Nacional
Autónoma de México, 1967.

García Márquez reads excerpts from his novel.

7. Corliss, Richard. "Eréndira." New York, NY: Time, v. 123, no. 4,
(July 23, 1984), p. 102.

A review of the Mexican movie Eréndira, a García Márquez story about
a young girl forced into prostitution by her grandmother.
Mr. Corliss compares Eréndira to a third world developing country
exploited by the conquistador and neo-colonialism.

8. Gabriel García Márquez: The Solitude of Latin America. Washington,
DC: National Public Radio, 1984, 60 min., sound cassette.

García Márquez reads excerpts from and discusses his works in this
recording of a National Public Radio Program.

9. "Una historia de García Márquez gana el certamen de Cartagena de
Indias." Madrid: El País, (June 12, 1981), p. 38.

At the 21st Festival Internacional de Cine at Cartagena de Indias,
Colombia, the Mexican movie María de mi corazón was awarded the
"Gran Premio India Catalina." This film was based on a story
recounted recently by García Márquez in the "Opinion" section of
the newspaper El País.

10. López de Martínez, Adelaida. "Gabriel García Márquez en la panta-
lla." Starksville, MS: Hispania, v. 67, no. 2, (May, 1984), pp.
285-286.

Reviews a film interpretation of the García Márquez story La viuda
de Montiel, commending the film as accurately reflecting the author
and his story.

11. La magia de lo real. Princeton, NJ: Films for the Humanities,
1984, p. 6

A 60 minute color videotape, available in both Spanish and English,
which portrays the world of One Hundred Years of Solitude and
which features García Márquez and the characters of his books.

12. Márceles Daconte, Eduardo. "El teatro mágico del Acto Latino."
Lawrence, KS: Latin American Theatre Review, v. 14, no. 1, (Fall,
1980), pp. 91-96.

A review of the production of García Márquez's short story, "Blacamán el bueno, vendedor de milagros," adapted for the theater by
the Acto Latino theater group.

13. McMurray, George R. "Un cuento de García Márquez filmado."
Boston, MA: Hispania, v. 65, no. 3, (September, 1982), p. 445.

The short story "La viuda de Montiel" is filmed in México with fi-
nancial aid from the Universidad Veracruzana and educational centers
of Colombia.

14. "El otoño del patriarca." In Archives of Hispanic Literature on
    Tape: Sound Recording: Colombia. Washington, DC: Library of
    Congress Motion Picture, Broadcasting, and Recorded Sound Division,
    Magnetic Recording Laboratory, 1977-, sound cassette: 1 7/8 ips,
    2 track, mono.

    Famous authors reading their own works. García Márquez reads the
    last chapter of El otoño del patriarca.

15. "El otoño del patriarca." In Narraciones: narración del autor.
    La Habana: Casa de las Américas, 1978, LD-CA-1-17, 12 in, 33 rpm.
    García Márquez reads fragments of his novel El otoño del patriarca.

16. Poesía trunca. La Habana: Casa de las Américas, 1978, LD-CA-1-20,
    12in, 33 rpm.

    This album of two records contains voice recordings of twelve Latin
    American writers, including García Márquez and readings of, or
    comments about, the works of sixteen other Latin Americans.

17. Rivera, Julius. "Cien años de soledad" by Gabriel García Márquez:
    A Personal Interpretation. El Paso, TX:  El Paso Public Library
    Book Club, 1979, 1 sound cassette, mono.

    A talk presented by the El Paso Public Library Book Club and
    recorded by its members.

18. Ruffinelli, Jorge. "La viuda de Montiel:"  guión cinematográfico
    sobre el cuento de Gabriel García Márquez. Textos de Jorge
    Ruffinelli, fotos de Julio Jaimes. Xalapa, Veracruz, México:
    Universidad Veracruzana, 1979, 68 p.

    A history with photographs of the filming of a movie based on the
    story "La viuda de Montiel" by García Márquez.

19. El secuestro:  guión cinematográfico. Bogotá:  Editorial La Oveja
    Negra, 1982, 124 p.

    A screenplay about José María Castillo Quant, a prominent Nicara-
    guan taken hostage by the Frente Sandinista de Liberación Nacional,
    who demand from Somoza the release of several political prisoners.

20. El secuestro:  relato cinematográfico. Salamanca, Spain:  Lóguez
    Ediciones, 1983, 143 p.

    The motion picture script of a movie based on the attack by the
    guerrillero, Juan José Quesada on the home of José María Castillo
    Quant in order to take him hostage for the release of political
    prisoners.

21. Segal, Aaron. "Si abuela ... García Márquez's Erotic Fairy Tale:
    Film Review." Miami, FL:  Caribbean Review, v. 13, no. 4, (Fall,
    1984), pp. 34-35.

    Review of the movie Eréndira based on a García Márquez novel.

22.  Twentieth-Century European Authors:  Spanish.  No. 3.  Márquez.
     A production of BBC.  Producer:  Christopher Stone.

     Tape no. TLN10208K001; Programme no. HFA208K001; Recording,
     Thursday, March 11, 1982, 1745-2045; Studio PP2; Broadcast
     April 18, 1982-1600-1630.  Presenter William Rowe.  Reader
     Michael Bryant.  Duration 27'23".  Production secretary, Salli
     Hornsby, 319 The Langham, PABX 5180/7684.

     This is the transcript of a taped discussion between William Rowe
     and Michael Bryant in which they read excerpts from and discuss
     García Márquez's One Hundred Years of Solitude.

23.  "La violencia, tema de la última novela de Gabriel García Márquez."
     Madrid:  El País, (September 23, 1980), p. 31.

     La increíble y triste historia de la cándida Eréndira y de su abue-
     la desalmada is made into a movie, entitled Eréndira, and co-
     produced by Spain and Venezuela.  This newspaper article also
     announces a forthcoming novel of García Márquez.

# Stories in Anthologies

1. "El ahogado más hermoso del mundo." In <u>Selección del cuento colombiano</u>. Cali, Colombia: Taller Gráfico, 1981, pp. 83-98.

2. "The Handsomest Drowned Man in the World; A Tale for Children." Gregory Rabassa, tr. In <u>The Eye of the Heart, Short Stories From Latin America</u>. Barbara Howes, ed. New York: The Bobbs-Merrill Company, 1973, pp. 351-256.

3. "Un día de estos." In <u>Antología de narrativa hispanoamericana</u>. Guatemala: Universidad de San Carlos, 1984, v. 1, pp. 11-14.

4. "Un día después del sábado." In <u>Los monstruos cuentan</u>, v. 1. Montevideo: Comentarios Bibliográficos Americanos, 1972, pp. 5-38.

5. "Un día después del sábado." In <u>Tres cuentos colombianos</u>. Bogotá: Editorial Minerva, 1954, pp. 7-11.

6. "One Day After Saturday." J. S. Bernstein, tr. In <u>The Borzoi Anthology of Latin American Literature</u>, v. 2. <u>The Twentieth Century -From Borges and Paz to Guimarães Rosa and Donoso</u>. Emir Rodríguez Monegal, ed. New York: Alfred A. Knopf, 1977. pp. 886-901.

7. <u>Los funerales de la Mamá Grande</u>. In <u>De lo real maravilloso</u>. Selections, prologue, and notes by Mercedes Santos Moray. La Habana: Editorial Gente Nueva, 1984, pp. 127-148.

8. <u>Los funerales de la Mamá Grande</u>. 18th ed. Buenos Aires: Editorial Sudamericana, 1976, 147 p.

    Contents: "La siesta del martes," "Un día de estos," "En este pueblo no hay ladrones," "La prodigiosa tarde de Baltazar," "La viuda de Montiel," "Un día después del sábado," "Rosas artificiales," and <u>Los funerales de la Mamá Grande</u>.

9. Los funerales de la Mamá Grande. In El cuento en hispanoamérica. Prologue, anthology, and bibliography by Mario Castro Arenas. Lima: Librería Studium Editores, 1974, pp. 110-131.

10. La hojarasca. In Dos novelas de Macondo. La Habana: Casa de las Américas, 1980, 303 p.

11. "Un hombre muy viejo con unas alas muy enormes." In Seis cuentos latinoamericanos. Montevideo: Editorial Sandino, 1969, pp. 5-10.

12. "Isabel viendo llover en Macondo." In "Los cuentos de Gabriel García Márquez o el trópico desembrujado." Bogotá: Eco, v. 7, no. 40, (1963), pp. 275-293.

13. La mala hora. In Dos novelas de Macondo. La Habana: Casa de las Américas, 1980, 303 p.

14. "Monólogo de Isabel viendo llover en Macondo." In Los cuentos de Gabriel García Márquez o El Trópico desembrujado. Buenos Aires: Editorial Estuario, 1967, 43 p.

15. "Monologue of Isabel Watching It Rain in Macondo." Gregory Rabassa, tr. In Latin-American Literature Today. Anne Fremantle, ed. New York, NY: New American Library, 1977, pp. 146-152.

16. "Ojos de perro azul." In Relato de un náufrago. La Habana: Editorial Arte y Literatura, 1981, pp. 110-213.

17. El otoño del patriarca. In Veinte jenerales en gefe y un sarjento desexperado. Mauro Bello, tr. Caracas: Ediciones La Draga y El Dragón, 1976, 74 p.

18. "Balthazar's Marvelous Afternoon." J. S. Bernstein, tr. In Contemporary Latin American Short Stories. Pat McNees Mancini, ed. Greenwich, CT: Fawcett Publications, 1974, pp. 281-290.

19. "La siesta del martes." In El cuento colombiano: antología, estudio histórico y analítico, v. 2. Eduardo Pachón Padilla. Comp. Bogotá: Plaza and Janes, 1980, pp. 15-22.

20. "La siesta del martes." In Los funerales de la Mamá Grande. Xalapa, Veracruz, México: Universidad Veracruzana, 1962, pp. 13-21.

21. "Tuesday Siesta." J.S. Bernstein, tr. In From Spain and the Americas: Literature in Translations. James E. Miller, Jr. et al, eds. Glenview, IL: Scott, Foresman and Company, 1970.

22. "El verano feliz de la señora Forbes." In El rastro de tu sangre en la nieve: Los últimos cuentos. Bogotá: William Dampier Editores, 1982, pp. 47-73.

# Translations

1. "El ahogado más hermoso del mundo."  (The Handsomest Drowned Man in the World).

   English:

   "The Handsomest Drowned Man in the World; A Tale for Children."
   Gregory Rabassa, tr.  In The Eye of the Heart, Short Stories From
   Latin America.  Barbara Howes, ed.  New York:  The Bobbs-Merrill
   Company, 1973, pp. 351-356.

2. Cien años de soledad.  (One Hundred Years of Solitude).

   Albanian:

   Njëqind vjet vetmi.  Ramiz Kelmendi, tr.  Prishtië:  Rilindja,
   1978, 438 p.

   Bulgarian:

   Sto godini samota.  Rumen Stojanov, tr.  Sofija:  OF, 1978 (2. ed.),
   527 p.

   Dutch:

   Honderd jaar eenzaamheid.  C. A. G. van den Broek.  Amsterdam:
   Meulenhoff, 1978 (9. ed.), 427 p.

   English:

   One Hundred Years of Solitude.  Middletown, PA:  Quality Paperback
   Books, 1984, 422 p.

   One Hundred Years of Solitude.  Gregory Rabassa, tr.  New York:
   The Limited Editions Club, 1982, 348 p.

One Hundred Years of Solitude.    Gregory Rabassa, tr.    London:    Pan
Books, 1978, 336 p.

One Hundred Years of Solitude.    Gregory Rabassa, tr.    New York:
Avon Books, 1972, 383 p.

Finnish:

Sadan vuoden yksinäisyys.    Matti Rossi, tr.    Porvoo:    Werner
Söderström, 1976, (4. ed.), 413 p.

German:

Hundert Jahre Einsamkeit.    Curt Meyer-Clason, tr.    Frankfurt am
Main:    Büchergilde Gutenberg, 1977, 476 p.

Hundert Jahre Einsamkeit.    Curt Meyer-Clason, tr.    Zürich:    Ex
Libris, 1976, 477 p.

Hundert Jahre Einsamkeit.    Curt Meyer-Clason, tr.    Reinbek bei
Hamburg:    Rowohlt, 1976, (6. ed.), 314 p.

Hundert Jahre Einsamkeit.    Curt Meyer-Clason, tr.    Köln:
Kiepenheuer and Witsch, 1971, 476 p.

Hungarian:

Száv êv magány.    Vera Székács, tr.    Budapest:    Magvető, 1975, (2.
ed.), 428 p.

Korean:

Baegnyeoneui godog.    Kim Byeong Ho, tr.    Seoul:    Yugmunsa, 1976,
2 v.

Norwegian :

Hundre års ensomhet.    Kjell Risvik, tr.    Oslo:    Gyldendal, 1978,
327 p.

Polish:

Sto lat samotności.    Grażyna Grudzinská and Kalina Wojciechowska,
tr.    Warsaw:    Państowowy Instytut Wydawniczy, 1975, 401 p.

Portuguese:

Cem anos de solidâo .    Eliane Zagury, tr.    Rio de Janeiro:    Record,
1984, (30a. ed.), 364 p.

Cem anos de solidâo:    romance.    Eliane Zagury, tr.    3. ed.
Portugal:    Mem Martins, Europa-América, 1979, 380 p.

Cem anos de solidâo.    Eliane Zagury, tr.    Rio de Janeiro:    Record,
1977-78 (19.20. ed.), 364 p.

Cem anos de solidão.  Eliane Zagury, tr.  Rio de Janeiro:  J.
Olympio, 1976, (17. ed.), 364 p.

Serbian:

Sto godina samoće:  roman.  Jasna Mimica Popovič, tr.  Belgrad:
Beogradski izdavačko-grafički zabod; Zagreb:  August Cesarec;
Ljubljana:  Mladinska knjiga, 1984. 341 p.

Sto godina samoće:  roman.  Jasna Mimica Popovič, tr.  Belgrad:
Beogradski izdavackografički zavod, 1978, 429 p.

Slovenian:

Sto let samote .  Alenka Bole-Vrabec, tr.  Ljubljana:  Mladinska
knjiga; Delo, 1978, 359 p.

Swedish:

Hundra år av ensamhet.  Karin Alin, tr.  Stockholm:  Wahlström and
Widstrand, 1982, 359 p.

3.    El coronel no tiene quien le escriba.  (No One Writes to the
       Colonel).

Croatian:

Pukovniku nema tko da piše.  Milivoj Telećan, tr.  Zagreb:  Znanje;
Ljubljana:  Delo, 1979, 1978, 108 p.

French:

Pas de lettre pour le colonel.  Paris:  Bernard Grasset, 1980,
125 p.

German:

Der Oberst hat niemand, der ihm schreibt.  Curt Meyer-Clason, tr.
Köln:  Kiepenheuer und Witsch, 1976, 126 p.

Hebrew:

En la-qolonel mi sheyyikhtov elaw.  Yosef Dayan, tr.  Tel-Aviv:
Sifriat Poalim, 1974, 203 p.

Hungarian:

Baljós óra.  Sópredék.  Az ezredes urnak nince, aki irjon.  Vilmos
Bencsik, László Scholz and György Margitai, tr.  Budapest:  Európa,
1975, 305 p.

Portuguese:

Ninguém escreve ao coronel.  New ed.  Protugal:  Mem Martins,
1981?, 95 p.

Ninguém escreve ao coronel. Danúbio Rodrigues, tr.    Rio de Janeiro:
J. Olympio, 1976 (4. ed.), 95 p.

Slovenian:

Polkovnik nima nikogar, ki bi mu pisal. Nina Kovic, tr.    Ljubljana:
Cankarjeva založba; Jože Moškrič, 1979, 122 p.

Swedish:

Oversten far inga brev.    Karin Alin, tr.    Stockholm:  Wahlström and
Widstrand, 1982, 91 p.

4.  Crónica de una muerte anunciada.    (Chronicle of a Death Foretold).

English:

Chronicle of a Death Foretold.    Gregory Rabassa, tr.    New York:
Ballantine Books, 1982, 1984, 143 p.

Chronicle of a Death Foretold.    Gregory Rabassa, tr.    Fernando
Gotero, il.    New York:  Vanity Fair. v. 46, no. 1, (March, 1983),
pp. 122-124.

Chronicle of a Death Foretold.    Gregory Rabassa, tr.    New York:  A.
Knopf, distributed by Random House, 1983, 120 p.

Chronicle of a Death Foretold.    Gregory Rabassa, tr.    London:
Picador, Pan Books, 1982, 1983, 122 p.

Chronicle of a Death Foretold.    Gregory Rabassa, tr.    London:  J.
Cape, 1982, 122 p.

Chronicle of a Death Foretold.    Gregory Rabassa, tr.    1.ed.    New
York:  Harper and Row, 1980,

French:

Chronique d'une mort annoncée.    Claude Couffon, tr.    Paris:  Bernard
Grasset, 1981, 200 p.

German:

Chronik eines angekündigten Todes.    Curt Meyer-Clason, tr.    Kholn:
Verlag Kiepenheuer and Witsch, 1981, 160 p.

Italian:

Cronaca di una morte annunciata.    Dario Puccini, tr.    Milano, Italy:
Mondadori Editore, 1983, 126 p.

Norwegian:

Beretningen om et varslet mord.    Kiell Risvik, tr.    Oslo, Norway:
Gyldendal Norsk, 1983, 1981, 115 p.

Portuguese:

Crónica de uma morte anunciada.  Fernando Assis Pacheco, tr.
Lisboa, Portugal:  O Jornal, 1983, 1981, 155 p.

Quechua:

Mushuc quellca huañuyta yachashpa huillarca.  Bogota:  Editorial
Oveja Negra, 1981, 133 p.

Slovenian:

Kronika napovedane amrti.  Nina Kovič, tr.  Murska Sobota:  Pomurska
založba; Ljubljana:  Jože Moškrič, 1982, 117 p.

Swedish:

Krönika om ett förebådat dödsfall.  Peter Landelius, tr.  Stockholm:
Wahlström and Widstrand, 1983, 143 p.

Ukranian:

"Khronika vbyvstva, pro aike vsi znaly zazdalehid."  Viktor Shovkun,
tr.  Ukrania:  Vsesvit , no. 11, (November, 1981),pp. 4-54.
(Portrait and short biographical sketch precedes translation).

5.    Cuando era feliz e indocumentado.

Dutch:

Toen ik nog gelukkig was en ongedocumenteerd.  Aline Glastra van
Loon, tr.  Amsterdam:  Meulenhoff, 1978, 139 p.

Italian:

Un giornalista felice e sconosciuto .  Enrico Cicogna, tr.  Milan:
Feltrinelli, 1974, 195 p.

6.    "Un día después del sábado."  (One Day After Saturday).

English:

"One Day After Saturday."  J. S. Bernstein, tr.  In The Borzoi
Anthology of Latin American Literature, The Twentieth Century -
from Borges and Paz to Guimarães Rosa and Donoso.  Emir Rodríguez
Monegal, ed.  New York:  Alfred A. Knopf, 1977, v. 2, pp. 886-901.

German :

Ein Tag nach dem Samstag.  Curt Meyer-Clason, tr.  Stuttgart:
Reclam, 1977, 75 p.

7.    Los funerales de la Mamá Grande.  (Big Mama's Funeral).

Dutch:

De uitvaart van Mamá Grande:    verhalen.    Amsterdam:    Meulenhoff
Editie, c1976, 150 p.

French:

Les funérailles de la Grande Mémé:    contes.    Paris:    B. Grasset,
1977, 156 p.

German:

Das Leichenbegängnis der Grossen Mama und andere Erzählungen.    Curt
Meyer-Clason, tr.    München:    Deutscher Taschenbuch-Verlag, 1979,
221 p.

Das Leichenbegängnis der Grossen Mama und andere Erzählungen.    Curt
Meyer-Clason, tr.    München:    Deutscher Taschenbuch-Verlag, 1977,
221 p.

Das Leichenbegängnis der Grossen Mama und andere Erzählungen.    Curt
Meyer-Clason, tr.    Köln:    Kiepenheuer and Witsch, c1974, 312 p.

Portuguese:

Os funerais da mamãe grande.    Edson Braga, tr.    Rio de Janeiro:
Sabía, 1970, 171 p.

Serbian:

Sahrana Velike Mame:    osam priča.    Jasna Mimica Popović, tr.    Gornji
Milanovac:    Dečje novine; Kragujevac:    Nikola Nikolić, 1979, 122 p.

8.    La hojarasca.    (Leaf Storm).

Hungarian:

Baljós óra.    Sópredék.    Az ezredes urnak nincs, aki írjon.    Vilmos
Bencsik, László Scholz and György Margitai, tr.    Budapest:    Európa,
1975, 304 p.

Italian:

Foglie morte.    Romanzo.    Angelo Morino, tr.    Milano:    Feltrinelli,
1977, 169 p.

Serbian:

Oharaska:    novela.    Jasna Mimica Popović, tr.    Gornji Milanovac:
Dečje novine; Kragujevac:    Nikola Nikolić, 1978, 107 p.

Slovenian:

Odvrzeni:    roman.    Nina Kovič, tr.    Murska Sobota:    Pomurska
založba; Ljubljana:    Jože Moškrič, 1982, 125 p.

Swedish :

Virvlande löv. Peter Landelius, tr.  Stockholm:  Wahlström and
Widstrand, 1983, 173 p.

9.  "Un hombre viene bajo la lluvia."

French:

"Un homme arrive sous la pluie." Jacques Gilard, tr.  Paris:  Silex,
no. 11, (March, 1979), pp. 26-29.  (Originally published in Bogota:
El Espectador, (May 9, 1954), pp. 16 and 31).

10.  La increíble y triste historia de la cándida Eréndira y de su abuela
desalmada.  (The Incredible and Sad Tale of the Innocent Eréndira
and Her Heartless Grandmother).

Dutch:

De ongelooflijke maar droevige geschiedenis van de onschuldige
Eréndira en haar harteloze grootmoeder:  en andere verhalen.  Barber
van de Pol, tr.  2. ed.  Amsterdam:  Meulenhoff Editie, c1975.
138 p.

English:

Innocent Eréndira and Other Stories.  Gregory Rabassa, tr.  London:
Jonathan Cape, 1979, 183 p.

Innocent Eréndira and Other Stories.  Gregory Rabassa, tr.  New
York:  Harper and Row, 1978, 183 p.

Contains:  "The Incredible and Sad Tale of Innocent Eréndira and Her
Heartless Grandmother," "The Sea of Lost Time," "Death Constant
Beyond Love," "The Third Resignation," "The Other Side of Death,"
"Eva is Inside Her Cat," "Dialogue with the Mirror," "Bitterness for
Three Sleepwalkers," "Eyes of the Blue Dog," "The Woman Who Came at
Six O'Clock," "Someone Has Been Disarranging These Roses," "The
Night of the Curlews."

French:

L'incroyable et triste histoire de la candide Eréndira et de sa
grandmère diabolique.  Claude Couffon, tr.  Paris:  B. Grasset,
1977, 164 p.

Romanian:

Fantastica şi trista poveste a Candidei Eréndira si a nesăbuitei
sale bunici.  Miruna and Darie Novaceanu, tr.  Bucuresti:  Univers,
1978, 208 p.

Fantastica şi trista poveste a Candidei Eréndira si a nesăbuitei sale
bunici.  Bucuresti:  Univers, 1980, 123 p.

Serbian:

Neverpvatna i tuzna istorija nevine Erendire i njene bezdusne babe: sedam prica. Jasna Mimica Popović, tr. Gornji Milanovac: Decje novine, 1978, 132 p.

11. La mala hora. (In Evil Hour).

English:

In Evil Hour. New York: Avon Bard, 1979, 183 p.

In Evil Hour. Gregory Rabassa, tr. 1.ed. New York: Harper and Row, 1979, 183 p.

In Evil Hour. Gregory Rabassa, tr. (Reprinted by Avon, 1980). New York: Harper and Row, 1979, 183 p.

German:

Die böse Stunde: Roman. Curt Meyer-Clason, tr. Köln: Kiepenheuer and Witsch, 1979, 229 p.

Hungarian:

Baljós óra. Sópredék. Az ezredes urnak nincs, aki irjon. Vilmos Bencsik, László Scholz and György Margitai, tr. Budapest: Európa, 1975, 305 p.

Slovenian:

Huda ura: roman. Nina Kovič, tr. Murska Sobota: Pomurska založba; Ljubljana: Jože Moškrič, 1982, 195 p.

Swedish:

Den onda timmen. Sonia Johansson, tr. Stockholm: Wahlström and Widstrand, 1982, 156 p.

12. Monólogo de Isabel viendo llover en Macondo. (Monologue of Isabel Watching It Rain in Macondo).

English:

"Monologue of Isabel Watching It Rain in Macondo." Gregory Rabassa, tr. In Latin-American Literature Today. Anne Fremantle, ed. New York: New American Library, 1977, pp. 146-152.

French:

"Monologue d'Isabelle regardant tomber la pluie à Macondo." Claude Couffon, tr. Paris: Silex, no. 11, (March, 1979), pp. 31-36. (Originally published in Bogota: Mito, año 1, no. 4, (October-November, 1955), pp. 221-225).

13.  "La noche de los alcaravanes."  (Night of the Curlews).

Hungarian:

A bölömbikak éjszakája:  elbeszélések.  Vilmos Benczik, tr.
Budapest:  Kozmosz Kiadó, 1977, 342 p.

14.  Ojos de perro azul.  (Eyes of the Blue Dog).

Dutch:

Ogen van een blauwe hond.  Mieke Westra, tr.  Amsterdam: Meulenhoff,
1978, 117 p.

German:

Die Nacht der Rohrdommen:  erste Erzählungen.  Curt Meyer-Clason,
tr.  Köln:  Kiepenheuer and Witsch, 1980, 166 p.

Polish:

Dialog lustra.  Zofia Chadzynska, tr.  Kraków:  Wydaw.  Liter.,
1976, 87 p.

Serbian:

Oči plavog psa.  Krinka Vidaković Petrov, tr.  Belgrade:  Rad, 1980,
116 p.

Oči plavog psa.  Krinka Vidaković Petrov, tr.  Belgrade:  Rad, 1979,
66 p.

Slovenian:

Kratka proza.  Nina Ković, tr.  Ljubljani:  Cankarjeva založba;
Delo, 1983, 299 p.

15.  El olor de la guayaba.  (The Fragrance of the Guava).

English:

The Fragrance of the Guava:  Plinio Apuleyo Mendoza in conversation
with Gabriel García Márquez.  London:  Verso, 1983.

The Smell of Guava.  Ann Wright, tr.  New York:  Perigee Books,
1984, 1982.

French:

Une odeur de goyave.  J. Gilard and P. Mendoza, tr.  Paris:
Belfond, 1982, 194 p.

16.  El otoño del patriarca.  (The Autumn of the Patriarch).

Dutch:

De herfist van de patriarch:  Roman.  Mariolein Sabarte Belacortu,
tr.  2. ed.  Amsterdam:  Meulenhoff, 1977, c1976, 248 p.

English:

The Autumn of the Patriarch.  Gregory Rabassa, tr.  London:  Pan
Books, 1978, 206 p.

The Autumn of the Patriarch.  Gregory Rabassa, tr.  New York:
Harper and Row, 1976, 251 p.

French:

L'automne du patriarche.  Claude Couffon, tr.  Paris:  B. Grasset,
1977, 317 p.

German:

Der Herbst des Patriarchen:  Roman.  Curt Meyer-Clason, tr.
München:  Deutscher Taschenbuch-Verlag, 1980, 266 p.

Der Herbst des Patriarchen:  Roman.  Curt Meyer-Clason, tr.  Berlin,
Weimar:  Aufbau-Verlag, 1979, 276 p.

Der Herbst des Patriarchen.  Curt Meyer-Clason, tr.  Köln:
Kiepenheuer and Witsch, 1978, 335 p.

Der Herbst des Patriarchen:  Roman.  Curt Meyer-Clason, tr.  Köln:
Kiepenheuer and Witsch, 1978, 335 p.

Hungarian:

A pátriárka alkonya.  István Dely, tr.  Budapest:  Magvető Kiadó,
1978, 275 p.

Portuguese:

O outono do patriarca.  Remy Gorga Filho, tr.  Rio de Janeiro:
Record, 1979, (4.ed.), 260 p.

O outono do patriarca.  Remy Gorga Filho, tr.  Rio de Janeiro:
J. Olympio, 1976, (2d.ed.), 260 p.

Russian:

Osen' patriarha.  V. Taras and K. Serman, tr.  Moskva:  Hudož,
1978, 270 p.

Serbian:

Jesen patrijarha:  Roman.  Milan Komnenič, tr.  Belgrad:  Prosveta;
Slobodan Jovič, 1982, 285 p.

Slovenian:

Patriarhova jesen. Alenka Bole Vrabčeva, tr. Ljubljana:
Cankarjeva Založba; Ljudska pravica, 1980, 274 p.

Swedish:

Patriarkens höst. Kjell A. Johansson, tr. Stockholm: Wahlström
and Widstrand, 1982, 215 p.

Patriarkens höst. Kjell A. Johansson, tr. Stockholm: Wahlström
and Widstrand, 1978, (New ed.), 215 p.

17. "La pesadilla." (The Nightmare).

French:

"Le Cauchemar." Jacques Gilard, tr. Paris: Silex, no. 11, (March,
1979), pp. 22-23. (Originally published in the column 'La Jirafa,'
under Gabriel García Márquez's pseudonym Septimus, Barranquilla,
Colombia: El Heraldo, (June 16, 1950), p. 3).

18. "La prodigiosa tarde de Baltazar." (Balthazar's Marvelous Afternoon).

English:

"Balthazar's Marvelous Afternoon." J. S. Bernstein, tr. In Doors
and Mirrors, selected and edited by Hortense Carpentier and Janet
Brof. New York: Grossman Publishers, 1972, pp. 258-265.

"Balthazar's Marvelous Afternoon." J. S. Bernstein, tr. In
Contemporary Latin American Short Stories, Pat McNees Mancini, ed.
Greenwich, CT: 1974, pp. 281-290.

Russian:

Nezabyvaemyj den'v zizni Bal'tasara. Rostislav Rybkin, tr. Moskva:
1978, 47 p.

19. "El rastro de tu sangre en la nieve." (The Trace of Her Blood in
the Snow).

French:

"Le Trace de ton sang dans la neige." Anne Morvan, tr. Paris: Le
Nouvel Observateur, (Saturday, December 26, 1981), pp. 12-18.

20. Relato de un náufrago. (The Story of the Shipwrecked Sailor).

Bulgarian:

Ispanski morski noveli. (Stories of the Sea; anthology). Includes
Relato de un náufrago by Gabriel García Márquez; Venko Kûnev, tr.;
and A ostra e vento by Mocir Costa Lopes; Todor Cenkov, tr. Varna:
G. Bakalov, 1976, 184 p.

French:

<u>Récit d'un naufragé</u>. Claude Couffon, tr.  Paris:  Bernard Grasset,
1979, 159 p.

Slovenian:

<u>Pripoved brodolomca</u>. Nadja Furlan, tr.  Ljubljani:  Cankarjeva
zaloŽba; Ljubljani:  Delo, 1983, 124 p.

21.  "La siesta del martes."  (Tuesday Siesta).

English:

"Tuesday Siesta."  J. S. Bernstein, tr.  In <u>From Spain and the
Americas; Literature in Translations</u>. James E. Miller, Jr. et al,
eds.  Glenview, IL:  Scott, Foresman and Company, 1970.

22.  "A la sombra del parque está el mono..."

French:

"Le Singe."  Jacques Gilard, tr.  Paris:  <u>Silex</u>, no. 11, (March,
1979), p. 21.  (Originally published in the column 'Punto y aparte,'
Cartagena, Colombia:  <u>El Universal</u>, (June 8, 1943), p. 4).

23.  "El último viaje del buque fantasma."  (The Last Voyage of the Ghost
Ship).

German:

<u>Die letzte Reise des Gespensterschiffs:  Erzählungen</u>. Curt Meyer-
Clason, tr.  Berlin, Weimar:  Aufbau-Verlag, 1978, pp. 1-

24.  <u>Collected Stories</u>. Gregory Rabassa and J. S. Bernstein, trs.
New York:  Harper and Row, 1984, 311 p.  (Contains twenty-six
stories written between 1947 and 1972).

FOOTNOTE:  (For additional translations see:  <u>Gabriel García Márquez:
An Annotated Bibliography, 1947-1979</u>, by Margaret Eustella
Fau.  Westport, CT:  Greenwood Press, 1980, pp. 21-31).

# SECONDARY SOURCES

# Bibliographies on Gabriel García Márquez

1. Benson, John. "García Márquez en Alternativa (1974-1979): Una bibliografía comentada." Chasqui: Revista de Literatura Latino-americana, v. 8, no. 3, (May, 1979), pp. 69-81.

   A bibliography containing articles by García Márquez published in Alternativa from February 15, 1974 to July 26, 1979, with brief comments about each. This bibliography also includes articles written about García Márquez.

2. Eyzaguirre, Luis B. and Carmen Grullón. "Gabriel García Márquez, contribución bibliográfica, 1955-1984." Providence, RI: INTI, Revista de Literatura Hispánica, Providence College, nos. 16-17, (Autumn, 1982 - Spring, 1983), pp. 175-193.

   A selective unannotated bibliography.

3. Fau, Margaret Eustella. Gabriel García Márquez: An Annotated Bibliography, 1947-1979. Westport, CT: Greenwood Press, 1980, 198 p.

   A book-length bibliography, the first of its kind, to deal exclusively with the Nobel Prize winner for literature.

4. "Gabriel García Márquez in Books Abroad 1963-1973." Norman, OK: Books Abroad, v. 47, no. 3, (Summer, 1973), p. 505.

   A short bibliography of articles and reviews about García Márquez, which appeared in Books Abroad.

5. Lozano, Stella. "Gabriel García Márquez: Novelist, Short-story Writer." In Selected Bibliography of Contemporary Spanish American Writers. Stella Lozano, compiler. Los Angeles, CA: Latin American Studies Center, 1979, pp. 61-72.

An unannotated bibliography of works by and about García Márquez, published between 1974-1978.

6.  Mena, Lucila Inés.  "Bibliografía anotada sobre el ciclo de la violencia en la literatura colombiana." Chapel Hill, NC: <u>Latin American Research Review</u>, v. 13, no. 3, (1978), pp. 95-107.

An introduction, followed by an annotated bibliography, on the cycle of violence as portrayed by García Márquez and other contemporary Colombian writers.

7.  Mena, Lucila Inés.  "Bibliografía anotada sobre el ciclo de violencia en la literatura colombiana." Austin, TX: <u>Latin American Research Review</u>, v. 13, no. 3, (1978), pp. 95-107.

An extensive general bibliography of books and articles on the cycle of violence in Colombia, which includes works by García Márquez.

8.  Rela, Walter.  <u>Spanish American Literature: A Selected Bibliography; Literatura Hispanoamericana: Bibliografía Selecta, 1970-1980</u>. East Lansing, MI: Michigan State University, 1982, 231 p.

Contains over fifty references to Gabriel García Márquez.

# Books, Dissertations and Theses on Gabriel García Márquez

1. Alfaro, Gustavo. <u>Constante de la historia de Latinoamérica en García Márquez</u>. Cali, Colombia: Biblioteca Banco Popular, 1979, 147 p.

   Explores themes of violence, political oppression, and imperialism in the works of Gabriel García Márquez.

2. Avila, Pablo Luis. <u>Gabriel García Márquez, I. B. Singer, N. V. Gogol: tres estructuras paralelas</u>. Granada, Spain: Universidad de Granada, 1980, 154 p.

   An intertextual analysis of García Márquez's, <u>El mar del tiempo perdido</u>, Isaac B. Singer's, <u>L'uomo venuto de Cracovia</u>, and N. V. Gogol's, <u>L'ispettore</u>.

3. Bedoya M., Luis Iván and Augusto Escóbar M. <u>Elementos para una lectura de "El otoño del patriarca."</u> Medellín, Colombia: Ediciones Pepe, 1979, 101 p.

   Analysis of the themes most prevalent in Gabriel García Márquez's works with special emphasis on <u>El otoño del patriarca</u> which focuses on power and solitude, life, death, and the conception of time.

4. Bedoya M., Luis Iván and Augusto Escóbar M. <u>"La mala hora" de Gabriel García Márquez: ficción y realidad</u>. Medellín, Colombia: Ediciones Hombre Nuevo, 1980, 197 p.

   In this second edition of the series on the novel of violence in Colombia, <u>La mala hora</u> is featured as the first successful attempt at integrating reality and fiction in this genre.

5. Box, J. B. H. <u>García Márquez: "El coronel no tiene quien le escriba."</u> London: Grant and Cutler, 1984, 109 p.

An intensive study which treats this novel from four elements: time, character, symbolism, and style.

6. Cartín de Guier, Estrella. Una interpretación de "Cien años de soledad." San José, Costa Rica: Editorial Costa Rica, 1981, 98 p.

   A thematic interpretation of One Hundred Years of Solitude, including an application to other works of García Márquez.

7. "Cien años de soledad," Gabriel García Márquez: estudio sobre Gabriel García Márquez y su época: sumario análisis de la obra y sinópsis y comentario. Barcelona: Editorial Vosgos, 1977, 101 p.

   As the title, taken from the cover of the book, implies, this is an intensive and critical study of García Márquez's major work.

8. Collazos, Oscar. García Márquez, la soledad y la gloria: su vida y su obra. Esplugues de Llobregat, Barcelona: Plaza y Janés, 1983, 248 p.

   Citing the scarcity of works which concentrate on García Márquez's life, this work traces the development of each one of his stories and novels, within the biographic framework.

9. Crovetto, Pier Luigi, ed. Gabriel García Márquez. Genoa: Tilgher, 1979, 173 p.

   The first collection of critical studies in Italian of the works of García Márquez.

10. Earle, Peter G., ed. Gabriel García Márquez. Madrid: Taurus Ediciones, 1981, 294 p.

    A collection of articles by various authors on Gabriel García Márquez.

11. Escóbar Mesa, Augusto. Imaginación y realidad en "Cien años de soledad:" estudio fenomenológico del espacio, el tiempo y el mito. Medellín, Colombia: Ediciones Pepe, 1981, 268 p.

    Elucidates through a study of the component elements of time, space, and myth the narrative structure of the novel of the "real maravillosa."

12. Estudios sobre Gabriel García Márquez y su época: sumario análisis de la obra y sinopsis y comentario de "Cien años de soledad." Barcelona: Editorial Vosgos, 1977, 101 p.

    Includes an introduction briefly describing the life of the author, summarizes his major works and presents a chapter by chapter synopsis and analysis of Cien años de soledad.

13. Farías, Víctor. Los manuscritos de Melquíades: "Cien años de soledad" burguesía latinoamericana y dialéctica de la reproducción ampliada de negación. Frankfort/M.: Verlag Klaus Dieter Vervuert, 1981, 404 p.

The author states that his book deals with loneliness as a political
concept opposed to solidarity, the latter being what most other
critics have dealt with. For Farías, this political loneliness as
the negation of solidarity is the true theme of Cien años de soledad.

14. Gabriel García Márquez, nuestro primer premio Nobel. Bogotá:
Imprenta de la Secretaría de Información y Prensa de la Presidencia
de la República, 1983, 113 p.

This publication in honor of Gabriel García Márquez's receipt of
the Nobel Prize, contains descriptive articles, speeches, and
literary essays about his works.

15. Gabriel García Márquez: Special Issue. Edited by Yvette E  Miller
and Charles Rossman. Pittsburgh, PA: University of Pittsburgh,
Latin American Literary Review, v. 13, no. 25, (January–June, 1985),
160 p.

A series of articles by authors and literary critics of García
Márquez and his works, some reminiscences, and an appeal in "Lost
Tales" by García Márquez for their sources, all of which have been
annotated separately, elsewhere in this book.

16. Halka, Chester S. Melquíades, Alchemy and Narrative Theory:  The
Quest for Gold in "Cien años de soledad." Lathrap Village, MI:
International Book Publishers, 1981, 197 p.

The quest for gold theme developed in Gabriel García Márquez's
Cien años de soledad traces the evolution of the theme both on the
literal and non-literal levels, and applies the analysis to an
interpretation and understanding of the work.

17. Janes, Regina. Gabriel García Márquez:  Revolution in Wonderland.
Columbia, MO: University of Missouri Press, 1981, 115 p.

Beginning with a biographical study of the novelist, the book
contains summaries of and critical comments on the short stories
and novels of Gabriel García Márquez.

18. Joset, Jacques. Gabriel García Márquez coetáneo de la eternidad.
Amsterdam: Rodopi, 1984, 79 p.

A series of interpretative essays covering such topics as the
picaresque nature of several of García Márquez's works, especially
"Blacamán el bueno, vendedor de milagros," the treatment of women,
and the mythological character of El otoño del patriarca and
Crónica de una muerte anunciada.

19. Kulin, Katalin. Creación mítica en la obra de García Márquez.
Budapest, Hungary: Akadémiai Kiadó, 1980, 270 p.

Characterizes the works of García Márquez, whose themes are solitude and death, where the real is confused with the imaginary, time
is abolished or juxtaposed, and the narrative structure is sub-
jected to fiction. Published also in Hungarian as, Mítosz és
valóság. Budapest: Akadémiai Kiadó, 1977.

20. León Guevara, Adelis. <u>Nacimiento y apoteosis de una novela</u>.
    Mérida, Colombia: Publicaciones del Consejo Científico Humanís-
    tico de la Universidad de los Andes, 1981, 107 p.

    An intensive study of García Márquez's narrative art and technique
    as applied to <u>Cien años de soledad</u> with parallels from his earlier
    works where themes of classical traditionalism, violence, and the
    time concept, are prevalent.

21. López Lemus, Virgilio. <u>García Márquez: una vocación incontenible</u>.
    La Habana: Editorial Letras Cubanas, 1982, 150 p.

    A study of the writings of Gabriel García Márquez, short stories,
    novels, essays, and newspaper articles, focusing upon such recur-
    ring themes as violence, economic conditions, and hope for Latin
    America.

22. Mena, Lucila Inés. <u>La función de la historia en "Cien años de</u>
    <u>soledad</u>." Barcelona: Plaza y Janes, 1979, 222 p.

    After examining <u>Cien años de soledad</u> in the context of its function
    as true history and not merely as a narrative, Mena concludes that
    this history is not only the history of the fictitious Macondo but
    of all Latin America as well.

23. Mendoza, Plinio Apuleyo. <u>La llama y el hielo</u>. Barcelona: Planeta,
    1984, 305 p.

    Revolving around five actual persons, prominent among them, Gabriel
    García Márquez, this autobiographical novel takes us through the
    author's experiences of Latin American politics, insurrections, and
    literature along the way.

24. Mercado Cardona, Homero. <u>Macondo: una realidad llamada ficción</u>.
    Barranquilla, Colombia: Ediciones Universidad del Atlántico, 1971,
    102 p.

    A descriptive analysis and study of the fictional city of Macondo
    created by Gabriel García Márquez throughout his works, as it
    demonstrates the author's success in expressing myth as reality.

25. Moreno Acero, Jorge Eduardo. <u>Vargas Vila, mejor que García</u>
    <u>Márquez</u>? Bogota: Ediciones Tercer Mundo, 1981, 109 p.

    Evaluates García Márquez relative to a fellow Colombian, Vargas
    Vila, who wrote fifty years earlier.

26. Oberhelman, Harley D. <u>The Presence of Faulkner in the Writings</u>
    <u>of García Márquez</u>. Lubbock, Texas: Texas Tech Press, 1980, 43 p.

    A comparative study of two novelists, García Márquez and William
    Faulkner, complete with a bibliography on pages 40-43.

27. Palencia-Roth, David Michael. <u>Gabriel García Márquez, la línea,</u>
    <u>el círculo y las metamorfosis del mito</u>. Madrid: Gredos, 1983,
    318 p.

In addition to presenting mythical and archetypal interpretations of Cien años de soledad and El otoño del patriarca, Palencia-Roth traces for the reader the roots and antecedents of these major works in García Márquez's previous stories.

28.  Paoli, Roberto. Invito alla lettura di Gabriel García Márquez. Milano: Mursia, 1981, 125 p.

This criticism of Cien años de soledad together with nine other works is complete, with a chronology, biographic notes, and a bibliography.

29.  Pastor, Ricardo, ed. Gabriel García Márquez: The Man and the Magic of His Writings. Symposium 1983. Saginaw Valley State College, Department of Modern Foreign Languages, University Center, MI: Special issue: Alèthea, no. 13 (Spring-Summer, 1984), 88 p.

The English and Spanish versions of articles by Ricardo Pastor, David Barker, Emilio Castañeda, Roberto Herrera, Pablo González, and Drew E. Hinderer.

30.  Pozanco, Víctor. García Márquez en "El Coronel." Barcelona: Ambito Literario, 1978, 75 p.

This intensive study of El coronel no tiene quien le escriba consists of two parts: first, an explanation of the basic theory that supports the type of analysis that the author considers to be effective, and second, an application of that analysis.

31.  Rama, Angel. Los dictadores latinoamericanos. Mexico: Fondo de Cultura Económica, 1976, 64 p.

Rama chooses for his essay three works: Yo el supremo, El recurso del método, and El otoño del patriarca to discuss the development of the theme of the "dictador" in the Latin American novel.

32.  Rentería Mantilla, Alfonso, ed. García Márquez habla de García Márquez, 33 reportajes. Bogota: Rentería Editores, 1979, 218 p.

A series of essays, articles, and interviews, taken from various periodicals, and written during the years 1967-1979. Each of these appears in this present bibliography.

33.  Sainte-Marie, A. Etude des Personnages Feminins de "Cien años de soledad" de Gabriel García Márquez. Toulouse-Le Mirail, France: Université de Toulouse-Le Mirail, Institut d'Etudes Hispaniques et Hispano-Americaines, 1983, 174 p.

The strength and influence of the feminine personalities in Cien años de soledad.

34.  Simón Martínez, Pedro, comp. Recopilación de textos sobre García Márquez. La Habana: Casa de las Américas, 1969, 259 p.

A collection of reports, essays, articles, and bibliographic reviews about the Colombian writer, Gabriel García Márquez.

35.  Sims, Robert Lewis.  The Evolution of Myth in Gabriel García
     Márquez: from "La hojarasca" to "Cien años de soledad."  Miami, FL:
     Ediciones Universal, 1981, 153 p.

     Gabriel García Márquez's efforts to create a universal narrative,
     which transcended the narrow bounds of reality hinted at in La
     hojarasca reached its successful culmination in his magic-realistic
     Cien años de soledad.

36.  Torrijos Herrera, Omar.  Respuestas a García Márquez.  Panamá:
     Ediciones Reforma Educativa, 1975, 101 p.

     Torrijos shares his political, economic, and social ideas with
     García Márquez in this volume.

37.  Viñas, David, et al.  Más allá del boom: literatura y mercado.
     Mexico: Marcha Editores, 1981, 326 p.

     In October of 1979, an international and multilingual group of
     intellectuals gathered at the Wilson Center in Washington, D.C.
     for a colloquium on the phenomenal surge in the literary world of
     Latin America known as "El boom."  Eleven of the essays in this
     book deal with García Márquez's role in that "boom" together with
     other Latin American writers.

38.  Williams, Raymond L.  Gabriel García Márquez.  Boston, MA:  Twayne
     Publishers, 1984, 176 p.

     The most complete work in English on Gabriel García Márquez to date.
     It contains a chronology, biography, chapters with analyses of the
     early works, the works before and after Cien años de soledad, and
     concludes with a chapter on Crónica de una muerte anunciada and
     the journalistic writings.  There is also a selected bibliography
     and index.

39.  Zuluaga, Conrado.  Puerta abierta a García Márquez, y otras puertas.
     Bogotá: La Editora, 1982, 198 p.

     Essays on articles and stories written by Gabriel García Márquez
     and once published in magazines such as Teorema, Correo de los
     Andes, and Los Cuadernos de Filosofía y Letras.


Doctoral Dissertations

1.   Abenoza, Bianca Ossorio de.  Gabriel García Márquez juzgado por la
     crítica: una bibliografía analítica y comentada, 1955-1974.  Ph.D.
     dissertation, Charlottesville, VA: University of Virginia, 1979,
     378 p.  (79-28007)

     "... The purpose of this dissertation is to catalogue and analyze
     the criticism published throughout the western world between the
     years 1955 and 1974 on García Márquez's novels and short stories."

2.  Antaki, Vivian Jane.  Beyond Political Perspectives: The Literary
    Craft of Carlos Fuentes, Mario Vargas Llosa and Gabriel García
    Márquez.  Ph.D. dissertation, Boulder, CO: University of Colorado
    at Boulder, 1978, 345 p.  (79-03017)

    A comparative analysis of one novel by each of the three authors
    mentioned.  In the case of García Márquez, the novel chosen was
    El otoño del patriarca.  The author specifically excludes the
    analysis of political elements in the works studied, in order to
    concentrate on the "literary and artistic preoccupations of the
    three novelists."

3.  Aronne —Amestoy, Lida Beatriz.  Utopía, paraíso e historia: tres
    versiones de la búsqueda mítica en el realismo fantástico hispano-
    americano.  Ph.D. dissertation, Storrs, CT: University of Con-
    necticut, 1982, 404 p.  (83-00118)

    This work consists of two interdependent studies: one involves the
    "synthesis of intrinsic and extrinsic views of literature on the
    basis of the archetypal structures of the text" and the other
    "applies that approach to the analysis and hermeneutics of 'El
    ahogado más hermoso del mundo' by García Márquez, Rulfo's Pedro
    Páramo, and Cortázar's Bestiario."

4.  Barsy, Kalman.  La estructura dialéctica de "El otoño del patriarca."
    Ph.D. dissertation, New York: New York University, 1981, 245 p.
    (81-15527)

    Barsy's study aims to probe the "inner structure" of the novel, in
    order to demonstrate that its originality lies not "in the theme
    but in it's peculiar structure, which hinges upon a complex system
    of dialectic opposites."

5.  Bass, Thomas Alden.  Fiction and History:  Essays on the Novels of
    Flaubert, García Márquez, Coover and Pynchon.  Ph.D. dissertation,
    Santa Cruz, CA: University of California at Santa Cruz, 1980,
    387 p.  (81-23244)

    An exploration of the problem of history as "central to a fiction
    that seeks both to write history and escape from it," a process
    the author considers as a constant in "literary modernism."  Gar-
    cía Márquez, Coover, and Pynchon are viewed as representatives of
    the "end of the modernist experiment."

6.  Bennett, Christine Elaine Harvey.  Satire and Irony in Two Works
    of García Márquez.  Ph.D. dissertation, Stanford, CA: Stanford
    University, 1975, 192 p.  (75-13487)

    Irony and satire in Cien años de soledad and Los funerales de la
    Mamá Grande, effectively portray man's helplessness in the
    presence of fate, his inability to decide his own destiny.

7.  Benson, John William.  Estructura de los cuentos de García Márquez.
    Ph.D. dissertation, Madison, WI: University of Wisconsin, 1977,
    252 p.  (77-23698)

This study sets forth a structural classification of García Márquez's short stories. The author's analysis reveals the presence of three underlying structures: 1) disjunctive; 2) transitional; and 3) conjunctive. The latter is considered the culmination of the novelist's narrative art, which the author considers clearly evident in the last two novels as well.

8.  Buchanan, Rhonda Lee Dahl. "El otoño del patriarca:" a Jungian Interpretation. Ph.D. dissertation, Boulder, CO: University of Colorado at Boulder, 1982, 421 p. (82-29815)

This dissertation intends to "reveal basic truths about the nature of the dictator and dictatorship in general," which in the author's view, is the intention of García Márquez in this particular novel.

9.  Craig, Barbara June. The Ironic Vision in the Fiction of Gabriel García Márquez and William Faulkner. Ph.D. dissertation, Norman, OK: University of Oklahoma, 1983, 204 p. (84-04554)

An examination of Gabriel García Márquez's and William Faulkner's use of irony in their major works which "debunk the myth of a heroic past" and "the brave new future."

10. Decker, Carmen Maldonado. Social and Political Alienation in the Novels of Gabriel García Márquez. Ph.D. dissertation, Riverside, CA: University of California, 1984, 325 p. (84-13178)

Each novel is a dramatization of all the forces which conspire to prevent man from being the instrument of his own fate.

11. Dixon, Paul Bergstrom. The Forms and Functions of Ambiguity in "Dom Casmurro," "Pedro Páramo," "Grande sertão: veredas" and "Cien años de soledad." Ph.D. dissertation, Chapel Hill, NC: University of North Carolina, 1981, 246 p. (81-25571)

Ambiguity as a vehicle for defining characters and situations in four Latin American novels.

12. Doyle, Linda Sheidler. A Study of Time in Three Novels: "Under the Volcano," "One Hundred Years of Solitude," and "Gravity's Rainbow." Ph.D. dissertation, South Bend, IN: University of Notre Dame, 1978, 186 p. (78-15535)

This study examines three visions of time in novels by Malcolm Lowry, Gabriel García Márquez, and Thomas Pynchon: the tension between cyclical and linear time in Under the Volcano, unconventional, repetitive time in One Hundred Years of Solitude, and cause and effect vs. non-sequential time in Gravity's Rainbow.

13. Frisch, Mark Frederic. Parallels between William Faulkner and Four Hispanic American Novelists. Ph.D. dissertation, Ann Arbor, MI: University of Michigan, 1985, 390 p. (85-12407)

A comparative study of William Faulkner, Eduardo Mallea, Agustín Yáñez, Manuel Rojas, and Gabriel García Márquez, and the reasons for the similarities among them. Of García Márquez, Frisch

comments, "one finds a conception of reality which is quite different from the Realism and Naturalixm of the nineteenth century."

14. Gantt, Barbara L. The Women of Macondo: Feminine Archetypes in
García Márquez's "Cien años de soledad." Ph.D. dissertation,
Tallahassee, FL: The Florida State University, 1977, 137 p.
(77-22109)
"The conclusion reached about the women of Macondo was that they
were better able to cope with their existence when they approached
the world as mothers ... The suggestion that selfish love leads to
solitude and selfless love leads to solidarity, friendship, or
union as a transpersonal experience was inherent throughout the
discussion of the feminine archetypes in the novel."

15. Green, Joan Rea. The Structure of the Narrator in the Contemporary
Spanish American Novel. Ph.D. dissertation, Austin, TX: University
of Texas, 1970, 247 p. (71-11545)

One novel, from each of twelve contemporary Latin American novelists, including García Márquez's, La hojarasca, has been dealt
with "in this study from the point of view of the narrator and the
narrative mode and, in a few cases, specifically with regard to
the use of time."

16. Hernández, Joan Lloyd. The Influence of William Faulkner in Four
Latin American Novelists (Yáñez, García Márquez, Cepeda Samudio,
Donoso). Ph.D. dissertation, Baton Rouge, LA: Louisiana State
University and Agricultural and Mechanical College, 1978, 282 p.
(79-11573)

A study of the influence of the American writer on the four novelists included in the title. Admits to being a continuation of
James East Irby's earlier work, La influencia de William Faulkner
en cuatro narradores hispanoamericanos.

17. Holt, Candace Kay. "Rayuela," "El obsceno pájaro de la noche" y
"El otoño del patriarca": nuevas formas de estructura narrativa.
Ph.D. dissertation, Iowa City, IA: University of Iowa, 1979, 202 p.
(80-12378)

The author departs from the premise of the existence of a "new
social conscience on the part of contemporary man", in order to
show how the three works studied represent the novelist's need to
"discover new literary forms for the artistic elaboration of this
new vision of reality".

18. Kent, Sarah. The Imagined Paradise: An Area of Meaning in the Fiction of Gabriel García Márquez. Ph.D. dissertation, Essex, England:
University of Essex, 1983, 124 p.

"Examines the ways in which this meaning (imaginative paradise)
manifests itself, and discusses its significance for the interpretation of his fiction. Attention is centered around Cien años de
soledad and El otoño del patriarca. . .".

19.  Mekled, Salomon.  Symbolism and Ideology in Gabriel García Márquez's, "Cien años de soledad":  Towards the deciphering of Melquiades. Ph.D. dissertation, Essex, England: University of Essex, 1982, 354 p.

A sociologic and psychoanalytic interpretation of García Márquez's masterwork.

20.  Medina, Elizabeth Ramos.  La muerte en las obras de Gabriel García Márquez.  Ph.D. dissertation, Boulder, CO:  University of Colorado, 1975, 232 p.  (76-11595)

García Márquez portrays death in his works as a "reality in which men are isolated, enclosed and condemned, without hope. . .".

21.  Palencia-Roth, David Michael.  Myth and the Modern Novel:  Gabriel García Márquez, Thomas Mann, James Joyce.  Ph.D. dissertation, Cambridge, MA: Harvard University, 1975, 392 p.

The central focus throughout this theoretical study is myth.  Each author, however, points in such different directions that contrasts proved more fruitful than comparisons.  Each novelist is seen to approach myth in the following way:  García Márquez through "primitivism" and "images"; Thomas Mann through "philosophy" and "dialectics"; James Joyce through "theology" and "the Word."

22.  Ramos, Juan Antonio.  Hacia "El otoño del patriarca":  La novela del dictador en Hispanoamérica.  Ph.D. dissertation, Philadelphia, PA: University of Pennsylvania, 1979, 266 p.  (79-19506)

Contrasting El otoño del patriarca with earlier treatments of the dictator, which he characterizes as more "schematic," the author concludes that this novel is the culmination of a process involving the "patient elaboration" of "a new symbol in universal literature," the Spanish American dictator.

23.  Ramos-Escobar, José L.  From Yoknapatawpha to Macondo:  A Comparative Study of William Faulkner and Gabriel García Márquez.  Ph.D. dissertation, Providence, RI: Brown University, 1980, 162 p. (81-11167)

In the light of numerous previous studies purporting to show the influence of William Faulkner upon García Márquez, this one sets out to "qualify the influence of Faulkner on García Márquez and to show in which way their narratives bear similar features and why."

24.  Richards, Timothy Albert Burton.  The Grotesque in the Contemporary Latin American Novel.  Ph.D. dissertation, Boulder, CO: University of Colorado, 1980, 208 p.  (81-03129)

Based on the premise that today's art forms show a more marked affinity with the grotesque than any previous time's productions, the author traces the treatment of the grotesque in El señor Presidente, Pantaleón y las visitadoras, and Cien años de soledad.

25. Rigg, Janet Louise. Tyranny of an Illusion: Romance and Historical Identity in the Fiction of Gabriel García Márquez. Ph.D. dissertation, Berkeley, CA: University of California, 1976.

    García Márquez establishes a relationship, by his choice of form, between a lack of a stable social order at the time of the conquistadors and Latin America's present failure to develop a viable social and historical identity.

26. Salazar, Carol Lacy. La cosmovisión primitiva del narrador magicorrealista. Ph.D. dissertation, Tempe, AZ: University of Arizona, 1984, 247 p. (85-00472)

    In analyzing four Spanish American novels, among which is Cien años de soledad the author points out that the distinguishing feature of these novels compared to other magical realist narratives is the "primitive world view expressed by the narrator."

27. Saldivar, José David. Claiming the Americas: Contemporary Third World Literature. Ph.D. dissertation, Stanford, CA: Stanford University, 1983, 192 p. (83-07210)

    Chapter II of this work explores Latin American history in Cien años de soledad from a Third World viewpoint.

28. Sierra Correa, Sylvia Rosa. Aproximación al mundo novelesco que crea Gabriel García Márquez en "Cien años de soledad." Ph.D. dissertation, Madrid: Universidad de Madrid, 1972, 50 p.

    Utilizes the text of One Hundred Years of Solitude in an attempt to understand the modern world.

29. Silverman, Daniel Albert. Media and Art as Cultural Data: An Exploration of Perceptual Fields Contained within the Novels of the Two Cultures. Ph.D. dissertation, Evanston, IL: Northwestern University, 1978, 315 p. (79-03364)

    "The study reveals the pervasive differences created by culture in respect to how a culture uses tradition as a context for the education of its members."

30. Velasco, Ana María. Función de lo mítico en "Cien años de soledad." Ph.D. dissertation, Los Angeles, CA: University of California, 1982, 250 p. (82-12885)

    The work proposes to analyze the role of the mythical elements present in the novel Cien años de soledad.

31. Vullin, Sylvie. Le baroque dans l'Oeuvre Romanesque de Gabriel García Márquez. Ph.D. dissertation, Nice, France: University of Nice, 1981, 285 p.

    The magic realism, the fantastic extending beyond the limits to the grotesque reaches its highest points in the works of García Márquez.

32. Zamora, Lois Parkinson. The Apocalyptic Vision in Contemporary American Fiction:  Gabriel García Márquez, Thomas Pynchon, Julio Cortázar, and John Barth. Ph.D. dissertation, Berkeley, CA: University of California, 1977, 314 p.  (77-31601)

The end of time as envisioned in the novels of four prominent authors.

## Master's Theses

1. Beason, Pamela S. The Dictator in "Yo el supremo," "El recurso del método" and "El otoño del patriarca." Master's thesis, Norman, OK: University of Oklahoma, 1980, 78 p.

A comparative study of the subject of the dictator in three Latin American novels.

2. Kemp, María M. Estudio crítico de "Los funerales de la Mamá Grande" de Gabriel García Márquez. Master's thesis, New Britain, CT: Central Connecticut State College, 1979, 156 p.

A critical study of short stories included in Los funerales de la Mamá Grande: "La siesta del martes," "Un día de éstos," "En este pueblo no hay ladrones," "Un día después del sábado," "Rosas articiciales," y "Los funerales de la Mamá Grande."

3. Molen, Patricia Hart. Humanizing Scatology ans Eschatology in Two Novels of Gabriel García Márquez. Master's thesis, Salt Lake City, UT: University of Utah, 1979, 30 p.

This study of The Autumn of the Patriarch and In Evil Hour, notes particularly the techniques used by García Márquez to present believable human beings who are at home with the fantastic.

4. Pérez, Luz R. El papel de la mujer en "Cien años de soledad." Master's thesis, El Paso, TX: University of Texas, 1981, 32 leaves.

The role of women in García Márquez's major work.

5. Roda F., Ana, y Ferro C., Juan Pablo. Recepción de la novela en algunos sectores del público bogotano: análisis del caso "Cien años de soledad." Master's thesis, Bogotá: Universidad de los Andes, 1981, 94 p.

Reactions and opinions of the natives regarding a novel situated in their area.

6. Rogers, Michelle Lee. Macondo and Yoknapatawpha County: Microcosmos of Society. Master's thesis, Memphis, TN: Memphis State University, 1984, 83 p.  (MA 1323923)

The Macondo of García Márquez's, One Hundred Years of Solitude, and Faulkner's Yoknapatawpha County depict the rural, simple lives of a people who labor on the land and the effects of the invasion of material progress.

7.  Smith Grillo, Dana Edward.  "El otoño del patriarca" by Gabriel
    García Márquez:  the Archetype of the Caudillo.  Master's thesis,
    College Station, TX: Texas A and M University, 1979, 99 p.

    The author "attempts to show how the patriarch of García Márquez's
    novel is in fact the archetype of the Latin American caudillo by
    discussing what appears to be the patriarch's archetypal qualities
    in the novel in relation to Jung's theory of archetypes and to the
    characteristics of Latin American society."


Research in progress

1.  Ariza González, Julio.  Gabriel García Márquez:  entre el mito y la
    otra realidad.  Kingston, Jamaica:  University of the West Indies,
    (1970-1985).

2.  Bell-Villada, Gene H.  Gabriel García Márquez:  the Man and His Work.
    Williamstown, MA:  Williams College, (1982-1986)

3.  Cardwell, Richard Andrew.  "Characterization in the Early Fiction of
    Gabriel García Márquez."  London, 1985.

    This work in progress will appear in a volume of essays on García
    Márquez.

4.  Gabriel García Márquez, Text and Intertext.  Julio Ortega, ed.
    Claudia Elliott, English language ed.  Austin, TX:  University of
    Texas Press.  (forthcoming)

5.  García Ramos, Juan Manuel.  La narrativa de Manuel Puig, Gabriel
    García Márquez y Juan Carlos Onetti.  Tenerife, Islas Canarias:
    Universidad de La Laguna, (1975-1984).

6.  Holdsworth, Carole A.  Persephone, Pökler and the Patriarch:  Study
    on García Márquez and Thomas Pynchon.  Chicago, IL:  Loyola
    University, (1983-1984).

7.  López de Martínez, Adelaida.  La narrativa de Gabriel García Márquez:
    Metaficción y carnaval.  College Station, TX:  Texas A and M
    University, (1981-1985).

# Chapters and Sections in Books

1. Aaron, M. Audrey. "García Márquez' mecedor as Link Between Passage of Time and Presence of Mind." In The Analysis of Literary Texts: Current Trends in Methodology, edited by Randolph D. Pope. Third and Fourth York College Colloquia. Ipsilanti, MI: Bilingual Press, 1980, pp. 21-30.

   Develops the concept of the rocking-chair as a poetic symbol in Cien años de soledad.

2. Acker, Bertie. "Religion in Colombia as Seen in the Works of García Márquez." In Religion in Latin American Life and Literature, edited by Lyce C. Brown and William F. Cooper. Waco, TX: Markham Press Fund of Baylor University Press, 1980, pp. 339-350.

   Acker discusses Roman Catholicism in Colombia as seen in the works of Gabriel García Márquez.

3. Alegría, Fernando. "Gabriel García Márquez." In Retratos Contemporáneos. New York, NY: Harcourt, Brace, Jovanovich, 1979, pp. 3-18.

   Describes the childhood of García Márquez, his life and works and writing style.

4. Arango, Manuel Antonio. "Gabriel García Márquez." In Gabriel García Márquez y la novela de la violencia en Colombia. México: Fondo de Cultura Económica, 1985, pp. 23-62.

   The title of this book is misleading since García Márquez is only one of eight Latin American novelists treated of in this book. However, the first section deals with violence as it occur in four of García Márquez's works: La hojarasca, El coronel no tiene quien le escriba, La mala hora, and Cien años de soledad.

5.  Arango L., Manuel Antonio.  "La temática y el aspecto social en
    Cien años de soledad de Gabriel García Márquez."  In his Aspectos
    sociales en ocho escritores hispánicos.  Bogotá:  Ediciones Tercer
    Mundo, 1981, pp. 161-175.

    Analyzes Macondo from a sociological viewpoint.

6.  Arce Vargas, Fernando Arturo.  "Gabriel García Márquez y el ciclo
    de Macondo."  In his Literatura hispanoamericana contemporánea:  una
    vision selectiva.  San José, Costa Rica:  Editorial Universidad
    Estatal Distancia, 1982, pp. 135-141.

    Critical discussion of four of García Márquez's works:  Cien años de
    soledad, El otoño del patriarca, Los funerales de la Mamá Grande,
    and the short story, "La siesta del martes."

7.  Ayala González-Nieto, Carlos.  "El autor y su obra."  In Cien años
    de soledad por Gabriel García Márquez.  Barcelona:  Círculo de
    Lectores, 1973, c1967, pp. 351-357.

    A summary of the life, times, and works of Gabriel García Márquez.

8.  Ayala Poveda, Fernando.  "Realismo mágico."  In his Manual de
    literatura colombiana.  Bogotá:  Educar Editores, 1984, pp. 320-345.

    A summary of Gabriel García Márquez's life and works, with an
    analysis of Cien años de soledad.

9.  Azancot, Leopoldo.  "GGM habla de política."  In García Márquez
    habla de García Márquez, 33 reportajes, edited by Alfonso Rentería
    Mantilla.  Bogotá:  Rentería Editores, 1979, pp. 37-40.

    García Márquez expresses his opinions on politics, critics and the
    present state of the Latin American narrative, in an interview from
    Indice, Madrid, 1968.

10. Bardelli, Fulvia.  "Il privilegio della memoria."  In Gabriel García
    Márquez.  Edited by Pier Luigi Crovetto.  Genoa:  Tilgher, 1977,
    pp. 145-158.

    The events in Cien años de soledad are magical illusions which have
    no existence in or relation to chronological time.

11. Bazán, Juan F.  "Cien años de soledad."  In La narrativa Latino-
    americana.  Asunción, Paraguay, 1970, pp. 42-56.

    Opinions of various critics regarding Cien años de soledad.

12. Bedoya M., Luis Iván.  "Cien años de soledad de Gabriel García Marque
    Márquez."  In Escritos sobre literatura colombiana.  Medellín,
    Colombia:  Edicones Pepe, 1980, pp. 79-84.

    Gabriel García Márquez's Cien años de soledad combines fantasy and
    myth with reality to portray life in the lower stratum of Latin
    American society.

13. Bedoya M., Luis Iván. "El coronel no tiene quien le escriba."
    In Escritos sobre literatura colombiana. Medellín, Colombia:
    Ediciones Pepe, 1980, pp. 62-79.

    Commentary upon and section by section illustration of the
    narrative progress of this novel of hopefulness.

14. Bedoya M., Luis Iván. "El otoño del patriarca de Gabriel García
    Márquez." In Escritos sobre literatura colombiana. Medellín,
    Colombia: Ediciones Pepe, 1980, pp. 84-88.

    A discussion of the hyperbole present in Gabriel García Márquez's
    El otoño del patriarca also includes a study of Mejía Duque's
    critique of the novel and mentions its shortcomings.

15. Bellini, Giuseppe. "Il mundo fantastico de Cien años de soledad."
    In Il Laberinto Magico: Studi sul Nuovo Romanzo Ispanoamericano.
    Milano: Cisalpino-Goliardica, 1973, pp. 181-225.

    The balance between fantasy and reality in Cien años de soledad is
    the element which binds the entire narrative structure of this
    novel together.

16. Benedetti, Mario. "García Márquez o la vigilia dentro del sueño."
    In Letras del continente mestizo. Montevideo: Editorial Arca,
    1967, pp. 145-154.

    Also in, El ejercicio del criterio. México: Editorial Nueva
    Imagen, 1981, pp. 253-261.

    Explores style and symbolism in the works of Gabriel García Márquez.

17. Bloch de Bejar, Lisa. "Una visión fabulosa que reconstruye la
    realidad." In Análisis de un lenguaje en crisis. Montevideo:
    Nuestra Tierra, 1969, pp. 125-141.

    An interpretation of the uses of humor in Cien años de soledad,
    referred to by the author as "one unique and extraordinary
    metaphor."

18. Boorman, Joan Rea. Rupturas temporales: La hojarasca - Simulta-
    neidad." In La estructura del narrador en la novela hispanoameri-
    cana contemporánea. Madrid: Hispanova de Ediciones, 1976,
    pp. 145-149.

    La hojarasca sets the stage for García Márquez's future works
    culminating in Cien años de soledad.

19. Burgos Ojeda, Roberto. "La magia como elemento fundamental en la
    nueva narrativa latinoamericana." In El ensayo y la crítica lite-
    raria en Iberoamérica. Memoria del XIV Congreso Internacional de
    Literatura Iberoamericana, Universidad de Toronto, Toronto, Canadá,
    24-28 de Agosto de 1969. Kurt L. Levy and Keith Ellis, eds.
    Toronto, Canada: University of Toronto, 1970, pp. 203-208.

    Concentrating on the element of magic in four contemporary Latin
    American novelists, Burgos Ojeda illustrates instances of

levitation in Cien años de soledad.

20.  Bosch, Juan.  Conferencias y artículos.  Santo Domingo:  Alfa y
     Omega, 1980, 253 p.

     In one article, Juan Bosch, personal friend of Gabriel García Már-
     quez, writes to the author after reading his short story La increí-
     ble y triste historia de la cándida Eréndira y de su abuela desal-
     mada, reflecting upon his reactions to the story and, the extreme
     amount of talent which he claims Gabriel García Márquez possesses,
     pp. 158-161.

     Also in a second article, Gabriel García Márquez's Cien años de
     soledad, the relationship between the novel and the author's other
     works is discussed, pp. 147-157.

21.  Bratosevich, Nicolás.  "La explosión rítmica en  El otoño del
     patriarca y su interpretación sociológica."  In Métodos de análisis
     literario.  Buenos Aires: Librería Hachette, 1980, pp. 209-220.

     The concept of "rhythm in the novel" using techniques such as
     "repetition in variation" in El otoño del patriarca.

22.  Brotherston, Gordon.  "García Márquez and the Secrets of Saturno
     Santos."  In Contemporary Latin American Fiction: Carpentier,
     Sábato, Onetti, Roa, Donoso, Fuentes, García Márquez.  Salvador
     Bacarisse, ed.  Edinburgh, Scotland: Scottish Academis Press,
     1980, 109 p.

     Refers to what Brotherston calls the "Indian engagement" in El
     otoño del patriarca and previous writings of García Márquez,
     particularly Cien años de soledad.

23.  Caballero, Oscar.  "Erase una dictadura..."  In García Márquez
     habla de García Márquez, 33 reportajes.  Alfonso Rentería Mantilla,
     ed.  Bogotá: Rentería Editores, 1979, pp. 119-125.

     The phenomenal success of El otoño del patriarca is the topic of
     this essay from Cambio, published in Madrid in 1975.

24.  Camerlingo, Emilio.  "Gabriel García Márquez: l'Avventura del
     racconto."  In La morte al presente: saggi sul nuovo romanzo lati-
     noamericano, a cura di Bruno Arpaia.  Napoli: T. Pironti Editore,
     1982? pp. 81-106.

     Included in this collection of essays which center on the state of
     the current Latin American novel, is one which defines the essence
     of García Márquez's writings, that is, the emphasis on magic
     realism, especially in Cien años de soledad and El otoño del
     patriarca.

25.  Campos, Jorge.  "Gabriel García Márquez," In Narrativa y crítica
     de nuestra América by Jaime Alazraki et al.  Compilation and
     introduction by Joaquín Roy.  Madrid: Editorial Castalia, 1978,
     pp. 317-350.

A short biography followed by summaries and critical commentaries on each of Gabriel García Márquez's works.

26.  Carrillo, Germán D. "Crónica de una muerte anunciada, de G. García Márquez: reportaje, profecía y recuento." In Literatures in Transition: The Many Voices of the Caribbean Area: A Symposium. Gaithersburg, MD: Hispamérica, (1982), pp. 77-83.

Focuses on the use of the first person as narrator, investigator, and interviewer in Chronicle of a Death Foretold.

27.  Céspedes, Diógenes. "Sistema de escritura y paralelismo cristiano en Crónica de una muerte anunciada de García Márquez." In Estudios sobre literatura, cultura e ideologías. Santo Domingo: Ediciones de Taller, 1983, pp. 161-163.

Indicates elements of the structure and characterization in Chronicle of a Death Foretold which were already foreshadowed in One Hundred Years of Solitude.

28.  Chao, Ramón. "Gabriel García Márquez y los presos políticos cubanos." In García Márquez habla de García Márquez, 33 reportajes, Alfonso Rentería Mantilla, ed. Bogotá: Rentería Editores, 1979, 173-177.

An important paper written by García Márquez is instrumental in securing the release of the political prisoner in Cuba, Reynold González as reported in Triunfo, from Madrid in 1978.

29.  Collazos, Oscar. "García Márquez y la nueva narrativa colombiana." In Actual narrativa latinoamericana, conferencias y seminarios. La Habana: Casa de las Américas, 1970, pp. 105-145.

A panel composed of Oscar Collazos, Angel Rama and Mario Benedetti concentrates on García Márquez's place in the new Colombian narrative and his influence on Colombian literature.

30.  Conte, Rafael. "Gabriel García Márquez o el mito." In Lenguaje y violencia. Madrid: M. Al-Borak, 1972, pp. 157-183.

Violence as portrayed in the Latin American novel is the subject of this book. The works of García Márquez are treated of in various pages throughout the book, especially in the section: "Gabriel García Márquez o el mito," which is a study of the creation of Macondo.

31.  Conti, Stefano. "Per l'analizi di un caso di scrittura collettiva." In Gabriel García Márquez. Pier Luigi Crovetto, ed. Genoa: Tilgher, 1977, pp. 87-100.

The literary concepts evident in La mala hora found their greater development in García Márquez's later novels, culminating in Cien años de soledad.

32. Córdova, José Hermán. "El otoño del patriarca de García Márquez
    o la poesía y la política de la narración." In Requiem for the
    Boom--Premature? Rose S. Minc and Marilyn R. Frankenthaler, eds.
    Montclair, NJ: Montclair State College, 1980, pp. 82-91.

    Deals with the poetic elements in a very political novel.

33. Correas de Zapata, Celia. "Estructuras míticas en Cien años de
    soledad." In Ensayos Hispanoamericanos. Buenos Aires: Ediciones
    Corregidor, 1978, pp. 77-121.

    In Cien años de soledad, García Márquez has utilized by demythi-
    cation and satirization, almost all of the known myths of the East
    and West down through the history of mankind.

34. Correas de Zapata, Celia. "La magia de Cien años de soledad en
    Los tumultos de María Granata." In Ensayos hispanoamericanos.
    Buenos Aires: Ediciones Corregidor, 1978, pp. 183-202.

    After stating that comparisons are odious, the author proceeds to
    contrast characters and situations from both novels.

35. Correas de Zapata, Celia. "Novelas arquetípicas de la dictadura:
    Carpentier, García Márquez y Roa Bastos." In Ensayos hispanoame-
    ricanos. Buenos Aires: Ediciones Corregidor, 1978, pp. 7-44.

    Enumerates the similarities and differences in this comparison of
    three novels whose protagonists are dictators: El recurso del
    método of Alejo Carpentier, Yo, el Supremo of Augusto Roa Bastos,
    and El otoño del patriarca of Gabriel García Márquez.

36. Crovetto, Pier Luigi. "Cien años de soledad: la coordinata della
    marginalita o la nostalgia della storia." In Gabriel García Már-
    quez. Genoa: Tilgher, 1977, pp. 101-144.

    An evaluative investigation of the interaction of the time and
    space elements in Cien años de soledad.

37. Crovetto, Pier Luigi. "El coronel no tiene quien le escriba o la
    memoria de Macondo." In Gabriel García Márquez. Pier Luigi
    Crovetto, ed. Genoa: Tilgher, 1977, pp. 67-86.

    The symbolism of solitude and hopelessness is the topic of this
    essay.

38. Delay, Florence. "Idées fausses et fausses idées." In La lette-
    ratura latino americana e la sua problematica europea. Elena
    Clementelli and Vittorio Minardi, eds. Rome: Istituto Italo-
    Latino Americano, 1978, pp. 75-86.

    In an effort to demonstrate how false ideas are projected from
    critics to readers, Florence Delay stresses the fact that Gabriel
    García Márquez is often compared to Faulkner for his invention of
    Macondo in many of his works.

39. Dessau, Adalbert. "El tema de la soledad en las novelas de
    Gabriel García Márquez." In El ensayo y la crítica literaria en
    Iberoamérica. Memoria del XIV Congreso Internacional de Literatura
    Iberoamericana, Universidad de Toronto, Toronto, Canadá, 24-28 de
    Agosto de 1969. Kurt L. Levy and Keith Ellis, eds. Toronto,
    Canada: University of Toronto, 1970, pp. 209-214.

    A comparison of the theme of loneliness in Cien años de soledad
    and in El coronel no tiene quien le escriba concluding that both
    are different solitudes.

40. Dessau, Adalbert. "Das Thema der Einsamkeit in Den Romanen von
    Gabriel García Márquez." In Geiträge zur Französischen Aufklärung
    und zur Spanischen Literatur. Berlin: Akademie-Verlag, 1971,
    pp. 517-522.

    Offers an analysis of the theme of loneliness in this comparison
    of Cien años de soledad with its fatalistic solitude of a whole
    people and the optimistic solitude of a single individual in
    El coronel no tiene quien le escriba.

41. Durán Luzio, Juan. "Cien años de soledad: quinientos años de
    historia hispanoamericana." In Creación y utopía: letras de his-
    panoamérica. San José, Costa Rica: Editorial de la Universidad
    Nacional, 1979, pp. 179-192.

    Views One Hundred Years of Solitude as a five hundred year history
    of the New World, mirroring the chronicle of the Buendía family,
    from their founding to their demise.

42. Equipo de Redacción de Seuil. "GGM: Al banquillo." In García
    Márquez habla de García Márquez, 33 reportajes. Alfonso Rentería
    Mantilla, ed. Bogotá: Rentería Editores, 1979, pp. 97-103.

    As vice-president of the Tribunal Russell, García Márquez de-
    nounces the persecution and repression in Latin America in this
    article taken from Seuil, Brussels, 1975.

43. Ezquerro, Milagros. "La fonction narratrice dans, El otoño del
    patriarca de Gabriel García Márquez." In Sujet et sujet parlant
    dans le texte (textes hispaniques). Toulouse: Université de
    Toulouse-Le Mirail, 1977, pp. 72-77.

    The exaggerated situations, characters and actions bound together
    in this prolonged metaphor is the underlying structure of El otoño
    del patriarca.

44. Ezquerro, Milagros. Théorie et fiction: Le nouveau roman hispano-
    americain. Montpellier, France: Centre d'Etudes et de Recherches
    Sociocritiques, Université Paul-Valéry, 1983, 255 p.

    Throughout this philosophical study of contemporary Latin American
    novelists and the use of the time and space elements, development
    of character and the narrative function employed by each, García
    Márquez's, El coronel no tiene quien le escriba and El otoño del
    patriarca are cited to illustrate various points.

45. Fiction et réalité: la littérature latino-americaine. Manuel Al-
    varez García, comp. Brussels: Editions de l'Université, 1983,
    127 p.

    A series of conferences given by Alejo Carpentier, Julio Cortázar
    and other Latin American authors. Contains the text of Velodia
    Teitelvoim's tribute to Gabriel García Márquez.

46. Flores, Angel. "Gabriel García Márquez." In Narrativa hispano-
    americana 1816-1981, historia y antología: v. 4; La generación de
    1940-1969. México: Siglo XXI Editores, 1982, pp. 429-448.

    This biographical summary of Gabriel García Márquez tracing the
    people and places which influenced his work from birth to 1975, is
    followed by a passage from The Autumn of the Patriarch, and
    includes an extensive bibliography.

47. Foster, David William. "The Double Inscription of the 'Narrataire'
    in Los funerales de la Mamá Grande." In Studies in the Contem-
    porary Spanish-American Short Story. Columbia, MO: University
    of Missouri Press, 1979, pp. 51-62.

    In Gabriel García Márquez's Los funerales de la Mamá Grande, one
    of the most salient features of the text is the "explicit pro-
    jection of an image of the reader and the bifurcation of that
    image into two conflicting and non-complementary modes."

48. Foster, David William. "García Márquez and the 'Ecriture' of Com-
    plicity: 'La prodigiosa tarde de Baltazar'." In Studies in the
    Contemporary Spanish-American Short Story. Columbia, MO: Univer-
    sity of Missouri Press, 1979, pp. 39-50.

    The relationship of the reader to the narrative in Gabriel García
    Márquez's "La prodigiosa tarde de Baltazar."

49. Franco, Ernesto. "Scrabble." In Gabriel García Márquez. Pier
    Luigi Crovetto, ed. Genoa: Tilgher, 1977, pp. 47-60.

    "Variant meanings of, and a play on the word 'casa' as illustrated
    in García Márquez's works, especially as employed in La hojarasca."

50. Franco, Jean. "La Prosa contemporánea ... Gabriel García Márquez."
    In Historia de la literatura hispanoamericana. Barcelona: Edito-
    rial Ariel, 1981, pp. 394-398.

    An overview of several of Gabriel García Márquez's major works and
    their recurring themes such as "the authenticity of an individual
    within an unjust world," and the isolation of Latin America as the
    result of the cycles of progress and neocolonialism.

51. Fuenmayor, Alfonso. "Gabito lee a Julio Mario." In Crónicas sobre
    el grupo de Barranquilla. Bogotá: Instituto Colombiano de Cultu-
    ra, 1981, pp. 169-180.

    Alfonso Fuenmayor speaks of the support given to Julio Mario Santo
    Domingo for his writing talent by the "Group of Barranquilla" and

tells of the episode when Gabriel García Márquez was asked to read
one of Santo Domingo's stories and to give his opinion.

52.  Gallo, Marta.  "El tiempo en Cien años de soledad, de Gabriel Gar-
     cía Márquez."  In Actas del Cuarto Congreso Internacional de His-
     panistas, v. 1.  Salamanca, August, 1971.  Salamanca: Asociación
     Internacional de Hispanistas, Consejo General de Castilla y León,
     Universidad de Salamanca, 1982, pp. 561-571.

     "The present work develops the following points: 1. The diversity
     of cyclic time and its many facets, 2. The finiteness of cyclic
     time, and 3. Abolition of the future."

53.  García Márquez, Eligio.  "Gabriel García Márquez:  el poder y la
     gloria."  In Son así:  reportaje a nueve escritores latinoamerica-
     nos.  Bogotá: Editorial La Oveja Negra, 1982, pp. 89-122.

     Section one examines García Márquez's own solitude, section two
     looks at his life in the public eye, and the final section
     discusses El otoño del patriarca.

54.  Gariano, Carmelo.  "Lo medieval en el cosmos mágico-fantástico de
     García Márquez."  In Otros mundos, otros fuegos:  fantasía y rea-
     lismo mágico en Iberoamérica.  Donald R. Yates, ed.  East Lansing,
     MI:  Michigan State University, Latin American Studies Center,
     1975, pp. 347-354.

     Medievalism in the "primitive, narrative, structure" of Cien años
     de soledad, is analyzed through "seven categories: time, space,
     existence, utopia, portent, prophecy, and eternity."

55.  Gerlach, John.  "The Logic of Wings:  García Márquez, Todorov, and
     the Endless Resources of Fantasy."  In Bridges to Fantasy.
     George E. Slusser, Eric S. Rabkin, and Robert Scholes, eds.
     Carbondale, IL:  Southern Illinois University Press, 1982, pp.
     121-129.

     Gerlach studies the correlation between fantasy and theme in Gar-
     cía Márquez's story, "A Very Old Man with Enormous Wings."

56.  Gilard, Jacques.  "Los suplementos literarios:  el caso de Colom-
     bia."  In Los escritores hispanoamericanos frente a sus críticos.
     Coloquio Internacional, Toulouse, 10-12 de marzo de 1982.
     Toulouse:  Université de Toulouse-Le Mirail, 1983, pp. 129-147.

     This article on the literary supplements to Colombian daily news-
     papers includes the contribution of García Márquez to the paper,
     El Espectador.

57.  Goić, Cedomil.  "Generación de 1957: I. Gabriel García Márquez."
     In Historia de la novela hispanoamericana.  Valparaíso, Chile:
     Ediciones Universitarias, 1972, pp. 245-260.

     Remarking that Cien años de soledad is an "encyclopedic concen-
     tration of the elements and persons of previous novels" Goić
     proceeds to analyze the work.

58.  Grossmann, Rudolf.  "Konventionelle und magische Zeit in dem Roman
     Cien años de soledad des Kolumbianers Gabriel García Márquez."
     In Romanica Europaea et Americana: Festschrift für Harri Meier, 8.
     Januar 1980.  Hans Dieter Bork, Artur Greive, and Dieter Woll, eds.
     Bonn: Bouvier Verlag Herbert Grundmann, 1980, pp. 217-224.

     The treatment of time in two radically different ways, conventional
     and magical, in One Hundred Years of Solitude as well as other
     elements of myth and reality in contemporary Latin American
     writers.

59.  Guibert, Rita.  "Algún día Estados Unidos hará su revolución so-
     cialista."  In García Márquez habla de García Márquez, 33 repor-
     tajes.  Alfonso Rentería Mantilla, ed.  Bogotá:  Rentería Editores,
     1979, pp. 75-78.

     First published in Guibert's book, 7 Voces (México:  Editorial
     Novaro, 1971), this interview gives us some revealing insights
     into García Márquez's personality.

60.  Guzman, Jorge.  "Cien años de soledad: en vez de dioses, el espa-
     ñol latinoamericano."  In Diferencias latinoamericanas.  Santiago,
     Chile:  Ediciones del Centro de Estudios Humanísticos, Universidad
     de Chile, 1984, pp. 79-127.

     Interprets Cien años de soledad in the light of the history of the
     narrative, indicating similarities and differences by comparing it
     to traditional world literature.  (Published also, in Acta Litera-
     ria, Concepción, Chile, no. 7, (1982), pp. 17-49).

61.  Hampares, Katherine J.  "North American Characters in the Spanish
     American Novel:  A Study of Satirical Mimicry."  In 1980 Pro-
     ceedings of the Rocky Mountain Council on Latin American Studies
     Conference, 28th Annual Meeting, April 3-5.  John J. Brasch and
     Susan R. Rouch, eds.  Santa Fe, NM: Rocky Mountain Council on La-
     tin American Studies, 198 , pp. 174-181.

     Discusses the presence of "foreigners in the Spanish American novel
     concluding with One Hundred Years of Solitude, and focusing on the
     banana company, and the destruction caused by the Americans.

62.  Holguín, Andrés.  "Gabriel García Márquez."  In Antología crítica
     de la poesía colombiana (1874-1974).  Tomo 2.  Bogotá:  Biblioteca
     del Centenario del Banco de Colombia, 1974, pp. 200-205.

     The works of Gabriel García Márquez have earned him a place within
     the generation of the Myth for his poetic vision of the world, his
     poetic use of language, and his fantastic talent to create myths.
     This brief article includes excerpts from his novel Cien años de
     soledad.

63.  Horányi, Mátyás, ed.  Actas del Simposio Internacional de Estudios
     Hispánicos, Budapest, 18-19 de agosto de 1976.  Budapest:  Akad.
     Kiadó, 1978, 523 p.

A collection of critical essays includes chapters which study various major works by Gabriel García Márquez.

64. "Into the Mainstream; (Colombia) Gabriel García Márquez." In An Outline History of Spanish American Literature. John E. Englekirk, chairman and editor. New York, NY: Irvington Publishers, 1980, pp. 247-249.

A biobibliography of García Márquez, together with a short list of bibliographical references.

65. Iribarren Borges, Ignacio. "El tiempo de García Márquez." In Escena y lenguaje. Caracas: Monte Avila Editores, 1981, pp. 161-163.

Power, time, and reality are compared in Cien años de soledad and El otoño del patriarca.

66. Janes, Regina. "García Márquez, Gabriel." In Contemporary Foreign Language Writers. James Vinson and Daniel Kirkpatrick, eds. New York, NY: St. Martin's Press, 1984, pp. 131-134.

A short biography, a bibliography of his major works, and a criticism of his magical realistic fiction.

67. Janik, Dieter. "Drei Zentralmotive der dichterischen Einbildungs- kraft des Erzählers Gabriel García Márquez: La casa - El Huracán - La muerte." In Homenaje a Gustav Siebenmann, tomo 1. Juan Manuel López de Abiada and Titus Heudenreich, eds. Munchen: Wilhelm Fink Verlag, 1983. Lateinamerika Studies, 13/1, pp. 369-387.

Home, storm, and death are three themes constantly present in the narrative art of García Márquez.

68. Jitrik, Noé. "La escritura y la muerte." In La memoria compartida. Xalapa, Veracruz, México: Universidad Veracruzana, 1982, pp. 215-254.

Centers on the various elements which make for unity in the works of García Márquez especially in Cien años de soledad.

69. Jitrik, Noé. "La perifrástica productiva en Cien años de soledad." In Melanges a la Mémoire d'André Joucla-Ruau, v. 2. Aix-en- Provence, Provence, France: Université de Provence, 1978, pp. 813-831.

From the numerous perspectives from which one can view this novel, Jitrik has chosen to analyze it from the idea which he terms, "productive paraphrasing."

70. Joset, Jacques. "Un sofocante aleteo de mariposas amarillas: lectura de un episodio de Cien años de soledad." In Actas del Simposio Internacional de Estudios Hispánicos, Budapest, 18-19 de agosto de 1976. Mátyás Horányi, ed. Budapest: Akadémiai Kiadó, 1978, pp. 421-427.

An allegorical and symbolic interpretation of the yellow butter- flies in Cien años de soledad.

71.  Joset, Jacques.  "'La mujer más bella del mundo:'  un narrema cons-
     tante en la obra de Gabriel García Márquez."  In Narradores latino-
     americanos 1929-1979.  Caracas:  Ediciones del Centro de Estudios
     Latinoamericanos Rómulo Gallegos, 1980, v. 2, pp. 207-218.

     The role of women in the novels and short stories of Gabriel Gar-
     cía Márquez.

72.  Jozef, Bella.  "Gabriel García Márquez."  In Historia da literatura
     hispano-americana.  Rio de Janeiro:  Francis Alves, 1982,
     pp. 310-313.

     Brief critical summaries of the major works of García Márquez.

73.  Kappeler, Susanne.  "Voices of Patriarchy: Gabriel García Márquez's
     One Hundred Years of Solitude."  In Teaching the Text.  Susanne
     Kappeler and Norman Bryson, eds.  London:  Routledge, 1983,
     pp. 148-163.

     Susanne Kappeler examines the epic features in Gabriel García
     Márquez's One Hundred Years of Solitude.

74.  Klein, Eduard.  "Ein sehr südamerikanisches Buch über Gabriel
     García Márquez."  In Schriftsteller über Weltliteratur:  Ansichten
     und Erfahrungen.  Berlin:  Aufbau-Verlag, 1979, pp. 72-77.

     Klein calls 100 Years of Solitude, which was published in German
     in 1975, "a very South American book."  It is full of the immensity
     of the tropics, of power, of fairy tales, of great robbers (the
     banana growers), and of cruelty, and hope.

75.  Kulin, Katalin.  "Mito y realidad en Cien años de soledad, de
     Gabriel García Márquez."  In Actas del Cuarto Congreso Internacional
     de Hispanistas, v. 2.  Salamanca, agosto, 1971.  Salamanca:
     Asociación Internacional de Hispanistas, Consejo General de Castilla
     y León, Universidad de Salamanca, 1982, pp. 91-100.

     Emphasizes the mythological aspects countered by reality in Cien
     años de soledad with a discussion of Faulknerian influences.

76.  Kulin, Katalin.  "El otoño del patriarca:  tema y mensaje."  In
     Actas del Simposio Internacional de Estudios Hispánicos, Budapest,
     18-19 de agosto de 1976.  Mátyás Horányi, ed.  Budapest:  Akadémiai
     Kiadó, 1978, pp. 429-433.

     The many symbols and representatins of power are explained and
     analyzed.

77.  Kulin, Katalin.  "Reasons and Characteristics of Faulkner's
     Influence on Juan Carlos Onetti, Juan Rulfo and Gabriel García
     Márquez."  In Proceedings of the 7th Congress of the International
     Literature Association, Milan V. Dimic and Juan Ferraté, eds.
     Toronto, Canada:  University of Toronto Press, The Canadian Review
     of Comparative Literature, v. 2, 1979, pp. 277-280.

In this comparative analysis of the techniques, language and
structure of the novels of three contemporary authors, Katalin
Kulin indicates various elements which demonstrate the Faulknerian
influence.

78.  Lamb, Ruth S.  "El mundo mítico en la nueva novela latinoamericana."
     In Actas del Cuarto Congreso Internacional de Hispanistas, v. 2.
     Salamanca, agosto, 1971.  Salamanca: Asociación Internacional de
     Hispanistas, Consejo General de Castilla y León, Universidad de
     Salamanca, 1982, pp. 101-108.

     Studies the contemporary Latin American novel, dwelling on time,
     mythical, historical, and cyclical in the structure of Cien años de
     soledad.

79.  Lecco, Margherita.  "Gabriel García Márquez e la definizione dell
     'eroe'."  In Gabriel García Márquez.  Pier Luigi Crovetto, ed.
     Genoa:  Tilgher, 1977, pp. 17-19.

     Fantasy as the underlying structure in García Márquez's works as
     compared to those of Arguedas, Asturias, and Carpentier.

80.  Levy, Kurt L.  "Planes of Reality in El otoño del patriarca."
     In Studies in Honor of Gerald E. Wade, Sylvia Bowman, Bruno M.
     Damiani, Janet W. Díaz, E. Michael Gerli, Everett Hesse, John E.
     Keller, Luis Leal, and Russell P. Sebold, eds. (Studia Humanitatis).
     Madrid:  Ediciones José Porrúa Turanzas, 1979, pp. 133-141.

     Views El otoño del patriarca from various planes of reality:
     philosophical, ideological, allegorical and verbal.

81.  Loveluck, Juan.  "The Magical World of Macondo."  In Dictionary of
     Literary Biography Yearbook:  1982.  Detroit, MI:  Gale Research
     Co., 1983, pp. 7-10.

     In this critique of the major works of García Márquez, Loveluck
     illustrates how in creating Macondo, García Márquez fulfilled his
     dreams, "his obsession to create a geographical and universal
     metaphor of the world."

82.  MacAdam, Alfred J.  "Gabriel García Márquez: A commodius vicus of
     recirculation."  In Modern Latin American Narratives:  The Dream
     of Reason.  Chicago, IL:  University of Chicago, 1977, pp. 78-87.

     Refers to García Márquez as "ironic magus" whose "action, is to
     appropriate myths, the plot of romance, and things as they are in
     a Spanish American country and bend them to show his personal
     vision."

83.  McMurray, George R.  "The Spanish American Short Story from Borges
     to the Present."  In The Latin American Short Story:  A Critical
     History.  Margaret Sayers Peden, ed.  Boston, MA:  Twayne
     Publishers, pp. 115-118 and pp. 130-131.

     Short critical studies of "Baltazar's Marvelous Afternoon" and
     "The Handsomest Drowned Man in the World."

84. Mañú Iragui, Jesús. "Aspectos del tiempo en Cien años de soledad." In Estructuralismo en cuatro tiempos; ensayos críticos sobre Darío, Cortázar, Fuentes y García Márquez. Caracas: Equinoccio, Ediciones de la Universidad Simón Bolívar, 1974, pp. 128-155.

    Elucidates the use of various time elements as they are reflected in the persons of Cien años de soledad.

85. Marcos, Juan Manuel. De García Márquez al postboom. Madrid: Orígenes, 1985, 184 p.

    García Márquez's influence on contemporary narrative writing.

86. Martínez Ruiz, Juan. "Hacia una distinción gramatical de las voces en la novela iberoamericana  a propósito de El otoño del patriarca de Gabriel García Márquez." In Estudios ofrecidos a Emilio Alarcos Llorach: Con motivo de sus XXV años de docencia en la Universidad de Oviedo, vol. 4. Oviedo: Servicio de Publicaciones, Universidad de Oviedo, 1979, pp. 495-508.

    Martínez Ruiz analyzes grammatically the use of dialogue in Iberoamerican Literature pointing to examples in García Márquez's El otoño del patriarca.

87. Maturo, Graciela. "Notas sobre literatura hispanoamericana: Fantasía y realismo en la literature." In La literatura hispanoamericana: de la utopía al paraíso. Buenos Aires: Fernando García Cambeiro, 1983, pp. 187-192.

    In her discussion of fantasy and reality in literature, Maturo mentions Gabriel García Márquez's works as examples of surrealism in Latin American literature, which differs from that of European writers.

88. Mauro, Walter. "Dal flaubertismo di Vargas Llosa al monólogo interiore di García Márquez." In La letteratura latino americana e la sua problematica europea, Elena Clementilli and Vittorio Minardi, eds. Rome: Istituto Italo-Latino Americano, 1978, pp. 127-135.

    The characters of Vargas Llosa's La casa verde and Conversaciones en la catedral are compared with those of García Márquez's in El otoño del patriarca.

89. Mejía Duque, Jaime. "Mito y realidad en Gabriel García Márquez." In Literatura y realidad, 2nd ed. Medellín, Colombia: Editorial La Oveja Negra, 1976, pp. 249-274.

    With a perception of time of chronological order, García Márquez introduces works of magical realism. Mejía Duque draws an analogy between García Márquez's "elevation" through One Hundred Years of Solitude to that of one of his own characters, Remedios la Bella. This article was published also in Mejía Duque's later work, Ensayos, Manizales, Colombia: Biblioteca de Escritores Caldenses, 1980, pp. 39-79. An earlier version of this article, under the same title, was published in Bogotá: Editorial La Oveja Negra, 1970.

90. Mejía Duque, Jaime. <u>Narrativa y neocoloniaje an América Latina</u>. Bogotá: Ediciones Tercer Mundo, 1977, 89 p.

Gleanings from <u>Cien años de soledad</u> are presented throughout this exploration of the neoclassic in Latin American fiction as examples which focus upon the many factors which contributed to the rise of a new literary movement.

91. Mejía Duque, Jaime. <u>Narrativa y neocolonialismo en América Latina</u>. Bogotá: Editorial La Oveja Negra, 1972, 94 p.

92. Mejía Duque, Jaime. <u>Narrativa y neocoloniaje en América Latina</u>. Buenos Aires: Ediciones de Crisis, 1974, 145 p.

Various references are made to García Márquez and his <u>Cien años de soledad</u> throughout this discussion of the Latin American novel, especially in the section entitled, "El 'boom' de la narrativa latinoamericana," in this expanded edition of the 1972 work.

93. Mejía Duque, Jaime. "<u>El otoño del patriarca</u> o la crisis de la desmesura." In <u>Literatura y realidad.</u> Medellín, Colombia: Editorial La Oveja Negra, 1976, pp. 275-301.

Mejía Duque states that the success of <u>El otoño del patriarca</u> rides on the fame of García Márquez's earlier novels. This article was published in Mejía Duque's later work, <u>Ensayos</u>, Manizales, Colombia: Biblioteca de Escritores Caldenses, 1980, pp. 81-118, as well as in <u>Cosmos</u> (n.d.), no. 16, pp. 3-15.

94. Mendoza, Plinio Apuleyo. <u>La llama y el hielo</u>. Barcelona: Planeta, 1984, 305 p.

Revolving around five actual persons, prominent among them, Gabriel García Márquez this autobiographical novel takes us through the author's experiences of Latin American politics, insurrections, revolutions, dropping names from the world of art, music, and literature along the way.

95. Mendoza, Plinio Apuleyo. "Retrato de García Márquez (fragmento)." In <u>Novísimos narradores hispanoamericanos en Marcha 1964-1980</u>. Angel Rama, ed. México: Marcha Editores, 1981, pp. 127-139.

A short personality sketch of García Márquez.

96. Mercado Cardona, Homero. <u>Macondo: una realidad llamada ficción</u>. Barranquilla, Colombia: Ediciones Universidad del Atlántico, 1971.

A descriptive analysis and study of the fictional city of Macondo created by Gabriel García Márquez throughout his works, and how it demonstrates the author's success in expressing myth as reality.

97. Millán J. Antonio and Covadonga López. "Lectura de <u>Cien años de soledad</u>, de Gabriel García Márquez." In <u>Cómo se analiza una novela</u>. Madrid: Editorial Alhambra, 1984, pp. 260-286.

Textual dynamics, theme, and repetition are explored on <u>Cien años de soledad</u>.

98.  Millington, M. I.  "Actant and character in García Márquez: _La_
     _increíble y triste historia ..._"  In Essays in Honour of R.B. Tate.
     Nottingham, England:  Nottingham University, 1984, pp. 32-39.

     The effectiveness of the understated cruelty in this short novel.

99.  Morón, Guillermo.  "Noticia sobre Gabriel García Márquez."
     In Escritores latinoamericanos contemporáneos.  Caracas:  Equi-
     noccio, Editorial de la Universidad Simón Bolívar, 1979, pp.
     309-326.

     Includes descriptive comments on the writing style, the works, and
     significant factors in Gabriel García Márquez's life.

100. Morrison, R. W.  "Literature in an Age of Specialization."  In
     Brave New Universe:  Testing the Values of Science in Society.
     Tom Henighan, ed.  Ottawa:  The Tecumseh Press, 1980, pp.
     112-124.

     The manner in which García Márquez portrays life in Macondo is
     used as an example of literature in an age of science and tech-
     nology which successfully depicts the whole range of the human
     experience.

101. Nazareth, Peter.  "Time in the Third World:  A Fictional Explora-
     tion."  In Awakened Conscience:  Studies in Commonwealth Litera-
     ture.  C. D. Narasimhaiah, ed.  New Delhi:  Sterling Publishers,
     1978, pp. 195-205.

     Time and reality as elements in the literature of the Third World,
     are illustrated by examples from One Hundred Years of Solitude
     and The Autumn of the Patriarch.

102. Neumeister, Sebastian.  "Die Auflösung der Phantastik:  Episte-
     mologische Anmerkungen zu Gabriel García Márquez' Roman Cien años
     de soledad."  In Phantastik in Literatur und Kunst.  Christian W.
     Thomsen and Jens Malte Fischer, eds.  Darmstadt, West Germany:
     Wissenschaftliche Buchgesellschaft, 1980, pp. 369-384.

     The use of fantasy or the fantastic, the "real maravilloso" as it
     occurs in Latin American literature and especially in Cien años
     de soledad.

103. Oberhelman, Harley D.  "Faulknerian Techniques in Gabriel García
     Márquez's Portrait of a Dictator."  In Ibero-American Letters in
     a Comparative Perspective.  Wolodymyr T. Zyla and Wendell M.
     Aycock, eds.  Lubbock, TX:  Texas Tech Press, 1978, pp. 171-181.

     The exterior relationships between Gabriel García Márquez and
     William Faulkner are discussed in this article focusing primarily
     on El otoño del patriarca as compared to several works of Faulkner.

104. Ondaatje, Michael.  "García Márquez and the Bus to Aracataca."
     In Figures in a Ground:  Canadian Essays on Modern Literature.
     Diane Bessai and David Jackel, eds.  Saskatoon, Canada:  Western
     Producer Prairie Books, 1978, pp. 19-31.

Commentaries on persons and incidents in One Hundred Years of
Solitude on a visit to Aracataca, the Macondo of the novel.

105. Ortega, Julio. "The Autumn of the Patriarch: Text and Culture."
In Poetics of Change: The New Spanish-American Narrative.
Austin, TX: University of Texas, 1984, pp. 96-119.

Ortega illustrates the debate between Latin American history and
culture through an analysis of The Autumn of the Patriarch "from
the perspective of a semiological approach to the literary text
within the sphere of culture."

106. Ortega, Julio. "Gabriel García Márquez: Cien años de soledad."
In La contemplación y la fiesta: ensayos sobre la nueva novela
latino-americana. Lima, Perú: Editorial Universitaria, 1968.
reimpr. Caracas: Monte Avila, 1969, pp. 44-58.

A survey of modern Latinamerican novels includes studies of works
by Juan Rulfo, Julio Cortázar, Gabriel García Márquez, Mario Vargas Llosa, Carlos Fuentes, Guillermo Cabrera Infante, and Néstor
Sánchez.

107. Ortega, Julio. "One Hundred Years of Solitude." In Poetics of
Change: The New Spanish-American Narrative. Austin, TX: University of Texas, 1984, pp. 85-95.

Examines "the relationships between different worlds and times"
which "form the central structure of the novel."

108. Ortega, José. "Siete variaciones del juego realidad-imaginación
en La increíble y triste historia de la cándida Eréndira y de su
abuela desalmada, de García Márquez." In Letras hispanoamericanas
de nuestro tiempo. Madrid: José Porrúa Turanzas, 1976, pp.
109-126.

The seven stories studied in this collection embody seven ways of
confronting reality. There is a fusion or confusion of the real
with the imaginary as the author sets out to prove in his treatment of each of these stories.

109. Osuña, Yolanda. "El incesto como línea accional en Cien años de
soledad." In Tres ensayos de análisis literario. Mérida: Grá-
ficos Universitarios, 1980, pp. 13-54.

An essay which treats the concept of incest and its medieval
repercussions.

110. Peden, Margaret Sayers. "The Arduous Journey." In The Teller and
the Tale: Aspects of the Short Story. 13th Symposium of Comparative Literature, 1980. Wendell M. Aynock, ed. Lubbock, TX:
Texas Tech Press, 1982, pp. 63-85.

The author selects a few prominent Latin American short story
writers including García Márquez and evaluates the successes,
failures, and difficulties in rendering their works into English.

66    Secondary Sources

111. Peel, Roger M. "Los cuentos de García Márquez." In El cuento hispanoamericano ante la crítica, directed by and with a prologue by Enrique Pupo-Walker. Madrid: Editorial Castalia, 1973, pp. 235-248.

A synopsis of the collections of short stories by Gabriel García Márquez comparing them to those of other authors, and demonstrating how his stories are an extension of his larger works, including the legend of Macondo, and other major themes.

112. Pérez Blanco, Lucrecio. "García Márquez, Gabriel." In Diccionario de Autores de las Literaturas Hispánicas. Emilio Palacios Fernández, ed. Madrid: Ediciones Orgaz, 1980, p. 126.

Brief biobibliographical sketch of García Márquez.

113. Pfeiffer, Erna. Literärische Strucktur und Realitatsbezug in kolumbianischen Violencia-Roman. Frankfurt/Bern: Peter Lang Verlag, 1984, 332 p.

Citations from La mala hora, introduced in various places throughout this work testify to the violence in Latin American literature.

114. Pritchett, Victor Sawdon. "Gabriel García Márquez: The Myth Makers." In The Myth Makers: Literary Essays. New York: Random House, 1979, pp. 164-173.

In Leaf Storm, García Márquez "sows the seed of a concern with memory, myth, and the nature of time which bursts into lovely blossom in his later book, One Hundred Years of Solitude."

115. Rama, Angel. La novela en América Latina: Panoramas (1920-1980). Bogotá: Procultura, 1982, 519 p.

This critical approach to contemporary Latin American fiction makes frequent mention of García Márquez and his relation to the "Grupo Barranquilla," his influence on "el boom" and includes an essay on El otoño del patriarca.

116. Rentería Mantilla, Alfonso. "En Moscú con el traductor de 'Cien años...' ¿Porqué mutilaron en Rusia, Cien años de soledad?" In García Márquez habla de García Márquez, 33 reportajes. Alfonso Rentería Mantilla, ed. Bogotá: Rentería Editores, 1979, pp. 127-131.

Valeri Stolbov explains his Russian translation of Cien años de soledad in this interview in Moscow in 1979.

117. Rentería Mantilla, Alfonso. "El viacrucis de un lector." In García Márquez habla de García Márquez, 33 reportajes. Alfonso Rentería Mantilla, ed. Bogotá: Rentería Editores, 1979, pp. 7-10.

Comments on El otoño del patriarca and García Márquez's political beliefs.

118.  Riley, Carol. Contemporary Literary Criticism. Detroit, MI:
      Gale Research Company, v. 3, 1975, pp. 179-183.

      A collection of criticisms of García Márquez and his works
      published in various periodicals, 1972-1973.

119.  Rogachevsky, Jorge R.  "Individualism and Imperialism in Cien
      años de soledad and El otoño del patriarca."  In Politics and the
      Novel in Latin America:  García Márquez and Asturias.  Amherst,
      NY:  State University of New York at Buffalo, 1980, pp. 1-24.

      Political philosophy as a tool of literature, as demonstrated in
      the imperialism of Cien años de soledad and the anarchism of
      of El otoño del patriarca.

120.  Roy, Joaquín, comp.  "GGM."  In Narrativa y crítica de nuestra
      America. Madrid: Editorial Castalia, 1978, pp. 317-350.

      A study and critique of Gabriel García Márquez's Cien años de
      soledad including background material on the novelist and the
      novel itself.

121.  Ruffinelli, Jorge.  "Gabriel García Márquez y el Grupo de Barran-
      quilla."  In Crítica en marcha. México: Premia, 1982, pp. 46-54.

      The evolution of the "Barranquilla Group" in Colombia, a collab-
      oration of writers once isolated politically, economically, and
      culturally, who influenced García Márquez's formative years.
      Also published in Bogotá: Eco, v. 28, no. 168, (October, 1974),
      pp. 606-617.

122.  Ruffinelli, Jorge.  "Un periodista llamado Gabriel García
      Márquez."  In Crítica en marcha. México: Premia, 1982, pp. 59-70.

      Cuando era feliz e indocumentado, an account of García Márquez's
      career as a journalist, gives context to his later works through
      the creation of themes for his narratives.

123.  Sacoto, Antonio.  Cinco novelas claves de la literatura hispano-
      americana.  Segunda parte.  Cuenca, Ecuador:  Casa de la Cultura
      Ecuatoriana "Benjamín Carrión," 1984, pp. 117-186.

      Three essays entitled respectively, "Cien años de soledad y la
      euforia narrativa," "Lo mítico," and "Tiempo," deal with such
      subjects as magical realism, mythological and biblical allusions,
      and time, mythical, historical and cyclical in García Márquez's
      classic work.

124.  Samper Pizano, Daniel.  "Gabriel García Márquez se dedicará a la
      música y compondrá un concierto para triángulo y orquesta."  In
      García Márquez habla de García Márquez, 33 reportajes.  Alfonso
      Rentería Mantilla, ed.  Bogotá:  Rentería Editores, 1979, pp.
      21-27.

      Biographical accounts and comments on the novels published in
      Bogotá: El Tiempo, (December, 1968).

125. Sarrailh, Michele. "Apuntes sobre el mito dariano en El otoño del patriarca." In Actas del Simposio Internacional de Estudios Hispánicos, Budapest, 18-19 de agosto de 1976. Mátyás Horányi, ed. Budapest: Akadémiai Kiadó, 1978, pp. 435-458.

   After establishing the prevalence of Rubén Darío in the modernist movement the author details attempts by García Márquez to distance himself from the darian influence in El otoño del patriarca.

126. Schoo, Ernesto. "La gran novela de América." In García Márquez habla de García Márquez, 33 reportajes. Alfonso Rentería Mantilla, ed. Bogotá: Rentería Editores, 1979, pp. 11-16.

   A series of biographical vignettes.

127. Schrader, Ludwig. "Aspekte der 'soledad' in der Lateinamerikanischen Literatur des 20. Jahrhunderts." In Homenaje a Gustav Siebenmann, tomo 2. José Manuel López de Abiada and Titus Heydeneich, eds. München: Wilhelm Fink Ferlag, 1983, Lateinamerika Studien, 13/2, pp. 811-830.

   Solitude as theme and its treatment by several Latin American writers in their works.

128. Schwartz, Ronald. "García Márquez, a New Colombian Cosmology." In Nomads, Exiles and Emigrés: The Rebirth of the Latin American Narrative, 1960-1980. Metuchen, NJ: Scarecrow, 1980, pp. 34-45.

   A chronological presentation with a brief criticism of Gabriel García Márquez's work.

129. Schwartz, Kessel. "Sexism in the Spanish American Novel, 1965-1975." In Studies on Twentieth-Century Spanish and Spanish American Literature. Lanham, MD: University Press of America, 1983, pp. 341-352.

   Although García Márquez is mentioned in various places throughout the book, this chapter dwells on his treatment of women and sex in his novels.

130. Scott, Nina M. "Vital Space in the House of Buendía." In Studies in 20th Century Literature. Manhattan, KS: Studies in Twentieth Century Literature, v. 8, no. 2, (1984), p. 265.

   Symbolism of the space theme as portrayed in Buendía's house.

131. Serra, Edelweis. "Narrema e isotopía en Cien años de soledad de Gabriel García Márquez." In El mensaje literario: estudios estilísticos y semiológicos. Rosario: Universidad Nacional de Rosario, 1979, pp. 119-141.

   Cien años de soledad can be read not only as a narrative of myth and fiction, but also as the history of Latin America, and that of contemporary humanity.

132. Shaw, Donald L. "El boom I." In Nueva narrativa hispanoamericana," Madrid: Ediciones Cátedra, 1981, pp. 108-118.

Although there are many references to Gabriel García Márquez
throughout the book, a chapter dedicated to the four most important authors of the "boom" period in Latin America: Julio Cortázar, Carlos Fuentes, Mario Vargas Llosa, and Gabriel García Márquez, examines the novels and short stories by Gabriel García
Márquez, with much emphasis given to an analysis of Cien años de
soledad.

133.  Siemens, William L.  "The Antichrist-Figure in Three Latin American Novels."  In The Power of Myth in Literature and Film.
Victor Carrabino, ed.  Tallahassee:  University Presses of Florida, 1980, pp. 113-121.

Colonel Aureliano Buendía from One Hundred Years of Solitude is
an example of an antichrist-figure in Latin American literature.

134.  Siemens, William L.  "Gabriel García Márquez, Cien años de soledad."  In Worlds Reborn:  The Hero in the Modern Spanish American Novel.  Morgantown, WV:  West Virginia University Press,
1984, pp. 109-137.

An intensive treatment of the roles of the hero-figures whose
solitude prevents them from achieving the renewal of their heroic
attributes.

135.  Sims, Robert L.  "Claude Simon and Gabriel García Márquez:  The
Conflicts between histoire-Histoire and historia-Historia."  In
Papers on Romance Literary Relations.  Cyrus Decoster, ed.
Evanston, IL:  Northwestern University, 1975, pp. 1-22.

"Although the novels of Claude Simon and Gabriel García Márquez
differ in many respects, they both explore the question of
history.  Each has his individual concept of history as con-
trasted with chronological history."

136.  Sturrock, John and Frank MacShane.  "Gabriel García Márquez ana-
lizado por The New York Times."  In García Márquez habla de García Márquez, 33 reportajes.  Alfonso Rentería Mantilla, ed.
Bogotá:  Rentería Editores, 1979, pp. 185-188.

This section is actually a republication of separate articles by
Sturrock and McShane, each appearing under their individual
bylines in the literary supplement to The New York Times, (July,
1978).

137.  Tauzin, Jacqueline.  "Un exemple de réalisme magique:  'Blacaman
le Bon, marchand de miracles'."  In Frontieres du conte.
Francois Marotin, ed.  Paris:  Editions du Centre national de la
recherche scientifique, 1982, pp. 137-144.

Jacqueline Tauzin chooses to analyze Gabriel García Márquez's
short story "Blacamán el bueno, vendedor de milagros," as an
example of such literary works which deal with "magic realism,"
a movement in literature which refers to the transposition of
reality.

138. Tobin, Patricia Drechsel. "'Everything is Known': Gabriel García Márquez, One Hundred Years of Solitude." In Time and the Novel. Princeton, NJ: Princeton University Press, 1978, pp. 164-191.

Departure from reality in the use of the "novelistic imagination" characterizes One Hundred Years of Solitude.

139. Todorov, Tzvetan. "Macondo a Paris (résumé)." In Littérature latinoaméricaine d'aujourd'hui: Colloque de Cerisy. Jacques Leenhardt, ed. Paris: Union Générale d'Editions, 1980, pp. 316-320.

Todorov comments on Gabriel García Márquez's Cien años de soledad, and speaks of the novel in a follow-up interview with Jacques Leenhardt.

140. Tolentino, Marianne de. "El otoño del patriarca de Gabriel García Márquez." In El dictador en la novela latinoamericana. Santo Domingo: Voluntariado de las Casas Reales, 1980, pp. 43-58.

In his elderly protagonist, García Márquez has created a prototype of the dictator with absolute power.

141. Tovar, Antonio. "G. García Márquez." In Novela española e hispanoamericana. Madrid: Alfaguara, 1972, pp. 225-230.

The narrative technique which captivates and absorbs the reader is present in these stories which constitute Los funerales de la Mamá Grande.

142. Trozos selectos de la literatura andiana. Bogotá: Secretaría Ejecutiva Permanente del Convenio "Andrés Bello," 1983, 465 p.

Contains a selection from Cien años de soledad on pages 125-163.

143. Vargas, Raúl. "El nuevo Quijote de la literatura española." In García Márquez habla de García Márquez, 33 reportajes. Alfonso Rentería Mantilla, ed. Bogotá: Rentería Editores, 1979, pp. 17-19.

This interview originally appeared in Pueblo, a Madrid evening newspaper, in 1968.

144. Vargas Llosa, Mario. "Réalité totale, roman total." Extract from García Márquez, historia de un deicidio. Albert Bensoussan, tr. Paris: Silex, no. 11, (March, 1979), p. 61. (Special issue: "Gabriel García Márquez - Amerique Latine").

For Mario Vargas Llosa, Cien años de soledad is a "total novel."

145. Vélez Serrano, Luis. "Función del espacio en El otoño del patriarca." In Homenaje a Gustav Siebenmann, tomo 2. José Manuel López de Abiada and Titus Heydenreich, eds. München: Vilhelm Fink Verlag, 1983, Lateinamerika Studien, 13/2, pp. 1017-1028.

Three elements, the syntactic, the semantic, and the pragmatic, and their interaction within the circular structure of The Autumn of the Patriarch.

146. Volkening, Ernesto. "Los cuentos de Gabriel García Márquez o el trópico desembrujado." In Isabel viendo llover en Macondo. Buenos Aires: Editorial Estuario, 1967, pp. 27-43.

Literary style, narrative expertise, character and plot development in the stories of García Márquez are topics for this literary criticism.

147. Walters, Marian. "García Márquez, Gabriel José." In Contemporary Authors. Ann Evory and Linda Metzger, eds. Detroit, MI: Gale Research, 1983, v. 10, pp. 190-192.

An introduction to the literature of Gabriel García Márquez includes listings of his writings, awards, and honors; facts on his career and personal life; critical notes on his major works; and a list of bibliographical sources.

148. Williams, Raymond Leslie. Una década de la novela colombiana: la experiencia de los setenta. Bogotá: Editores-Colombia, 1980, 228 p.

This study of Colombian novels of the 70's includes an analytical commentary on the major work of each year. Chapter seven discusses Gabriel García Márquez's El otoño del patriarca, pp. 109-131.

149. Williams, Raymond Leslie. La novela colombiana contemporánea. Bogotá: Plaza y Janes, 1976, 93 p.

In this history of the contemporary Colombian novel, several authors are treated in length, including García Márquez, pp. 76-87.

150. Zalamea, Jorge. "La actual literatura de Colombia." In Panorama de la actual literatura latinoamericana. Centro de Investigaciones Literarias de Cuba, ed. Caracas: Editorial Fundamentos, 1971, pp. 88-97.

Commenting upon contemporary Colombian literature, in light of the political violence and injustice prevalent in this country, Zalamea places García Márquez at the forefront of the authors who have contributed to the flourishing narrative literature.

151. Zuluaga, Conrado. Novelas del dictador, dictadores de novela. Bogotá: Carlos Valencia Editores, 1977, 125 p.

A collection of essays and articles about novels which describe dictators and their relation to the people of Latin America. Three novels most frequently cited are: El recurso del método; Yo, el Supremo; and El otoño del patriarca.

# Critical Articles

1.  Aaron, M. Audrey. "Remedios, la bella, and 'The Man in the Green Velvet Suit'." Madison, WI: Chasqui, v. 9, nos. 2-3, (February-May, 1980), pp. 39-43.

    Essays to illustrate from one narrated incident in Cien años de soledad the common sense and feminine independence of Remedios, la bella.

2.  Aguirre, C., Alberto. "El otoño del patriarca: la anatomía del poder en América Latina." Medellín, Colombia: Cuadro, v. 20, (July-September, 1975), pp. 97-108.

    After commenting on the literary style, the humor, the contrast between the real and the imaginary in El otoño del patriarca, Aguirre judges it to be a master work.

3.  Alfaro, Gustavo A. Cien años de soledad y la violencia en Colombia. Bogotá: Correo de los Andes, v. 2, no. 1, (January, 1980), pp. 78-81.

    Violence throughout the history of Colombia is depicted in Gabriel García Márquez's works, here his ultimate message to his readers is clear. "It is imperative to stop the vicious circle of vengeance, of the foolish hatred among members of national families."

4.  Alfaro, Gustavo. "La nave del imperialismo en El otoño del patriarca." Bogotá: Eco, v. 32, no. 195, (January, 1978), pp. 325-334.

    Maintains that The Autumn of the Patriarch features two tyrants: the dictator himself and the Yankee imperialists.

5.  Alstrum, James J. "Los arquetipos en La increíble y triste historia de la cándida Eréndira y de su abuela desalmada de Gabriel García Márquez." Seattle, WA: Proceedings of the Pacific Northwest Conference on Foreign Languages, v. 29, no. 1, (1968), pp. 140-142.

The author argues that <u>La increíble y triste historia de la cándida Eréndira y de su abuela desalmada</u> should receive more attention and therefore literary criticism because of its rich use of mythical archetypes.

6. Alvarez-Borland, Isabel. "From Mystery to Parody:  (Re) Readings of García Márquez's <u>Crónica de una muerte anunciada</u>." Washington, D.C.: Symposium, v. 38, no. 4, (Winter, 1984-1985), pp. 278-286.

In this novel of temporal ambiguity, "Ironic parady, the main impediment to a comfortable reading of this slippery text, can thus be seen on two levels:  as a parody of the institutions and morals at the textual level, and as a parody of the classic detective structure at the artistic level."

7. Amate Blanco, Juan José. "La novela del dictador en hispanoamérica." Madrid:  <u>Cuadernos Hispanoamericanos</u>, no. 370, (April, 1981), pp. 85-102.

Absolute power and its political overtones in many Hispanic American novels is evident in Gabriel García Márquez's <u>El otoño de patriarca</u> among others.

8. Amoretti, María H. "<u>Un día de estos</u>'de García Márquez:  un desafortunado proceso de venganza." San José, Costa Rica: <u>Literatura Latinoamericana</u>, v. 7, no. 1, (1983), pp. 35-42.

The theme of revenge in this short story will be elaborated upon in future works.

9. Annino, Antonio. "Centroamerica, Macondo in estinzione." Firenze, Italy:  <u>Il Ponte-Revista Mensile di Politica e Letteratura</u>, v. 35, nos. 203, (1980), pp. 133-136.

Political violence is alive and present in Central America, Chile, Argentina. . . as it was in Macondo of <u>One Hundred Years of Solitude</u>.

10. Aponte, Barbara B. "El rito de la iniciación en el cuento hispano-americano." Philadelphia, PA:  <u>Hispanic Review</u>, v. 51, no. 2, (1983), pp. 129-146.

Aponte studies the theme of the rite of initiation of a child into the world, and among various examples, sights Gabriel García Márquez's <u>La increíble y triste historia de la Cándida Eréndira y de su abuela desalmada</u>.

11. Arciniegas, Germán. "Aracataca es Macondo." Bogotá:  <u>Correo de los Andes</u>, no. 17, (September-October, 1982), pp. 33-48.

In this article, complete with illustrations, we are made aware that the spirit of Aracataca is rampant in the Macondo of García Marquez's works.

12. Arenas Saavedra, Anita. "El tiempo:  engranaje de una generación ausente en <u>Cien años de soledad</u>." Maracaibo, Venezuela:  <u>Revista de Literatura Hispanoamericana</u>, v. 3, (July-December, 1972), pp. 67-79.

Emphasizes the time elements in Gabriel García Márquez's <u>Cien años</u> <u>de soledad</u>, as each meshes with previous events and integrates aspects of our society such as solitude, anguish, pain, and death.

13. Ariza González, Julio. "La espera en <u>El coronel no tiene quien le</u> <u>escriba</u>." San Juan, Puerto Rico: <u>Sin Nombre</u>, v. 4, no. 3, (1973-1974), pp. 3-29.

The themes of hopefulness, expectation and hunger and their social implications in <u>El coronel no tiene quien le escriba</u>.

14. Aronne-Amestoy, Lida Beatriz. "Fantasía y compromiso en un cuento de Gabriel García Márquez." Washington, D.C.: <u>Symposium</u>. v. 38, no. 4, (Winter, 1984-1985), pp. 287-297.

Diagrammatically explains the relationship between fantasy and compromise in García Márquez's short story, "The Handsomest Drowned Man in the World."

15. Aronne-Amestoy, Lida Beatriz. "<u>La mala hora</u> de los géneros: Gabriel García Márquez y la génesis de la nueva novela." Providence, RI: <u>INTI, Revista de Literatura Hispánica</u> , nos. 16-17, (Autumn, 1982 - Spring, 1983), pp. 27-36.

<u>La mala hora</u> has set the pattern for the detective-type narratives which seems to form the basis for García Márquez's later fiction.

16. Arrigoitia, Luis de. "Tres cuentos de Gabriel García Márquez: 'Monólogo de Isabel viendo llover en Macondo' (1955), 'La siesta del martes' (1957), 'Los funerales de la Mamá Grande' (1959)." Río Piedras, Puerto Rico: <u>Revista de Estudios Hispánicos</u>, v. 6, (1979), pp. 132-152.

Three of García Márquez's earlier stories best reveal the evolution of the novelist's narrative art.

17. Asiain, Aurelio. "<u>Crónica de una muerte anunciada</u>." México: <u>Vuelta</u>, v. 5, no. 58, (September, 1981), pp. 32-33.

Aurelio Asiain writes about Gabriel García Márquez' recent novel <u>Crónica de una muerte anunciada</u> and discovers in it, elements from the author's previous works.

18. Athas, Daphne. "'The Beauty' in <u>The Sheltered Life</u>: A Moral Concept." Durham, NC: <u>The South Atlantic Quarterly</u>, v. 80, no. 2, (Spring, 1981), pp. 206-221.

In her analysis of "The Beauty" in <u>The Sheltered Life</u>, Athas cites "Remedios the beauty" of <u>One Hundred Years of Solitude</u> and states that ". . .The infusion of the South Americans in the current fiction scene admits the idea of the beauty free of Puritan morality."

19. Avila, Pablo Luis. "Una lectura de <u>Crónica de una muerte anunciada</u>." La Habana: <u>Casa de las Américas</u>, v. 24, no. 140, (September-October, 1983), pp. 28-40.

Many of the characteristics of García Márquez's earlier works appear in this recent novel, Chronicle of a Death Foretold.

20. Barilli, Renato. "La narrativa di García Márquez tra Centro e Nord-America." Bologna, Italy: Il Mulino, v. 32, no. 3, (May-June, 1983) 1983), pp. 492-498.

Short summaries of García Márquez's latest works: El otoño del patriarca, and Crónica de una muerte anunciada with indications of similarities in other contemporary novels.

21. Barros-Lémez, Alvaro. "Beyond the Prismatic Mirror: One Hundred Years of Solitude and Serial Fiction." Las Cruces, NM: Studies in Latin American Popular Culture, v. 3, (1984), pp. 105-114.

An analysis of serial fiction technique used by García Márquez in writing One Hundred Years of Solitude.

22. Barsy, Kalman. "Retroactividad del discurso en El otoño del patriarca." San Juan, Puerto Rico: Sin Nombre, v. 13, no. 1, (October-December, 1982), pp. 36-49.

In the text of The Autumn of the Patriarch the "absolute narrator" is used throughout.

23. Basalisco, Lucio. "Da Cien años de soledad a El otoño del patriarca: Aspetti e temi dell'arte narativa di Gabriel García Márquez." Naples, Italy: Annali, v. 21, no. 2, (July, 1979), pp. 425-438.

An in-depth exploration of One Hundred Years of Solitude and The Autumn of the Patriarch in the context of García Márquez's use of theme and narrative art.

24. Bell-Villada, Gene H. "García Márquez and the Novel." Pittsburgh, PA: Latin American Literary Review, Special Issue Gabriel García Márquez, v. 13, no. 25, (January-June, 1985), pp. 15-23.

"García Márquez has done the most so far to save the novel from itself, to rescue it from the narrow impasses and byways into which it had taken refuge and set up shop."

25. Bell-Villada, Gene H. "Names and Narrative Pattern in One Hundred Years of Solitude." Pittsburgh, PA: Latin American Literary Review, v. 9, no. 18, (Spring-Summer, 1981), pp. 37-46.

Bell-Villada stresses the pattern of names used in Gabriel García Márquez's Cien años de soledad.

26. Bellini, Giuseppe. "El coronel no tiene quien le escriba o i riti della miseria." Milan: Studi di letteratura Ispano-Americana, no. 15-16, (1983), pp. 203-215.

Poverty, anxiety, and survival are themes present in El coronel no tiene quien le escriba.

27.  Benedetti, Mario.  "Il ricorso del supremo patriarca."  Firenze,
     Italy:  Il Ponte-Revista Mensile di Politica e Letteratura, v. 35,
     no. 1, (1979), pp. 107-124.

     Similarities and differences in the novels of three Latin American
     authors:  El recurso del método of Alejo Carpentier, Yo, el Supremo
     of Augusto Roa Bastos, and El otoño del patriarca of Gabriel García
     Márquez.

28.  Benedetti, Mario.  "Tres dictadores:  El recurso del método, Yo, el
     Supremo y El otoño del patriarca."  Cali, Colombia:  El Pueblo;
     Semanario Cultural, (November 6, 1976), pp. 1-5.

     Contrasts the narrative structure of three novels dealing with
     dictators.

29.  Benítez Rojo, Antonio e Hilda O. Benítez.  "Eréndira liberada:  la
     subversión del mito del macho occidental."  Madrid:  Revista Ibero-
     americana, nos. 128-129, (July-December, 1984), pp. 1057-1075.

     A study of the mythical subversion quality, and the meaningful
     allegories of Colombia as seen in Gabriel García Márquez's La
     increíble y triste historia de la cándida Eréndira y de su abuela
     desalmada.

30.  Bensoussan, Albert.  "Macondo, l'espace de l'imaginaire."  Paris:
     Silex, no. 11, (March, 1979), pp. 62-64.  (Special issue:  "Gabriel
     García Márquez - Amerique Latine.")

     The effects of "Macondo" on the dreams, thoughts, and imagination
     of García Márquez as seen through his works.

31.  Bensoussan, Albert.  "Le premier roman de García Márquez."  Paris:
     La Quinzaine Litteraire, no. 390, (March 16-31, 1983), pp. 10-11.

     The Macondo of La hojarasca is featured in many of García Márquez's
     later novels.

32.  Berroa, Rei.  "Sobre Muerte constante más all del amor."  Stillwater,
     OK:  Discurso Literatio:  Revista de Temas Hispánicos, v. 1, no. 1,
     (Fall, 1983), pp. 5-15.

     Interprets the symbolism and significance of the title of this story
     with its lyrical qualities in relation to the characters.

33.  Bjornson, Richard.  "Cognitive Mapping and the Understanding of
     Literature."  Madison, WI:  Sub-stance, A Review of Theory and
     Literary Criticism, no. 30, (1981), pp. 51-62.

     Uses the development of themes in Gabriel García Márquez's works as
     an example to explain how a writer's conception of the events,
     experiences or perceptions are translated into plans for the comple-
     tion of his works.

34.  Bollettino, Vicenzo.  "El concepto trágico en La hojarasca de Gabriel
     Carcía Márquez."  Chapel Hill, NC:  Hispano, 53, (January, 1975)
     pp. 49-50.

For Bollettino, La hojarasca and El coronel no tiene quién le escriba
are the two works of García Márquez that most closely deal with the
concept of tragedy.

35.  Borgeson, Paul W.  "Los pobres ángeles de Gabriel García Márquez y
     Joaquín Pasos."  Johnson City, TN:  Crítica Hispánica, v. 3, no. 2,
     (1981), pp. 111-123.

     A comparison between El ángel pobre by Joaquín Pasos and "Un hombre
     muy viejo con unas alas enormes" by Gabriel García Márquez.

36.  Boschetto, Sandra María.  "El texto matriarcal y la fatalidad del
     cronista en Crónica de una muerte anunciada."  Corvallis, OR:
     Selecta, Journal of the Pacific Northwest Council on Foreign
     Languages, v. 5, (1984), pp. 103-109.

     A discussion of the roles of men and women in Chronicle of a Death
     Foretold, concluding that if this novel is "a denunciation of
     'machismo' it will be, also" a denunciation "of the matriarchal
     society that permitted it."

37.  Botond, Annaliese.  "Gabriel García Márquez:  Cien años de soledad
     o la historia como jeroglífico."  Tübingen:  Iberoromania, no. 5,
     (1980), pp. 112-131.

     Botond equates the popularity of García Márquez's Cien años de
     soledad with the extreme identification by most Latin Americans with
     characters and situations in the novel.

38.  Brushwood, John S.  "Reality and Imagination in the Novels of García
     Márquez."  Pittsburgh, PA:  Latin American Literary Review, Special
     Issue Gabriel García Márquez, v. 13, no. 25, (January-June, 1985),
     pp. 9-14.

     In commenting about the differences which separate Latin American
     countries from others, Brushwood explains that García Márquez has
     searched out the "essential quality of difference" and that "his
     greatest gift to us is that, in making reality larger than life, he
     makes it big enough for us to see."

39.  Brushwood, John S.  "José Félix Fuenmayor y el regionalismo de García
     Márquez."  Xalapa, Veracruz:  Texto crítico, v. 3, no. 7, (May-August,
     1977), pp. 110-115.

     García Márquez follows tradition in his coastal writings illustrated
     by his mimetic regionalism and imagination.

40.  Buchanan, Rhonda Lee.  "The Cycle of Rage and Order in García
     Márquez's, El otoño del patriarca."  Louisville, KY:  Perspectives
     in Contemporary Literature, v. 10, (1984), pp. 75-85.

     Demonstrates by use of several concepts from Jungian psychology the
     relationship between rage and order in García Márquez's novel about
     an aging general.

41.  Burgos, Fernando.  "Hacia el centro de la imaginación:  La increíble
     y triste historia de la cándida Eréndira y de su abuela desalmada."
     Providence, RI:  INTI, Revista de Literatura Hispánica, nos. 16-17,
     (Autumn, 1982 - Spring, 1983), pp. 71-81.

     Employs the space theme as a basis for the study of the title story
     as well as the other stories in this collection.

42.  Caballero Calderón, Enrique.  "El Nuevo Mundo de García Márquez."
     Bogotá:  Correo de los Andes, no. 17, (September-October, 1982),
     pp. 31-32.

     Considers El otoño del patriarca to be the most meritorious of all
     of García Márquez's novels and most representative of the Latin
     American spirit.

43.  Caicedo Jurado, Cecilia.  "Lo fantástico en Cien años de soledad."
     Pasto, Colombia:  Meridiano, v. 3, no. 5, (December, 1969), pp. 78-
     84.

     Analyzes the fantastic and the mythic elements which make One Hundred
     Years of Solitude unsurpassable.

44.  Caicedo Jurado, Cecilia.  "El machismo en la narrativa de Gabriel
     García Márquez."  Pasto, Colombia:  Meridiano, año 6, no. 17,
     (October, 1973), pp. 66-76.

     A study of machoism as it occurs in García Márquez's five works:
     One Hundred Years of Solitude, La mala hora, Los funerales de la
     Mamá Grande, "En este pueblo no hay ladrones" and "Muerte constante
     más allá del amor."

45.  Calasans Rodrígues, Selma.  "Cien años de soledad y las crónicas de
     la conquista."  México:  Revista de la Universidad de México, v. 38,
     nueva época, no. 23, (March, 1983), pp. 13-16.

     The interweaving of history, imaginary and real in Cien años de
     soledad.

46.  Campanella, Hortensia.  "De la literatura a la literatura."  Madrid:
     Cuadernos Hispanoamericanos, no. 383, (May, 1982), pp. 423-428.

     García Márquez's novel, Crónica de una muerte anunciada encompasses
     a narrative with a tense and significant prose, and a demonstration
     of verb tenses which function along these narrative lines.

47.  Campos, Jorge.  "Una novela y un cuento de Gabriel García Márquez."
     Madrid:  Insula, v. 36, no. 420, (November, 1981), p. 11.

     Recurring themes in various works of García Márquez.

48.  Campra, Rosalba.  "Las técnicas del sentido en los cuentos de Gabriel
     García Márquez."  Madrid:  Revista Iberoamericana, nos. 128-129,
     (July-December, 1984), pp. 937-955.

The works of Gabriel García Márquez are viewed as a self-sufficient and self-generated system where each additional story relates to those already written.

49. Canfield, Martha L. "El otoño del patriarca." Bogotá: Eco, v. 41/6, no. 252, (October, 1982), pp. 567-602.

Examines the polyvalence of the language in the style of The Autumn of the Patriarch.

50. Canfield, Martha L. "El patriarca de García Márquez:  padre, poeta y tirano." Madrid: Revista Iberoamericana, no. 128-129, (July-December, 1984), pp. 1017-1056.

A perceptive, thorough analysis of the elements which combine to make of El otoño del patriarca, a most successful novel.

51. Carballo, Emmanuel. "Gabriel García Márquez, ayer y hoy." México: Diálogos, v. 19, no. 2 (110), (March-April, 1983), pp. 12-19.

A brief history of and commentary on the writing style, technique, and characteristics apparent in García Márquez's works.

52. Cardozo Morón, Luis Alberto.  "El mundo ancestral del 'patriarca'." Bogotá: El Espectador; Magazine Dominical, (May 25, 1975), pp. 7-8.

Parallels are drawn between that in The Autumn of the Patriarch and the numerous dictatorships during the tempestuous history of Latin America.

53. Castillo, Rafael C. "Recommended:  Gabriel García Márquez." Urbana, IL:  The English Journal; The High School Organ of the National Council of Teachers of English, v. 73, no. 6, (October, 1984), pp. 77-78.

These summaries of García Márquez's works are presented in order to familiarize the English speaking reader with this Latin American novelist and encourage their use in the classroom.

54. Castro-Klarén, Sara. "The space of solitude in Cien años de soledad." Washington, D.C.:  Wilson Center, Working Paper, no. 18, 1978, 26 p.

Focuses on solitude as it occurs in physical space, social space, and inner space.

55. Chase, Victoria F.  "(De) mitificación en Los funerales de la Mamá Grande." México: Texto Crítico, año VI, nos. 16-17, (January-June, 1980), pp. 233-247.

García Márquez declares that he wrote Los funerales de la Mamá Grande as a reaction against Latin American rhetoric and maintained that this story was a burlesque of the "official rhetoric of Colombian periodical literature."

56. Christen, María. "Cien años de maravilla." Veracruz, México: La Palabra y el Hombre, no. 44, (October-December, 1982), pp. 29-44.

Mythological and historical allusions abound in this extensive discussion of Macondo.

57. Clark, John R. "'Pangs Without Birth, and Fruitless Industry': Redundancy in Satire." East Lansing, MI: Centennial Review, v. 26, no. 3, (Summer, 1982), pp. 239-255.

In discussing the redundancy in the satire of various literary works, Clark mentions Gabriel García Márquez's story Big Mama's Funeral.

58. Clark, Stella T. "Cien años de soledad: A Texte de plaisir, a Texte de jouissance." Clear Creek, IN: The American Hispanist, v. 4, nos. 30-31, (November-Decmeber, 1978), pp. 17-19.

Cien años de soledad is a "novel that reads easily but at the same time suggests a complex and mysterious reality."

59. Cobo Borda, Juan Gustavo. "La cocina literaria de Gabriel García Márquez." Bogotá: Eco, v. 43/1, no. 259, (May, 1983), pp. 1-13.

The works of García Márquez reveal his tremendous literary background, for in the reading of his novels one can ascertain influences of Kafka, Faulkner, Hemingway, and others.

60. Cobo Borda, Juan Gustavo. "Crónica de una muerte anunciada: la nueva novela de Gabriel García Márquez." Bogotá: Eco, v. 38/6, no. 234, (April, 1981), pp. 605-612.

García Márquez's literary background is reflected in his novels as is evident in Crónica de una muerte anunciada.

61. Concha, Jaime. "Entre Kafka y el Evangelio." Pamplona, Spain: Araucaria de Chile, no. 21, (1983), pp. 105-109.

Some parallels drawn from Kafka's, The Castle and García Márquez's, Chronicle of a Death Foretold, with their endless digressions.

62. Cope, Jackson I. "Generic Geographies." Chicago, IL: Genre, v. 14, no. 1, (Spring, 1981), pp. 151-161.

Geography, fictitious and real in the works of Borges, Lowery, Malcolm and García Márquez.

63. Copeland, John G. "Pedro Prado, Gabriel García Márquez y el hombre con alas." San Juan, Puerto Rico: Revista/Review Interamericana, v. 6, (1976), pp. 321-334.

A comparative study of the works of Pedro Prado and Gabriel García Márquez depicting the authors' struggle to give artistic and esthetic expression to human existence.

64. Cornejo Polar, Antonio. "El indigenismo y las literaturas heterogéneas: su doble estatuto socio-cultural." Lima: Revista de Crítica Literaria Latinoamericana, año 4, nos. 7-8, (1978), pp. 7-21.

Examines One Hundred Years of Solitude together with other Latin American works in the context of their socio-cultural impact.

65. Corvalán, Octavio. "Faulkner y García Márquez:  una aproximación."
    Buenos Aires:  Sur, no. 349, (July-December, 1981), pp. 71-38.

    Compares and contrasts works by William Faulkner and Gabriel García
    Márquez, focusing on stylistic, narrative, and thematic elements in
    their works.

66. Costantini, Alessandro.  "L'ideologia formale ne El otoño del
    patriarca."  Milano:  Studi de Letteratura Ispano-Americana, v. 9,
    (1979), pp. 63-69.

    In this unique model of works dealing with dictatorships, that of
    El otoño del patriarca emerges as a global structure that voids all
    spatio-temporal dimensions.

67. Crovetto, Pier Luigi.  "L'ultimo Gabriel García Márquez, tra fato e
    'detection'."  Torino, Italy:  Quaderni Ibero-Americani, ciclo 15,
    v. 7, nos. 55-56, (December, 1982 - June-December, 1983), pp. 381-
    386.

    An in-depth analysis of Chronicle of a Death Foretold, with a
    detailed commentary on excerpts from the book, and a comparison of
    it with other works by García Márquez, principally The Autumn of the
    Patriarch, and No One Writes to the Colonel.

68. Cuervo Hewitt, Julia.  "La dictadura en 'El otoño del patriarca'."
    México:  Plural, Segunda época, v. 14-11, no. 167, (August, 1985),
    pp. 16-20.

    A comparative study of the historical and literary images and myths
    used in El otoño del patriarca while describing the patriarch with
    the images of truth and reality as opposed to fable.

69. Cuervo Hewitt, Julia.  "Nuestra América en El otoño del patriarca:
    ecos populares y textos históricos en la invención de América."
    Stillwater, OK:  Discursos Literarios, v. 1, no. 2, (Spring, 1983),
    pp. 143-158.

    Commenting on Martí's Nuestra América, Cuervo Hewitt discusses among
    other works, The Autumn of the Patriarch stressing the analogy
    between the discovery of America and the invention of its history.

70. Cullhed, Anders.  "Myt och fiktion:  Om nyöversatt litteratur fran
    Latinamerika."  Stockholm:  BLM-Bonniers Litterara Magasin, v. 53,
    no. 1, (February, 1984), pp. 54-58.

    Allusions to various mythological persons and entities as they appear
    in One Hundred Years of Solitude.

71. Da Vita Di Febo, Giuliana:  "La componente mágica en Cien años de
    soledad di Gabriel García Márquez."  Catania, Italy:  Siculorum
    Gymnasium, v. 23, nos. 1-2, (1970), pp. 102-128.

    "Magical realism" as the main ingredient in One Hundred Years of
    Solitude.

72.  Dauster, Frank.  "Ambiguity and Indeterminacy in Leafstorm."
     Pittsburgh, PA:  Latin American Literary Review, Special Issue
     Gabriel García Márquez, v. 13, no. 25, (January-June, 1985), pp. 24-
     28.

     The formal characteristics of Leafstorm, according to Dauster, are:
     "1. extreme use of the 'dato escondido', the withholding of informa-
     tion so that the novel is like a mystery which can never be solved;
     2. the deliberate use of intertextuality; and, 3. the radical
     perspectivism of technique, complicated by an extensive use of
     chronological leaps."

73.  Delgado Senior, Igor.  "Realidad y fantasía en tres cuentos de
     Gabriel García Márquez."  Caracas:  Letras, v. 32-33, (1976), pp.
     113-141.

     The relationship between reality and fantasy with reference to
     history is discussed in Gabriel García Márquez's three short stories:
     "Un señor muy viejo con unas alas muy enormes" (1968), "El ahogado
     más hermoso del mundo" (1968), and "Blacamán el bueno vendedor de
     milagros" (1968).

74.  Dellepiane, Angela B.  "Tres novelas de la dictadura:  El recurso
     del método, El otoño del patriarca, Yo, el Supremo."  Toulouse,
     France:  Cahiers du Monde Hispanique et Luso-Brésilien Caravelle,
     no. 29, (1977), pp. 65-87.

     Three modern Latin American novels about dictators including Gabriel
     García Márquez's El otoño del patriarca are considered in the light
     of the differences between the recent dictator novels and those from
     past Latin American novelists.

75.  Dessau, Adalbert.  "Zur weltliterarischen Bedingtheit, Geltung und
     Wirkung der Literaturen Asiens, Afrikas und Lateinamerikas."  E.
     Berlin, German Democratic Republic:  Weimarer Beiträge, v. 9, (1980),
     pp. 5-32.

     For Dessau, García Márquez and other similar writers represent the
     democratic and socialist tendency in Latin American literature and
     enrich these tendencies in world literature.

76.  Dill, Hans-Otto.  "'Hundert Jahre Einsamkeit' oder die Faszination
     preolischer Subjektivität."  E. Berlin, German Democratic Republic:
     Weimarer Beiträge, 30, (1984), pp. 1335-1352.

     One Hundred Years of Solitude with its collection of numerous
     characters spanning generations, interwoven with events from history,
     mythology and the Bible can truly be called the Latin American epic.

77.  Dilmore, Gene.  "One Hundred Years of Solitude:  some translation
     corrections."  Philadelphia, PA:  Journal of Modern Literature, no.
     11, (July, 1984), pp. 311-314.

     A word clarification list for the Gregory Rabassa translation of
     Cien años de soledad.

78.  Earle, Peter G. "Utopía, Universópolis, Macondo." Philadelphia,
     PA: Hispanic Review, v. 50, no. 2, (Spring, 1982), pp. 143-157.

     The mythical village of Macondo becomes an "inverted Utopia" one of
     "continuing paradox of harmony and struggle."

79.  Ekstrom, Margaret V. "Los Márquez en Macondo: Surnames for a Family
     of Characters." Brockport, NY: Literary Onomastics Studies, v. 7,
     (1980), pp. 235-255.

     Examines the etymology of the surnames of characters in Cien años de
     soledad.

80.  Eminescu, Roxana. "Los emperadores de la lluvia: Dumitru Radu
     Pepescu y Gabriel García Márquez." Bucharest: Synthesis: Bulletin
     du Comité National de Littérature Comparée de la République
     Socialiste de Roumanie, v. 7, (1980), pp. 115-122.

     Details the mythical significance of rain in One Hundred Years of
     Solitude.

81.  Epshtein, M. and E. Yukina. "The World and Man - On the Artistic
     Possibilities of Contemporary Literature." Moscow: Novyi Mir, no.
     4, (1981), pp. 236-248.

     Written in the Russian language, this is a comparison of García
     Márquez and Cortázar in their use of "fantastic reality."

82.  Epstein, Joseph. "How Good is Gabriel García Marquez?" New York,
     NY: Commentary, v. 75, no. 5, (May, 1983), pp. 59-65.

     Commenting briefly on each of García Márquez's works, the author
     answers his question. . . "he is, in the strict sense of the word,
     marvelous. The pity is that he is not better."

83.  Eyzaguirre, Luis Bernardo. "La espera en El coronel no tiene quien
     le escriba." San Juan, Puerto Rico: Sin Nombre, v. 4, no. 3,
     (1973-1974), pp. 13-29.

     Eternal hope and patience as a test of man's character is the theme
     of El coronel no tiene quien le escriba.

84.  Ezquerro, Milagros. "El otoño del patriarca: Mythe du pouvoir et
     pouvoir du mythe." Montpellier, France: Imprévue, special volume
     1977, pp. 3-35.

     Uses diagrams to illustrate the time-space concepts in this exhaus-
     tive study of El otoño del patriarca.

85.  Farías, Víctor. "La dialéctica de la solidaridad." Pamplona,
     Spain: Araucaria de Chile, no. 21, (1983), pp. 110-121.

     Through analyzing García Márquez's thoughts and statements about
     life, writing, politics, etc., gleaned from his works and interviews,
     Farias determines what García Márquez perceived as solitude and
     solidarity.

86.  Faris, Wendy B.  "Icy solitude: Magic and Violence in Macondo and
     San Lorenzo."  Pittsburgh, PA:  Latin American Literary Review,
     Special Issue Gabriel García Márquez, v. 13, no. 25, (January–June,
     19u5), pp. 44–54.

     In comparing García Márquez's, One Hundred Years of Solitude and
     Vonnegut's, Cat's Cradle, Faris considers the ice images present in
     each as symbols for "a solitude which contributes to man's final
     eclipse at the end of both texts."

87.  Fernández, Jesse.  "La ética del trabajo y la acumulación de la
     riqueza en Cien años de soledad."  Gaithersburg, MD:  Hispamérica:
     Revista de Literatura, año 13, no. 37, (April, 1984), pp. 73–79.

     An analysis of the socio–economic aspects of Gabriel García Marquez's
     Cien años de soledad, including the distribution of wealth, the
     accumulation of capital, and how these factors create the social
     classes and relationships, and the entire social organism.

88.  Fernández, Margarita.  "El personaje feminino en Cien años de
     soledad.  Bogotá:  Revista del Convenio Andrés Bello, (August, 1981),
     pp. 59–81.

     García Márquez's depiction of women, especially in Cien años de
     soledad as ideal positive types, primarily concerned with the
     struggle to maintain the stability of the family.

89.  Ferrari, Américo.  "L'épique et le lyrique dans Cent ans de
     solitude."  Paris:  Silex, no. 11, (March, 1979), pp. 72–76.
     (Special issue:  "Gabriel García Márquez - Amerique Latine.")

     An analysis of the lyrical poetry in García Márquez's One Hundred
     Years of Solitude as a privileged element, an "extra," which makes
     the novel come to life.

90.  Fogel, Jean-François.  "La longue marche vers Macondo."  Paris:
     Magazine Littéraire, no. 178, (November, 1981), pp. 28–30.

     Macondo, according to García Márquez symbolizes the "state of spirit."

91.  Foster, David William.  "García Márquez and the 'Escritura' of
     Complicity: 'La Prodigiosa Tarde bel Baltazar'."  Newberry, SC:
     Studies in Short Fiction, v. 16, no. 1, (Winter, 1979), pp. 33–40.

     Shows how Gabriel García Márquez's "Escritura" technique establishes
     a close bond between the author and reader, making the reader
     essentially an accomplice.

92.  Foster, David William:  "Latin American Documentary Narrative."
     New York, N.Y.:  PMLA-Publications of the Modern Language Associa-
     tion of America, v. 99, no. 1, (January, 1984), pp. 41–55.

     Among works dealing with the documentary narrative, García Márquez's
     Relato de un náufrago figures prominently as an "appropriate example
     of Latin American documentary narrative."

93. Fouques, Bernard. "La autopsia del poder según Roa Bastos, Carpentier y García Máruqez." México: Cuadernos Americanos, v. 222, no. 1, (January-February, 1979), pp. 83-111.

The anatomy of power in the Latin American novel, focusing in great detail on The Autumn of the Patriarch.

94. Forgues, Roland. "Le printemps des peuples." Paris: Silex, no. 11, (March, 1979), pp. 125-131. (Special issue: "Gabriel García Márquez - Amerique Latine.")

Points out the political implications of the works of Gabriel García Márquez.

95. Fowles, John. "The Falklands, and a Death Foretold." Athens, GA: Georgia Review, v. 36, no. 4, (Winter, 1982), pp. 721-728.

The Falklands War is compared to the tragic death of Santiago Nasar in Gabriel García Márquez's Chronicle of a Death Foretold in that both disasters were the results of a traditional way of thinking.

96. Franco, Jean. "From Modernization to Resistance: Latin American Literature 1959-1976." Riverside, CA: Latin American Perspectives, v. 5, no. 1, issue 16, (Winter, 1978), pp. 77-97.

An analysis of Latin American literature after the "boom" of the sixties. The author reviews attempts of modern Latin American writers to bridge the gulf between the old "realism" and the new politicized "avant-garde."

97. Franco, Jean. "Les limites de l'imagination libérale: A propos de Nostromo de Joseph Conrad et de Cent ans de solitude." Paris: Silex, no. 11, (March, 1979), pp. 65-71. (Special issue: "Gabriel García Márquez - Amerique Latine.")

The article is a study of liberalism and imagination in Nostromo by Joseph Conrad and One Hundred Years of Solitude.

98. Fraser, Howard M. "The Cockfight Motif in Spanish American Literature." Washington, DC: Revista Interamericana de Bibliogra Bibliografía-Inter-American Review of Bibliography, v. 31, no. 4, (1981), pp. 514-523.

Among various works cited, García Márquez's El coronel no tiene quien le escriba, illustrates the evolution of the cockfight from a cultural symbol of bravery and heroism to its present representation of violence and gruesome death.

99. Fuenmayor, Emerita. "Histoire d'un paradoxe." Paris: Silex, no. 11, (March, 1979), pp. 94-99. (Special issue: "Gabriel García Márquez - Amerique Latine.")

Highlights the prominent themes, language usage, and narrative style in Cien años de soledad.

100.  "Gabriel García Márquez - Amerique Latine." Paris:  Silex, no. 11,
      (March, 1979), 141 p.  (Special issue:  "Gabriel García Márquez -
      Amerique Latine.")

      This sisue of Silex is dedicated to aspects of the works of Gabriel
      García Márquez, his formative years and additional notes on some
      artists who are different but whose contrasting style provides a
      counterpoint for the benefit of an expanded audience.

101.  Gallo, Marta .  "El futuro perfecto de Macondo."  New York, NY:
      Revista Hispánica Moderna, v. 38, no. 3, (1974-1975), pp. 115-135.

      The confusion of time and the use of tense is explained with
      diagrams, in this study of Cien años de soledad.

102.  Galvada, Brigitte.  "Macondo, de urbe condita."  Paris:  Silex,
      no. 11, (March, 1979), pp. 77-83.  (Special issue:  "Gabriel García
      Márquez - Ameríque Latine.")

      Galvada describes the city of Macondo in One Hundred Years of
      Solitude, remarking on its dynamic archetypes, themes, literary
      reminiscences, and cultures.

103.  Garavito P., Edgar León.  "La parábola del cometa cautivo."
      Bogotá:  Boletín Cultural y Bibliográfico, v. 16, (April, 1979),
      pp. 166-180.

      Examines power and its control over the main character in The
      Autumn of the Patriarch.

104.  García, Emilio.  "La noción existencial del absurdo en Cien años de
      soledad."  Providence, RI:  INTI, Revista de Literatura Hispánica,
      Providence College, nos. 16-17, (Autumn, 1982 - Winter, 1983),
      pp. 125-134.

      García considers Cien años de soledad to be an expression of the
      absurdity of the human condition, the existencial anguish of man.

105.  Gariano, Carmelo.  "Humorismo erótico en Cien años de soledad."
      Stanford, CA:  Vortice, v. 1, (1974), pp. 17-21.

      Points out the various instances of erotic humor which are employed
      to "translate the energy, dogmatism and narcissism of humanity into
      compression, repression and intensification."

106.  Gariano, Carmelo.  "El humor numérico en Cien años de soledad."
      Worcester, MA:  Hispania, v. 61, no. 3, (September, 1978), pp. 443-
      450.

      Numeric humor as comic relief is present in the exaggerated
      eroticism, equivocation of persons and places, drunks and victims
      of other excesses, abusers of power, even in the "macabre realiza-
      tion of individual and collective death."

107. Gateau, Jean-Charles. "Deux épopées de la décrépitude." Paris: Silex, no. 11, (March, 1979), pp. 119-224. (Special issue: "Gabriel García Márquez - Amerique Latine.")

Comparative study of El otoño del patriarca and Roa Bastos' Yo, el Supremo.

108. Ghose, Zulfikar. "Lila of the Butterflies and Her Chronicler." Pittsburgh, PA: Latin American Literary Review, Special Issue Gabriel García Márquez, v. 13, no. 25, (January-June, 1985), pp. 151-157.

Impressions while on a visit to Quito, which are reminiscent of scenes in García Márquez's books.

109. Gilard, Jacques. "García Márquez: Quatre textes de jeunesse." Paris: Silex, no. 11, (March, 1979), pp. 19-20. (Special issue: "Gabriel García Márquez - Amerique Latine.")

Gilard examines four texts of García Márquez's earlier works: "Le Singe," "Le cauchemar," "Notes," and "Un homme arrive sous la pluie."

110. Gilard, Jacques. "Pistes temporelle de García Márquez." Paris: Silex, no. 11, (March, 1979), pp. 37-44. (Special issue: "Gabriel García Márquez - Amerique Latine.")

Gilard analyzes the development of the ideology, symbols, and style of García Márquez in his works.

111. González, Eduardo. "Beware of Gift-Bearing Tales: Reading García Márquez According to Mauss." Baltimore, MD: MLN (Modern Language Notes), v. 97, no. 2, (March, 1982), pp. 347-364.

The ideals and symbolism of Gabriel García Márquez in his short story "La prodigiosa tarde de Baltazar" parallel those of Marcel Mauss.

112. González, Pablo. "Cien años de soledad: Una interpretación colombiana." University Center, MI: Alèthea, no. 13, (Spring-Summer, 1984), pp. 27-37. (Special issue: Gabriel García Márquez: The Man and the Magic of His Writings.)

Elaborates on the first paragraph of Cien años de soledad which resembles a fairy tale, but is in reality, the day-to-day life in any small town of the Caribbean region or the interior of Colombia.

English version: "One Hundred Years of Solitude: A Colombian Approach." pp. 69-78.

113. González Echeverría, Roberto. "Cien años de soledad: The Novel as Myth and Archive." Baltimore, MD: MLN (Modern Language Notes), v. 99, no. 2, (March, 1984), pp. 358-380.

While Latin American history in Cien años de soledad "may be mired in myth, it cannot be turned to myth" since "its newness makes it impervious to timelessness, circularity, or any such delusion."

114.  Gonzalez Echeverría, Roberto.  "The Dictatorship of Rhetoric/The
      Rhetoric of Dictatorship:  Carpentier, García Márquez and Roa
      Bastos."  Chapel Hill, NC:  Latin American Research Review, v. 15,
      no. 3, (1930), pp. 205-228.

      Prominent in the literature of Latin America is the dictator theme
      which is evidenced in the in-depth study of Carpentier's El recurso
      del método, García Márquez's El otoño de patriarca, and Roa Bastos'
      Yo, el Supremo.

115.  González Echevarría, Roberto.  "With Borges in Macondo."   Ithaca,
      NY:  Diacritics, v. 2, (Spring, 1972), no. 1, pp. 57-60.

      Quoting from various works by Borges, the author of this essay
      intimates that "García Márquez had taken a stroll through one or
      several corridors of that Borgesian library that define's writing's
      universe and chosen . . . elements for the invention of Macondo."

116.  Gordon, Ambrose.  "The Seaport Beyond Macondo."  Pittsburgh, PA:
      Latin American Literary Review, Special Issue Gabriel García
      Márquez, v. 13, no. 25, (January-June, 1985), pp. 79-89.

      In The Autumn of the Patriarch and Chronicle of a Death Foretold,
      Gordon concentrates not on the magic present in the works but on
      the ability of García Márquez to hold the attention of his readers
      by his magical skill with narrative technique, to present unreality
      as reality.

117.  Gutiérrez Mouat, Ricardo.  "Carnivalización de la literatura en
      Casa de campo y Cien años de soledad."  San Juan, Puerto Rico:
      Sin Nombre, v. 13, no. 1, (October-December, 1982), pp. 50-64.

      Compares One Hundred Years of Solitude, by Gabriel García Márquez
      with Casa de Campo, by Donoso, examining their common language
      which is that of the carnival.

118.  Hampares, Katherine J.  "Gabriel García Márquez:  a Synthesis on
      Inter-American Reality."  Providence, RI:  INTI, Revista de
      Literatura Hispánica, nos. 16-17, (Autumn, 1982 - Winter, 1983),
      pp. 111-123.

      García Márquez "has accomplished the aesthetic and political
      culmination of social protest literature by endowing it with a
      universal dimension that gives every reader a new view of the human
      condition."

119.  Hancock, Joel.  "Gabriel García Márquez's Eréndira and the Brothers
      Grimm."  Lincoln, NE:  Studies in Twentieth Century Literature,
      v. 3, no. 1, (Fall, 1978), pp. 43-52.

      The narrative structed in Eréndira resembles those of the fairy
      tale genre.

120.  Harrison, Keith.  "'One Hundred Years of Solitude':  the Only
      Mystery."  Frederickton, New Brunswick, Canada:  The International
      Fiction Review, v. 12, no. 1, (Winter, 1985), pp. 47-49.

Analyzes the character of Rebeca and her murder of José Arcadio in
One Hundred Years of Solitude.

121.    Hart, Stephen.  "Magical Realism in Gabriel García Márquez's Cien
        años de soledad."  Providence, RI:  INTI, Revista de Literature
        Hispánica, nos. 16-17, (Autumn, 1982-Spring, 1983), pp. 37-52.

        Hart discusses Cien años de soledad, in the light of an established
        fact that "the world of magical realism is at once natural and
        supernatural."

122.    Hedeen, Paul M.  "Gabriel García Márquez's Dialectic of Solitude."
        Dallas, TX:  Southwest Review, v. 68, no. 4, (Autumn, 1983), pp.
        350-364.

        An examination of the various nuances of solitude as portrayed in
        One Hundred Years of Solitude.

123.    Heise, Hans-Jürgen.  "Episch mündiges Lateinamerika:  Zu Büchern
        von Gabriel García Márquez und Mario Vargas Llosa."  Frankfurt:
        Die Neue Rundschau, S. Fischer Verlag, v. 85, no. 4, (1974), pp.
        684-689.

        The two most important modern representatives of Latin American
        prose, according to Heise, are Gabriel García Márquez and Mario
        Vargas Llosa.

124.    Hinderer, Drew E.  "The Short Stories of García Márquez."  Univer-
        sity Center, MI:  Alèthea, no. 13, (Spring-Summer, 1984), pp. 79-86.
        (Special issue:  Gabriel García Márquez:  The Man and the Magic of
        His Writings.)

        Three collections of short stories in English:  Innocent Eréndira,
        No One Writes to the Colonel, and Leaf Storm and Other Stories,
        all, translated by Gregory Rabassa, are evaluated in this article.

125.    Holt, Candace K.  "El otoño del patriarca:  una perspectiva
        hegeliana."  Stillwater, OK:  Discursos Literarios:  Revista de
        Temas Hispánicos, v. 1, no. 1, (Fall, 1983), pp. 23-35.

        Discusses The Autumn of the Patriarch from a stylistic point of
        view, applying theories of Hegel and George Wilhelm Friedrich.

126.    Howard, David C.  "Mind as Reality:  Borges' 'The Circular Ruins'
        and García Márquez' One Hundred Years of Solitude."  Atlanta, Ga:
        CLA Journal, v. 23, no. 4, (June, 1980), pp. 409-415.

        Examines the idea of the world as a dream or illusion through the
        joint analysis of Borges' The Circular Ruins and Gabriel García
        Márquez's One Hundred Years of Solitude.

127.    Huerta, Albert.  "O tempo fantástico e o espaço dos espelhos:
        Gabriel García Márquez, Premio Nobel de Literatura 1982."
        Petrópolis, Brazil:  Vozes, v. 77, no. 2, (March, 1983), pp. 85-96.

The idea of a Latin American reality as defined by a fantastic time
and space of mirrors in Cien años de soledad is presented, where
characters like pieces of a broken mirror never cease reflecting
unforgettable truths.

128.  Hughes, Psiche.  "The Concept of Suicide in Borges' Stories in
      Relation to the Themes of Destiny and Aggression."  Chapel Hill,
      NC:  Hispanófila, no. 67, (September, 1979), pp. 61-71.

      The problem of suicide in Borges' stories is the topic of this
      article with a mention of its treatment by Gabriel García Márquez
      in Cien años de soledad.

129.  Ivanovici, Victor.  "The Colonel's Phantom:  Aureliano Buendía and
      the 'Patchwork' of Fantasy."  Bucharest:  Romanian Review, nos. 2-
      3, (1983), pp. 182-187.

      Although García Márquez refuses to be labeled as a writer of
      fantastic literature, a study of the Colonel Aureliano Buendía
      within the works of Gabriel García Márquez, especially in Cien años
      de soledad depicts him as such.

130.  Jaksić, Iván.  "La lógica del terror en la novela latinoamericana
      contemporánea sobre dictadura."  Sacramento, Ca:  Explicación de
      Textos Literarios, v. 12, no. 2, (1983-1984), pp. 37-48.

      The logistics of the political influence, specifically that of the
      dictator in Latin American Literature is studied, together with
      examples from Facundo:  civilización y barbarie, El Señor presidente,
      Oficio de difuntos, and El otoño del patriarca.

131.  Janes, Regina.  "Liberals, Conservatives, and Bananas:  Colombian
      Politics in the Fiction of Gabriel García Márquez."  Chapel Hill,
      NC:  Hispanófila, no. 82, (September, 1984), pp. 79-102.

      Latin American politics and social issues, specifically those of
      Colombia are integrated satirically in García Máruqez's novels.

132.  Jelinski, J. B.  "Memory and the Remembered Structure of Cien años
      de soledad - García Márquez."  Alabama:  Revista de Estudios
      Hispánicos, v. 18, no. 3, (October, 1984), pp. 323-333.

      The vehicle of memory and recall becomes the structural connection
      in the narration of Cien años de soledad.

133.  Jitrik, Noé.  "L'écriture entre la censure et la clandestinité."
      (extract)  Paris:  Silex, no. 11, (March, 1979), pp. 49-51.
      (Special issue:  "Gabriel García Márquez - Amerique Latine").

      A study of the role of censorship, politics, and war in various
      works by Gabriel García Márquez.  The article was translated by
      Roland Forgues.

134.  Jofré, Manuel.  "La imaginación realista de García Márquez."  Los
      Angeles, CA:  Literatura Chilena en el Exilio, v. 2, no. 3, (July.
      1978), pp. 9-13.

The stories which comprise, Los funerales de la Mamá Grande integrate the romantic-symbolic tradition with the natural-realistic.

135. Joset, Jacques. "José Donoso, Gabriel García Márquez: dos cultos fracasados." Madrid: Revista Iberoamericana, nos. 130-131, (January-June, 1985), pp. 241-247.

In this comparison of the beatification-canonization theme of Donoso's, El obsceno pájaro de la noche and García Márquez's, El otoño del patriarca Jacques views the passing of domination in Latin America from the Church to secular institutions and ideologies.

136. Joset, Jacques. "Le paradis perdu de Gabriel García Márquez." Brussels: Revue des Langues Vivantes, v. 37, no. 1, (1971), pp. 81-90.

Summarizes and compares the relative merits of several of García Márquez's novels.

137. Joset, Jacques. "Un sofocante aleteo de mariposas amarillas: Lectura de un episodio de Cien años de soledad." Washington, DC: Organization of American States, Revista Interamericana de Bibliografía (Inter-American Review of Bibliography), v. 28, no. 2, (April-June, 1978), pp. 149-155.

Comments on the symbolism of the apparition of yellow butterflies in One Hundred Years of Solitude, relating them to the calamaties and death which ensue.

138. Juárez, Hildebrando. "Radiografiá de la soledad a través de El coronel no tiene quien le escriba." El Salvador: Aura, año 1, no. 3, III trimestre, (1983), pp. 2-5.

The sadness, mystery, nostalgia, loneliness, the hopeless solitude of the Latin American people are embodied in the person of the Colonel.

139. Kercher, Dona M. "García Márquez's Crónica de una muerte anunciada (Chronicle of a Death Foretold): Notes on Parody and the Artist." Pittsburgh, PA: Latin American Literary Review, Special Issue Gabriel García Márquez, v. 13, no. 25, (January-June, 1985), pp. 90-103.

In this critique of the first English translation of Chronicle of a Death Foretold, published in Vanity Fair, Kercher relates the illustration by Fernando Botero to the actual text of the novel.

140. Kersten, Raquel. "Gabriel García Márquez y el arte de lo verosímil." Pittsburgh, PA: Revista Iberoamericana, v. 46, no. 110-111, (January-June, 1980), pp. 195-204.

Examines the technique of making the narrative credible through various stylistic aspects of One Hundred Years of Solitude.

141.  King, Lloyd.  "Cien años de soledad y la transformación instantánea
      de la historia."  San Juan Puerto Rico:  Sin Nombre, v. 13, no. 1,
      (October-December, 1982), pp. 28-35.

      Lloyd King discusses Gabriel García Márquez's use of history and
      memory in his novel Cien años de soledad.

142.  Kirsner, Robert.  "Four Colombian Novels of 'La violencia'."
      Gaithersburg, MD:  Hispania, v. 49, (1966), pp. 70-74.

      The treatment of violence as it occurs in Ernesto León Herrera's,
      Lo que el cielo no perdona, Eduardo Caballero Calderón's, El Cristo
      de espaldas, Gabriel García Márquez's, La mala hora, and Manuel
      Mejía Vallejo's, El día señalado.

143.  Knowlton, Edgar C.  "García Márquez's One Hundred Years of
      Solitude."  Washington, DC:  The Explicator, v. 38, no. 3, (Spring,
      1980), pp. 37-39.

      Knowlton draws a parallel between the unsuccessful suicidal attempt
      of Aureliano Buendía in the novel and the suicide of the poet, José
      Asunción Silva, raising the question of whether the fictional
      suicide attempt copies the real-life suicide of Silva.

144.  Kulin, Katalin.  "Cien años de soledad:  Aspectos de su mundo
      mítico."  Madrid:  Anales de Literatura Hispanoamericana, nos. 2-3,
      (1973-1974), pp. 677-685.

      A comparative study, emphasizing the mythological aspects of the
      writings of García Márquez.

145.  Kulin, Katalin.  "García Márquez:  El otoño del patriarca."
      San Juan, Puerto Rico:  Sin Nombre, v. 8, no. 1, (April-June, 1977),
      pp. 20-34.

      A section by section commentary on El otoño del patriarca with
      comparisons to Cien años de soledad.

      Spanish version of the original article, published in Neohelicon,
      v. 4, nos. 1-2, (1971), pp. 147-169.

146.  Kulin, Katalin.  "García Márquez:  El otoño del patriarca"
      (versión española revisada por la autora).  Xalapa, Veracruz,
      México:  Texto crítico, 111, 8, (September-December, 1977), pp. 88-
      103.

      Katalin Kulin compares the novel to other works of Gabriel García
      Márquez, and states that as with many of Gabriel García Márquez's
      works, El otoño de patriarca was based on a vision.

147.  Kuteishchikova, Vera.  "Gabriel García Márquez Visits Moscow."
      Moscow:  Soviet Literature, v. 4, no. 385, (1980), pp. 145-152.

      Gabriel García Márquez is enthusiastically received by his Russian
      readers as numerous interviews indicate.  This visit prompted the
      author of this article to view in retrospect the criticisms of
      various Russian writers about García Márquez's works.

148. Kutzinski, Vera M. "The Logic of Wings: Gabriel García Márquez and Afro-American Literature." Pittsburgh, PA: Latin American Literary Review, Special Issue Gabriel García Márquez, v. 13, no. 25, (January-June, 1985), pp. 133-146.

Although García Márquez never actually wrote about blacks in his novels Kutzinski illustrates instances in which he did make use of Afro-American history and myth in his writings.

149. Levine, Suzanne Jill. "A Second Glance of The Spoken Mirror: Gabriel García Márquez and Virginia Woolf." Providence, RI: INTI, Revista de Literatura Hispánica, nos. 16-17, (Autumn, 1982 - Spring, 1983), pp. 53-60.

A comparative study of Cien años de soledad by García Márquez and Virginia Woolf's, Orlando.

150. Lloreda, Waldo César. "García Márquez y la historia." Santa Catarina Mártir, Puebla, México: Perspectivas, (Spring, 1983), pp. 14-21.

Emphasizes the importance of Gabriel García Márquez's works and his contribution and influence upon the depiction of the historical theme in Latin American novels.

151. López Baralt, Mercedes. "Cien años de soledad: Cultura e historia latinoamericanas replanteadas en el idioma del parentesco." Piedras, Puerto Rico: Revista de Estudios Hispánicos, v. 6, (1979), pp. 153-175.

Kinship and the family become the metaphor through which García Márquez recounts the history and cultural development of Latin America.

152. Luchting, Wolfgang A. "¿Quién escribe los pasquines?" Bogotá: El Café Literario, v. 5, nos. 29-30, (September-December 1982), pp. 13-20.

The lampoons In Evil Hour become a metaphorical device for fiction.

153. Lucyga, Christine. "Gabriel García Márquez: el compromiso estético con la solidaridad." Santa Clara, Cuba: Islas, no. 76, (September-December, 1983), pp. 145-158.

The real and the imaginative as they compliment each other in García Márquez's works.

154. Lucyga, Christine. "Probleme des Realismus in den Romanen Gabriel García Máruqez." Rostock, German Democratic Republic: Lateinamerica, (Spring, 1970), pp. 31-52.

The real world of Aracataca, Colombia becomes the Macondo of several of García Márquez's works where magical realism introduces the co-existence of the modern with the anachronistic.

155. Luna, Norman. The Barbaric Dictator and the Enlightened Tyrant in
     El otoño del patriarca and El recurso del método. Pittsburgh, PA:
     Latin American Literary Review, v. 8, no. 15, (Fall–Winter, 1979),
     pp. 25–32.

     Contrasts the elements of Latin American dictatorship in Alejo
     Carpentier's Recurso del método and Gabriel García Márquez's
     El otoño del patriarca.

156. McGowan, John P. "A la recherche du temps perdu in One Hundred
     Years of Solitude." Purdue University, West Lafayette, IN:
     Modern Fiction Studies, v. 28, no. 4, (Winter, 1982–1983), pp. 557–
     567.

     Contrasts García Márquez's use of the techniques of time with that
     of Proust.

157. McGrady, Donald. "Dos sonetos atribuídos a Gabriel García Marquez."
     Philadelphia, PA: Hispanic Review, v. 51, no. 4, (Autumn, 1983),
     pp. 429–434.

     Evaluates two sonnets, "Amor" and "Niña" written by García Márquez
     in his youth.

158. McMurray, George R. "The Aleph and One Hundred Years of Solitude:
     Two Microcosmic Worlds." Pittsburgh, PA: Latin American Literary
     Review, Special Issue Gabriel García Márquez, v. 13, no. 25,
     (January–June, 1985), pp. 55–64.

     In this comparative study of Borges' The Aleph and García Márquez's
     One Hundred Years of Solitude, McMurray demonstrates how each author
     strove "to depict a total universe."

159. McNerney, Kathleen and Martin, John. "Alchemy in Cien años de
     soledad." Morgantown, WV: West Virginia University Philological
     Papers: Special Medieval Issue. Morgantown, WV: West Virginia
     University, v. 27, (1981), pp. 106–112.

     Presents alchemy as a leitmotif in Cien años de soledad and shows
     how it is closely interwoven with two of the most prominent themes,
     time and solitude.

160. Mallett, Brian J. "El ajeno albedrío: Crónica de una muerte
     anunciada y su contexto Ibérico." Bogotá: Eco, v. 43/1, no. 259,
     (May, 1983), pp. 27–41.

     Commenting on the political and subversive overtones of Chronicle
     of a Death Foretold, Mallett concludes that the novel is "an
     important contribution to the 'decolonization' of Latin America."

161. March, Kathleen N. "Crónica de una muerte anunciada: García
     Márquez y el género policiaca." Providence, RI: INTI, Revista de
     Literatura Hispánica, nos. 16–17, (Autumn, 1982–Spring, 1983),
     pp. 61–70.

     Characterizes Crónica de una muerte anunciada as a police or
     detective story as it adequately follows the formula for such.

162.  Marcos, Juan Manuel.  "García Márquez y el arte del reportaje:  de
      Lukacs al 'postboom'."  Providence, RI:  INTI, Revista de Literatura
      Hispánica, nos. 16-17, (Autumn, 1982 - Spring, 1983), pp. 147-154.

      Discusses the emergence of the political and social protest
      literature and its flowering in the present in Latin America.

163.  Marcos, Juan Manuel.  "Isabel viendo llover en Barataria."
      Poughkeepsie, NY:  Revista de Estudios Hispánicos, v. 19, no. 2,
      (May, 1985), pp. 129-137.

      Compares Isabel Allende's, La casa de los espíritus to Gabriel
      García Márquez's Cien años de soledad, indicating similarities and
      differences, and pointing out the fact that Isabel Allende was
      inspired by García Márquez's book.

164.  Masoliver, Juan Antonio.  "Los cien engaños de García Márquez."
      Oxford, England:  Bulletin of the Society for Latin American Studies,
      no. 31, (October, 1979), pp. 23-37.

      Maintains that the various artifices and deceptions employed in
      Cien años de soledad, explain the novel's success, both on a popular
      and a critical level.

165.  Maturo, Graciela.  "El sentido religioso de La Hojarasca de Gabriel
      García Márquez."  Bogotá:  Eco, v. 24, 3/4, nos. 141-142, (January-
      February, 1972), pp. 216-235.

      Examines the imagery of Christianity and the role it plays in
      La hojarasca.

166.  Meckled, S.  "The Theme of the Double:  An Essential Element
      throughout García Márquez's Works."  Dublin, Ireland:  Crane Bag,
      v. 6, (1982), pp. 108-117.

      The use of doubles in Gabriel García Márquez's stories is studied,
      and in particular, the four pairs of doubles in One Hundred Years
      of Solitude, and the one pair in Autumn of a Patriarch.

167.  Megenney, William W.  "The Origin of Francisco el Hombre in Cien
      años de soledad."  Frankfurt am Main:  Romanische Forschungen,
      v. 92, nos. 1-2, (1980), pp. 132-133.

      The origin of Gabriel García Márquez's character Francisco el
      Hombre in One Hundred Years of Solitude reveals that Gabriel García
      Márquez, probably borrowed this figure from existing folklore which
      tells the tale of a man defeating the devil.

168.  Meise, Hans-Jürgen.  "Über den Nobelpreisträger fur Literatur,
      1982."  Gutersloh, W. Germany:  Neue Deutsche Hefte, v. 30, no.
      177, (1983), pp. 28-43.

      A critique of Gabriel García Márquez's works, his literary
      techniques, personality, as well as the writers who have influenced
      his literary development.

169. Mena, Lucila Inés. "Bibliografía anotada sobre el ciclo de
     violencia en la literatura colombiana." Austin, TX: Latin American
     Research Review, v. 13, no. 3, (1978), pp. 95-107.

     An extensive bibliography of books and articles on violence in
     Colombia is preceded by an explanatory essay on the causes and
     results of Colombian violence, as portrayed in the novels of
     contemporary authors of that country, including García Márquez.

170. Mendez, José Luis. "El discurso del método literario latino-
     americano: a propósito de Gabriel García Márquez." (fragmento)
     Providence, RI: INTI, Revista de Literatura Hispánica, nos. 16-17,
     (Autumn, 1982 - Spring, 1983), pp. 155-161.

     Comments on García Márquez's acceptance speech on receiving the
     Nobel Prize for Literature, concentrating on the sociology of
     literature.

171. Molen, Patricia Hart. "Potency vs. Incontinence in The Autumn of
     the Patriarch of Gabriel García Márquez." Tempe, AZ: Rocky
     Mountain Review of Language and Literature, v. 33, no. 1, (Winter,
     1979), pp. 1-6.

     A study of power, and lack of self restraint in man as viewed
     through the character of the Patriarch in Gabriel García Márquez's
     novel The Autumn of the Patriarch.

172. Monleón, José. "Historia de una contraducción." San Diego, CA:
     Maize, (Spring-Summer, 1980), pp. 17-22.

     States that Cien años de soledad is a history of contradictions and
     sets out to prove that the entire narrative revolves around this
     element.

173. Montes, Arturo. "La route de Macondo." Paris: Silex, no. 11,
     (March, 1979), pp. 84-93. (Special issue: "Gabriel García Marquez
     - Amerique Latine").

     Emphasizes the urbanization and the social and political changes
     that occur in the city of Macondo in One Hundred Years of Solitude.

174. Mora, Gabriela. "'La prodigiosa tarde de Baltazar': problema del
     significado." Providence, RI: INTI, Revista de Literatura
     Hispánica, nos. 16-17, (Autumn, 1982 - Spring, 1983), pp. 83-93.

     Characterizes this short story as a parable, and sets out to prove
     this statement.

175. Morello-Frosch, Marta. "Función de lo fantástico en La increíble
     y triste historia de la cándida Eréndira y de su abuela desalmada
     de Gabriel García Márquez." Washington, DC: Symposium, v. 38,
     no. 4, (Winter, 1984-1985), pp. 321-330.

     Fantasy, so prevalent in the stories in this collection is made
     acceptable because it does not supplant or dominate reality.

176. Moreno Turner, Fernando. "El tiempo del mar perdido." Madrid: Araucaria de Chile, no. 21, (1983), pp. 121-130.

A study of the symbolic meaning of the 'lost sea' within Gabriel García Márquez's El otoño del patriarca. Also in: Budapest: Acta Litteraria Academiae Scientiarum Hungaricae, v. 23, nos. 3-4, (1981), pp. 341-350.

177. Muñoz, Willy Oscar. "Sexualidad y religión: crónica de una rebelión esperada." Providence, RI: INTI, Revista de Literatura Hispánica, nos. 16-17, (Autumn, 1982 - Spring, 1983), pp. 95-109.

Chronicle of a Death Foretold is "the seed of a new carnal, temporal, liberating part that is substituted for the ancient, spiritual, eternal and oppressive."

178. Natella, Arthur. "Aspectos neomedievales de la nueva narrativa latinoamericana." Madrid: Cuadernos Hispanoamericanos, no. 411, (September, 1984), pp. 166-174.

A primary element of the medieval mentality is the use of symbolism as is evident in the novels of contemporary Latin American authors, among whom is García Márquez.

179. Neghme Echeverría, Lidia. "Lo verosímil y la intertextualidad en El otoño del patriarca." Gaithersburg, MD: Hispamérica: Revista de Literatura, v. 12, no. 36, (December, 1983), pp. 87-99.

The interpenetration of the real into the fabric of fiction creates for the reader the ability to foresee the probable outcome of the novel.

180. Nelson, William. "The Humor and Humanizing of Outrage." Ottawa: Thalia, v. 2, nos. 1-2, (1979), pp. 31-34.

The use of comic relief in Gabriel García Márquez's One Hundred Years of Solitude, and Thomas Pynchon's The Crying of Lot 49.

181. Neves, Eugenia. "Variaciones sobre Gabriel García Márquez: sus novelas, ficción y realidad en América Latina." Madrid: Araucaria de Chile, no. 21, (1983), pp. 131-140.

An exposition of One Hundred Years of Solitude and The Autumn of the Patriarch through Latin American history, literature and social conditions, in order to determine what is fiction and what is reality in García Márquez's works.

182. Ocampo de Gómez, Aurora Naura. "Mito y realidad en Cien años de soledad." Xalapa, Veracruz, México: Texto Crítico, v. 5, no. 13, (April-June, 1979), pp. 175-179.

Cien años de soledad, the novel of magic realism par excellence is the epitome of surrealism.

183.  Onstine, Roberto.  "Forma, sentido e interpretación del espacio en
      El otoño del patriarca."  Madrid:  Cuadernos Hispanoamericanos,
      v. 106, no. 317, (November, 1976), pp. 428-433.

      A critique of Gabriel García Márquez's El otoño del patriarca which
      interprets the use of myth and imaginary space throughout the novel.

184.  Ordoñez, Montserrat.  "Crónica de una muerte anunciada."  Toulouse,
      France:  Caravelle, no. 37, (1981), pp. 187-190.

      The use of dialogue and the powerful effects the dialogue has over
      the characters, and other themes in Gabriel García Márquez's
      Crónica de una muerte anunciada is studied in detail.

185.  Ortega, Julio.  "Ciclo y errancia en Cien años."  Providence, RI:
      INTI, Revista de Literatura Hispánica, nos. 16-17, (Autumn, 1982 -
      Spring, 1983), pp. 3-8.

      The use of time as a structural vehicle in Cien años de soledad.

186.  Ortega, Julio.  "El otoño del patriarca:  texto y cultura."  Bogotá:
      Eco, 32/6-33/1-2, nos. 198-200, (April, May, June, 1978), pp. 678-
      703.

      A thorough analysis of García Márquez's El otoño del patriarca
      including studies of the political themes, social structure,
      mythology, collective narration, and writing style.

187.  Ortíz Domínguez, Efrén.  "La cándida Eréndira":  una lectura mítica.
      Xalapa, Veracruz, México:  Texto Crítico, v. 6, no. 16-17, (January-
      June, 1980), pp. 248-254.

      Traces mythical elements in the García Márquez novel, La increíble
      y triste historia de la cándida Eréndira y su abuela desalmada.

188.  Ospovata, L.  "Gabriel García Márquez on Literature, Himself, and
      His Work."  New York, NY:  Soviet Studies in Literature, v. 16, no.
      4, (Fall, 1980), pp. 46-77.  (Originally published in Russian in
      Voprosy literatury, 1980, no. 3, pp. 159-176).

      A thorough study of Gabriel García Márquez's literary and political
      writings, comparing the renowned Colombian author to Hemingway,
      Faulkner, and Kafka, and including interviews with Luis Suárez and
      Manuel Pereira, two Latin American journalists who discuss Gabriel
      García Márquez's works.

189.  Oviedo, José Miguel.  "A la (Mala) hora señalada."  México:
      Revista de la Universidad de México, vol. 36, no. 7, 1981, pp. 38-
      42.

      Concentrates on the Greek tragedy fatalism present in Crónica de una
      muerte anunciada.

190.  Oviedo, José Miguel.  "García Márquez:  La novela como taumaturgia."
      Cleark Creek, IN:  The American Hispanist, v. 1, no. 2, (1975),
      pp. 4-9.

Examines The Autumn of the Patriarch, the work written after One
Hundred Years of Solitude, and concludes that it can only be
understood by first studying it independently of the earlier novel.
Once accomplished the two can then be studied together, examining
them as two contrasting works.

191.  Palencia-Roth, David Michael.  "El círculo hermenéutico en El otoño
      del patriarca."  Madrid:  Revista Iberoamericana, no. 128-129,
      (July-December, 1984), pp. 999-1000.

      In Gabriel García Márquez's El otoño del patriarca "there is always
      another version behind the one received or read," another truth
      behind the truth. . . the truth of the text. . . (which) only comes
      gradually, and finally, not partially."

192.  Palencia-Roth, David Michael.  "La imagen del uroboros:  el incesto
      en Cien años de soledad ."  México:  Cuadernos Americanos, v. 237,
      no. 4 (July-August, 1981), pp. 67-81.

      Freud, Sophocles, and myth are cited and employed in an analysis of
      the incestuous behavior and instincts of the Buendía family.

193.  Palencia-Roth, Michael.  "Los pergaminos de Aureliano Babilonia."
      Pittsburgh, PA:  Revista Iberoamericana, v. 49, no. 123, (1983),
      pp. 403-417.

      An investigation into the significance of the manuscripts of
      Aureliano Babilonia in Gabriel García Márquez's Cien años de soledad.

194.  Pancorbo, Luis.  "Tres tristes tiranos."  Madrid:  Revista de
      Occidente, 3ra época, no. 19, (May, 1977), pp. 12-16.

      Demonstrates how political issues are confronted in the modern Latin
      American novel, by discussing the dictator characters in Yo, el
      Supremo, by Augusto Roa Bastos; El recurso del método, by Alejo
      Carpentier; and El otoño del patriarca by Gabriel García Márquez.

195.  Pankow, Gisela.  "L'homme absurde et son espace."  Paris:  Esprit,
      no. 1, (January, 1984), pp. 96-108.

      Compares A House for Mr. Biswas by V. S. Naipaul with García
      Márquez's Crónica de una muerte anunciada.

196.  Paoli, Roberto.  "Carnavalesco y tiempo cíclico en Cien años de
      soledad."  Madrid:  Revista Iberoamericana, no. 128-129, (July-
      December, 1984), pp. 979-998.

      In Cien años de soledad we learn that ". . .one of the essential
      components of the art of Gabriel Márquez. . . is that of 'lo
      carnavalesco, (carnival-like)', . . . a vision of life by the lower
      classes who make fun of idealism, of etiquette, and of the good
      manners of the high classes."

197.  Parkinson-Zamora, Lois.  "The End of Innocence:  Myth and Narrative
      Structure in Faulkner's Absalom, Absalom! and García Márquez's Cien
      años de soledad."  Indiana, PA:  Hispanic Journal, v. 4, no. 1,
      (Fall, 1982), pp. 23-40.

The similarities of myth and narrative structure within Faulkner's
Absalom, Absalom! and Gabriel García Márquez's Cien años de soledad,
are brought out.

198.  Parkinson Zamora, Lois.  "Ends and Endings in García Márquez's
Crónica de una muerte anunciada (Chronicle of a Death Foretold)."
Pittsburgh, PA:  Latin American Literary Review, Special Issue
Gabriel García Márquez, v. 13, no. 25, (January–June, 1985), pp.
104–116.

Chronicle of a Death Foretold, which reveals García Márquez's
journalistic background, takes its place beside his other novels
which are "apocalyptic in nature."

199.  Pastor, Ricardo.  "No One Writes to the Colonel."  University
Center, MI:  Alèthea, no. 13, (Spring-Summer, 1984), pp. 63–68.

Pastor, Ricardo.  "El coronel no tiene quien le escriba."
University Center, MI:  Alèthea, no. 13, (Spring-Summer, 1984),
pp. 21–26.  Special issue:  Gabriel García Márquez:  The Man and
the Magic of His Writing).

Pastor chooses for his presentation:  El coronel no tiene quién le
escriba as the novel which represents best the essence of García
Márquez's writings, "which does not present the deeds of great
heroes;  but rather relates the life of the common man."

200.  Peña Gutiérrez, Isaías.  "Carpentier and García Márquez:  Genesis,
Foundation and Apocalypse in Los perdidos and Cien años de soledad."
La Habana, Cuba:  Casa de las Américas, no. 143, (1983), pp. 125–132.
132.

The element of progression is the basis for this comparative literary study of Carpentier and García Márquez in which Peña Gutiérrez
traces the evolution of Macondo from primitive beginnings to a place
dominated by capitalism and industrialization.

201.  Penuel, Arnold M.  "Death and the maiden demythologization of
virginity in García Márquez's Cien años de soledad."  University,
MS:  Hispania, v. 66, no. 4, (December, 1983), pp. 552–560.

Analyzes the character of Amaranta from One Hundred Years of
Solitude and the effects of her narcissism, which ultimately leads
her to the solitude of death.

202.  Popeanga, Eugenia.  "Formule narative in romanul latino-american
contemporan."  Bucarest:  Revista de Istorie si Teoríe si literara,
v. 22, no. 3, (1973), pp. 397–402.

Commenting on the narrative structure of present day Latin American
fiction, Popeanga finds elements of the Faulknerian style in the
novels, especially those of García Márquez.

203.  Popeanga, Eugenia.  "Romanul latino-american contemporan."
Bucarest:  Revista de Istorie si Teorie Literara, v. 21, no. 2,
(1972), pp. 347–353.

In the literary world of Latin America, García Márquez excels as the writer who best employs, myth, symbolism, and a phenomenal imagination.

204. Porter, Laurence M., and Laurel. "Relations with the Dead in Cien años de soledad." Winnepeg, Canada: Mosaic, v. 15, no. 1, (Winter, 1982), pp. 119-127.

The problem and mystery of death and García Márquez's manner of dealing with it in his books.

205. Predmore,Richard L. "El mundo moral de Crónica de una muerte anunciada." Madrid: Cuadernos Hispanoamericanos, no. 390, (December, 1982), pp. 703-712.

The moral issues become a major factor in Crónica de una muerte anunciada.

206. Putzeys Alvarez, Guillermo. "100 años de soledad de Gabriel García Márquez." San Salvador: La Universidad, año 95, no. 2, (March-April, 1970), pp. 13-28.

The contemporaneity of Cien años de soledad was perhaps the most single contributing factor to its universal appeal.

207. Rabia, Abdelkader. "Gabriel García Márquez et sa fortune dans les pays arabes." Paris: Recherches et Etudes Comparatistes Ibéro-francaises de la Sorbonne Nouvelle Paris, no. 3, (1981), pp. 95-103.

A comparison between García Márquez's, Cien años de soledad and Rachid Boudjera's Les Mille et Une Années de la Nostalgie as to nuances in cultures, politics and style of writing. Discusses García Márquez's literary reception in Arab countries.

208. Rama, Angel. "De Gabriel García Márquez a Plinio Apuleyo Mendoza." Bogotá: Eco, v. 32/6, no. 198, (April-May, 1978), v. 33/1-2, nos. 199-200, (June, 1978), pp. 837-859.

The political and social unrest and violence in Latin America is reflected in the writings of its authors, especially in those of Gabriel García Márquez.

209. Rama, Angel. "García Márquez entre la tragedia y la policial o crónica y pesquisa de la Crónica de una muerte anunciada. San Juan, Puerto Rico: Sin Nombre, v. 13, no. 1, (October-December, 1982), pp. 7-27.

Gabriel García Márquez's Crónica de una muerte anunciada is viewed as both an historical tale, and an informative article in that it "observes the order of events," and also treats real life themes.

210. Rama, Angel. "El puesto de Gabriel García Márquez." Bogotá: Eco, v. 42/3, no. 255, (January, 1983), pp. 225-237.

García Márquez's winning of the Nobel Prize has enkindled interest in Latin American culture and caused writers to search among their own cultures for inspiration.

211.   Rama, Angel. "La tecnificación narrativa." Gaithersburg, MD:
       Hispamérica-Revista de Literatura, año 10, no. 30, (December, 1981),
       pp. 29-82.

       Gabriel García Márquez's utilization of imagination and the un-
       believable in One Hundred Years of Solitude is discussed in this
       article on the contemporary Latin American narrative and its
       salient characteristics.

212.   Ramos Escóbar, José L. "Cien años de soledad: Juegos ad infinitum."
       San Juan, Puerto Rico: Revista/Review Interamericana, v. 11, no. 3,
       (Fall, 1981), pp. 444-452.

       Opening with a quote from García Márquez, Ramos Escóbar perceives
       Cien años de soledad as a literary game.

213.   Ramos Escobar, Jose L. "La voz comunal en la narrativa de Gabriel
       García Márquez." San Juan, Puerto Rico: Sin Nombre, v. 13, no. 1,
       (October-December, 1982), pp. 65-71.

       Communal solidarity and individual alienation are evident in Cien
       años de soledad and other works of Gabriel García Márquez.

214.   Reid, Alastair. "García Márquez: A Brief Note." Pittsburgh, PA:
       Latin American Literary Review, Special Issue Gabriel García
       Márquez, v. 13, no. 25, (January-June, 1985), p. 148.

       The reader's personal relationship to the writings of García
       Márquez.

215.   Reid, Alastair. "The Latin-American Lottery." New York, NY:
       The New Yorker, v. 56, no. 49, (January 26, 1981), pp. 106, 109-111.

       A study of the "Boom" period of Latin American literature centers
       upon Gabriel García Márquez, among several authors, his major works,
       and his search for fiction which creates "the marvellous in the
       real."

216.   Reis, Roberto. "O fantastico do poder e o poder do fantastico."
       Minneapolis, MN: Ideologies and Literature, v. 3, no. 13, (June-
       August, 1980), pp. 3-22.

       In explaining fantastic literature and the relationship between
       literature and reality, Gabriel García Márquez becomes himself the
       link between narration and reality in Latin American literature.

217.   Riquelme Austin, Sonia. "La función de la repetición en Cien años
       de soledad." Panamá: Revista Lotería, no. 318-319, (October,
       1982), pp. 97-103.

       Repetition in García Márquez's literary style is examined in Cien
       años de soledad.

218.   Rojas, Mario. "Tipología del discurso del personaje en el texto."
       Ann Arbor: Dispositio: Revista Hispánica de Semiótica Literaria,
       v. 1, 506, no. 15-16, (Fall, 1980 - Winter, 1981), pp. 19-55.

Quotations from works of García Márquez together with contemporary
Latin American novelists are cited as illustrations of the typology
of character discourse.

219.  Sklodowska, Elzbieta.  "Aproximaciones al discurso histórico en la
      nueva novela hispanoamericana."  México: Plural, Segunda época,
      v. 14/4, no. 160, (January, 1985), pp. 11-19.

      Examines the state of the novel of the "boom," as a departure from
      the traditional novel, in the light of the historic theme contained
      in García Márquez's works, as well as in the works of the other
      contemporary Latin American writers.

220.  Romero, Armando.  "Gabriel García Márquez, Alvaro Mutis, Fernando
      Botero:  tres personas distintas, un objectivo verdadero."
      Providence, RI:  INTI, Revista de Literatura Hispánica, nos. 16-17,
      (Autumn, 1982 - Spring, 1983), pp. 135-146.

      Having selected three Colombian artists, the painter, Fernando
      Botero, the poet Alvaro Mutis, and the novelist García Márquez,
      Romero indicates and illustrates the similarities and differences
      in their works.

221.  Rosa Sierra, Sylvia.  "Tres figuras femeninas de Cien años de
      soledad."  Panamá: Lotería, no. 277, (March, 1979), pp. 55-67.

      Woman's role in Gabriel García Márquez's Cien años de soledad.

222.  Ruíz Gómez, Darío.  "Cien años de soledad y Rayuela, los dos polos
      de la novela latinoamericana."  Medellín, Colombia:  UDEM, Revista
      de la Universidad de Medellín, v. 13, no. 14, (1968), pp. 159-163.

      On being compared with Cortázar's Rayuela, One Hundred Years of
      Solitude is described as a novel which "surpasses provincialism to
      become one of the most lucid and beautiful testimonies of man and
      society."

223.  Rumazo, Lupe.  "En Las pequeñas estaturas: vigor polémico de
      Alfredo Pareja."  Quito, Ecuador:  Letras del Ecuador, no. 149,
      (April, 1971), pp. 5, 28.

      Parallels the theme, characters, fantasy, myth and magic in Las
      pequeñas estaturas of Alfredo Pareja and Cien años de soledad of
      Gabriel García Márquez.

224.  Saldívar, Dasso.  "Acerca de la función política de la soledad en
      El otoño del patriarca."  Madrid:  Estafeta literaria, no. 561,
      (April 1, 1975), pp. 4-5.

      Characterizes El otoño del patriarca as a great work of philosophy,
      a political, social and historic novel portraying the solitude of
      power.

225.  Saldívar, José David.  "Ideology and Deconstruction in Macondo."
      Pittsburgh, PA:  Latin American Literary Review, Special Issue
      Gabriel García Márquez, v. 13, no. 25, (January-June, 1985), pp.
      29-43.

"What finally makes reading One Hundred Years of Solitude so
unforgettable is the harrowing power with which García Márquez
convinces us of the essential history of solitude and alienation in
the Americas, and how it must be deconstructed."

226. Sexson, Michael. "Postmodern paradigms: the enchantment of realism
in the fiction of Italo Calvino and Gabriel García Márquez."
London: Journal of Social and Biological Structures, v. 6, no. 2,
(April, 1983), pp. 115-121.

The fictional works of Italo Calvino and Gabriel García Márquez are
cited in an effort to redefine the meaning of Postmodernism.

227. Silva, Maria Aparecida da. "García Márquez e a Função Crítica da
Escritura." Belo Horizonte, Brazil: Minas Gerâis, Suplemento
Literário, v. 14, no. 754, (March 14, 1981), pp. 4-5.

Silva states that García Márquez's style assumed a metalinguistic
function by restructuring the dynamics of language through expand-
ing the meaning of words in this criticism of La increíble and
triste historia de la cándida Eréndira y de su abuela desalmada.

228. Sims, Robert L. "The Banana Massacre in Cien años de soledad: A
Micro-structural Example of Myth, History and Bricolage."
Williamsburg, VA: Chasqui, v. 8, no. 3, (May, 1979), pp. 3-23.

A study of the banana massacre in Gabriel García Márquez's Cien años
de soledad, suggests that there are many levels on which the novel
can be read, from plot to myth.

229. Sims, Robert L. "Theme, Narrative, Bricolage and Myth in García
Márquez." Manhattan, KS: Journal of Spanish Studies: Twentieth
Century, v. 8, nos. 1-2, (Spring-Fall, 1980), pp. 145-159.

"This study examines the evolution of myth in Gabriel García Márquez
by analyzing the interrelationship between theme and narration in
La hojarasca, Los Funerales de la Mamá Grande, and Cien años de
soledad."

230. Solotorevsky, Myrna. "Crónica de una muerte anunciada, la escritura
de un texto irreverente." Madrid: Revista Iberoamericana, no. 128-
129, (July-December, 1984), pp. 1077-1091.

An investigation of the ambiguous and open narration of Gabriel
García Márquez's Crónica de una muerte anunciada which fluctuates
between two extremes: the mythical text and the chronicle.

231. Solortorevsky, Myrna. "El otoño del patriarca: Texto ambiguo."
Buenos Aires: Megafón, año 4, no. 7, (June, 1978), pp. 141-169.

This is an extensive and perceptive study of García Márquez's
El otoño del patriarca which analyzes the ambiguity of the intention
of the narrative structure of the novel.

232. Stevens, L. Robert and G. Roland Vela. "Jungle Gothic:  Science, Myth, and Reality in One Hundred Years of Solitude." West Lafayette, IN:  Modern Fiction Studies, v. 26, no. 2, (Summer, 1980), pp. 262-266.

Stevens and Vela discuss the mixture of reality and illusion in Gabriel García Márquez's Cien años de soledad.

233. Suárez, Pedro Alejandro. "Obsesión, símbolo y mito en Cien años de soledad." Bogotá:  Revista Javeriana, v. 72, no. 358, (September, 1969), pp. 286-295.

An analysis of the various types of symbolism; biblical, spiritual, love, animal, weather, etc. as they occur in Cien años de soledad.

234. Tittler, Jonathan. "Paisajes figurales en tres novelas colombianas." Bogotá:  El Café Literatio, (April-June, 1984), pp. 26-31.

Regionalism with similarities and differences in the novels of three Colombian authors:  Jorge Isaac's Maria, José Rivera's La Voragine, and Gabriel García Márquez's El otoño del patriarca.

235. Tobin, Patricia. "The Autumn of the Signifier:  The Deconstructionist Moment of García Márquez." Pittsburgh, PA:  Latin American Literary Review, Special Issue: Gabriel García Márquez, v. 13, no. 25, (January-June, 1985), pp. 65-78.

Referring to The Autumn of the Patriarch as "a book for the head, a book that allows us to think the thought of the times," Tobin goes on to explain the role of the protagonist, to whom she refers to as the "Signifier."

236. Todorov, Tzvetan. "Macondo en París." Xalapa, Veracruz, México:  Texto Crítico, v. 11, (1978), pp. 36-45.

Todorov cites examples from García Márquez's Cien años de soledad as he contrasts modern Latin American literature with that of past generations.

237. Toro, Alfonso de. "Estructura narrativa y temporal en Cien años de soledad." Madrid:  Revista Iberoamericana, no. 128-129, (July-December, 1984), pp. 957-978.

A study of the temporal dimension and narrative procedure in Gabriel García Márquez's Cien años de soledad.

238. Tyler, Joseph. "The Cinematic World of García Márquez." Providence, RI:  INTI, Revista de Literatura Hispánica, nos. 16-17, (Autumn, 1982 - Spring, 1983), pp. 163-171.

Examines García Márquez's experiences and associations with the film world about which García Márquez once remarked, "I can't live with it and I can't live without it."

239.  Ugalde, Sharon Keefe. "Ironía en El otoño del patriarca."
      Providence, RI: INTI, Revísta de Literatura Hispánica, nos. 16-17,
      (Autumn, 1982 - Spring, 1983), pp. 11-26.

      The circular structure of the time element in this novel of
      dictatorship intensifies the general irony and satirization of the
      abuse of power in Latin American history.

240.  Urza, Carmelo. "Lo maravilloso en el Amadis, el Quijote y Cien
      años de soledad: un juego perspectivista." Sacramento, CA:
      Explicación de Textos Literarios, v. 10, no. 1, (1981), pp. 101-109.

      A discussion of the "marvelous" as it appears in One Hundred Years
      of Solitude, illustrating how García Márquez uses narrative tech-
      niques and irony to unite the unbelievable, magic, or "marvelous"
      to the elements which constitute reality.

241.  Vázquez-Ayora, Gerardo. "Estudio estilístico de Cobra de Severo
      Sarduy." Takoma Park, MD: Hispamérica: Revista de Literatura,
      año 9, nos. 23-24, (January-March, 1980), pp. 35-42.

      Sarduy's literary style in Cobra is compared to García Márquez's
      in El otoño del patriarca.

242.  Vidal, Hernán. "Narrativa de mitificación sátirica: equivalencias
      socio-literarias." Gaithersbury, MD: Hispámerica: Revista de
      Literatura, supp., (1975), pp. 57-72.

      Considers satirical mythification in three novels: El lugar sin
      límites by José Donoso; Pedro Páramo by Juan Rulfo; and Cien años
      de soledad by Gabriel García Márquez.

243.  Volkening, Ernesto. "Los cuentos de Gabriel García Márquez o el
      trópico desembrujado." Bogotá: Eco, v. 7, no. 40, (1963), pp.
      275-293.

      Evaluative study of the short stories. "Isabel viendo llover en
      Macondo" is included in its entirety.

244.  Wilkie, James W., Edna Monzón de Wilkie, and María Herrera-Sobek.
      "Elitelore and Folklore: Theory and a Test Case in One Hundred
      Years of Solitude." Los Angeles, CA: Journal of Latin American
      Lore, v. 4, no. 2, (Winter, 1978), pp. 183-223.

      Illustrates the relationship between "elitelore" and folklore using
      as a case study the village life of Macondo.

245.  Williams, Raymond Leslie. "Los comienzos de un Premio Nobel: La
      tercera resignación." Bogotá: El Café Literario, v. 5, nos. 29-30,
      (September-December, 1982), pp. 39-41.

      La tercera resignación, García Márquez's first story is studied
      within the context of his later and more successful works.
      Williams also comments upon the reasoning behind the award of the
      Nobel Prize.

246. Williams, Raymond Leslie. "García Márquez y Gardeazábal ante
     Cien años de soledad:  un desafío a la interpretación crítica."
     Pittsburgh, PA:  Revista Iberoamericana, v. 47, no. 116-117, (July-
     December, 1981), pp. 165-174.

     Studying the after-effects of the "Macondo phenomenom" in Colombia,
     Williams focuses on the direction Colombian literature has taken
     since One Hundred Years of Solitude.

247. Williams, Raymond Leslie. "An Introduction to the Early Journalism
     of García Márquez:  1948-1958." Pittsburgh, PA:  Latin American
     Literary Review, Special Issue:  Gabriel García Márquez, v. 13,
     no. 25, (January-June, 1985), pp. 117-132.

     Noting that Chronicle of a Death Foretold, points to García
     Márquez's training as a journalist, Williams presents a study that
     "will provide a descriptive overview and analysis of his journalist
     writing from 1948 to 1958 within the context of his total fiction."

248. Williams, Raymond Leslie. "El tiempo en la novela:  Observaciones
     en torno al tiempo en la novela colombiana contemporánea."
     Sacramento, CA:  Explicación de Textos Literarios, v. 11, no. 2,
     (1982-1983), pp. 11-28.

     Discusses, El bazar de los idiotas and Dabeiba by Gustavo Alvarez
     Gardeazábal and his treatment of space and time elements in
     comparison with García Márquez's Cien años de soledad and El otoño
     del patriarca, and Soto Aparicio's, Viaje a la claridad.

249. Yurkievich, Saul. "La fiction somatique." Translated from the
     Spanish by Pierre Rivas.  Paris:  Silex, no. 11, (March, 1979),
     pp. 112-118. (Special issue:  "Gabriel García Márquez-Amerique
     Latine.")

     Yurkievich studies various works of fiction by García Márquez,
     describing them as novels of extended metaphor.

250. Yviricu, Jorge. "Las pistas falses de un cuento de Gabriel García
     Márquez." Forest Hills, NY:  Enlace, (March-June, 1985), pp. 20-23.

     The influence of the Bible and biblical allusions in the short
     story, "Un señor muy viejo con unas alas enormes."

251. Zemskov, Valeri.  "¿Quién mató a Santiago Nasar?" Moscow:  America
     Latina, no. 4, (1982), pp. 76-78.

     The last two novels, El otoño del patriarca and Crónica de una
     muerte anunciada reveal the maturing of García Márquez as an artist
     and an artisan of the written word.

252. Zverev, A. "A Presentiment of Epics - Latin-American Prose and the
     Course of the Contemporary Novel." Moscow:  Novyi Mir, no. 9,
     (1980), pp. 220-236.

Zverev, A.  "Predchuvstvie epiki:  Latinoamerikanskaia proza i puti sovremennogo romana."  Moscow: <u>Novyi Mir</u>, no. 9, (1980), pp. 220-236.

In these pages, the author represents the Latin American writer as a social novelist.  He maintains that Gabriel García Márquez is the brightest Latin American novelist and cites <u>One Hundred Years of Solitude</u> as a prime example of a Baroque novel.  He also contrasts the element of tragedy in <u>Autumn of the Patriarch</u> to <u>All The Kings Men</u>, by Robert Penn Warren.

# Interviews

1. Arroyo, Frances. "Gabriel García Márquez habla de las posibilidades novelísticas de recientes sucesos españoles." Madrid: El País, (November 26, 1981), p. 33.

   An interview in which García Márquez comments on possible themes for future novels.

2. Caballero, Antonio, Enrique Santos Calderón, Hernando Corral, and Jorge Restrepo. "'La realidad se ha vuelto populista'." In García Márquez habla de García Márquez, 33 reportajes, Alfonso Rentería Mantilla, ed. Bogotá: Rentería Mantilla, 1979, pp. 189-194.

   Latin American politics and García Márquez's views are the topics of this interview published in Alternativa in November of 1978.

3. Calderón, Enrique Santos and Jorge Restrepo. "'Estoy comprometido hasta el tuétano con el periodismo político'." In García Márquez habla de García Márquez, 33 reportajes, Alfonso Rentería Mantilla, ed. Bogotá: Rentería Editores, 1979, pp. 105-110.

   This interview which appeared in García Márquez's Colombian based newspaper, Alternativa, in 1975 explains his leftist position in the world of politics.

4. Ceberio, Jesús. "Ez a legjobb regényem: Beszélgetés Gabriel García Marquezzel." Budapest, Hungary: Nagyvilág, (July, 1932), pp. 1049-1052.

   García Márquez considers Crónica de una muerte anunciada to be his "best book yet" in this article for a Hungarian periodical.

5. Ceberio, Jesús. "Mon meilleur roman." Albert Bensoussan, tr. Paris: Magazine Littéraire, no. 178, (November, 1981), pp. 26-27.

In an interview with Jesús Ceberio, Gabriel García Márquez discusses why he feels that his latest novel, Crónica de una muerte anunciada is his best ever and how he was able to create such a masterpiece.

6.  Cobo Borda, J. G.  "Bate-papo literário com García Márquez."  São Paulo, Brazil:  Leia Livros, año 4, no. 41, (November, 1981), pp. 14-15.

    García Márquez answers questions about his novels, poetry, and the writers who have influenced him in his literary career.

7.  "Colombian writer and political activist Gabriel García Márquez interviewed."  New York, NY:  The New York Times, v. 2, no. 3, (May 22, 1980), p. 18.

    The political activities of García Márquez as seen through his works.

8.  Conte, Rafael.  "Gabriel García Márquez publica su novela 'Crónica de una muerte anunciada'."  Madrid:  El País, (January 22, 1981), p. 25.

    García Márquez speaks of his new novel and the economics of publishing a book.  A short biography of García Márquez follows.

9.  Couffon, Robert.  "A Bogotá chez García Márquez."  Paris:  L'Express, no. 1332, (January 17-23, 1977), pp. 70-78.

    García Márquez speaks of his family life, political involvement and other influences upon his writings.

10. Dreifus, Claudia.  "Playboy Interview:  Gabriel García Márquez."  Chicago, IL:  Playboy, v. 30, no. 2, (February, 1983), pp. 65-67.

    García Márquez talks about his novels, his friend Fidel Castro, and life, love, and revolution in Latin America.

11. Durán, Armando.  "Conversaciones con GGM."  In García Márquez habla de García Márquez, 33 reportajes, Alfonso Rentería Mantilla, ed. Bogotá:  Rentería Editores, 1979, pp. 29-35.

    "Nothing in this world pleases me more than to write," states García Márquez in this conversation with Durán, reprinted from the Revista Nacional de Cultura of Caracas, September, 1968.

12. Equipo de Redacción de "El Manifiesto."  "El viaje a la semilla."  In García Márquez habla de García Márquez, 33 reportajes, Alfonso Rentería Mantilla, ed.  Bogotá:  Rentería Editores, 1979, pp. 159-167.

    In response to a variety of questions, García Márquez expresses his preferences among his writings and mentions events from his youth which influenced his later works.  Taken from El Manifiesto of Bogotá in 1977.

13. Erofeeva, G.  "Obraz prevyshe vsego."  Moscow:  Voprosy Literatury, v. 10, (October, 1982), pp. 191-195.

García Márquez explains his method of writing and the influence of other writers, such as Rubén Darío, on his work.

14.  "Gabriel García Márquez:  '...mucho de lo que he contado es la primera vez que lo digo...'."  (Interview).  Moscow: América Latina, no. 1, (1980), pp. 79-105.

    García Márquez states that much of what he has said to his interviewers has never been said by him before.  His Cien años de soledad and El otoño del patriarca are subjects for discussion.

15.  "García Márquez interrogado por otros escritores."  Panamá:  Hombre de Mundo, v. 2, no. 5, (1973), pp. 80-93.

    In this joint interview, García Márquez expresses his opinion on various topics.

16.  García Márquez, Gabriel.  "Impresiones (ante la muerte de Alejo Carpentier)."  La Habana:  Casa de las Américas, v. 21, no. 121, (July-August, 1980), p. 13.

    A brief interview with García Márquez reveals the novelist's views on Alejo Carpentier's use of magical realism and political overtones in his works.

17.  García Márquez, Gabriel.  "Making of a Classic:  Excerpts from an Interview."  New York, NY:  Atlas, v. 26, no. 7, (July, 1979), p. 50.

    Interviewed while in México, by O Pasquim of Rio de Janeiro, García Márquez states that "...for me, what matters is that One Hundred Years of Solitude has passed from one generation to another."

18.  Gilio, María Esther.  "'Escribir bien es un deber revolucionario'."  In García Márquez habla de García Márquez, 33 reportajes.  Alfonso Rentería Mantilla, ed.  Bogotá:  Rentería Editores, 1979, pp. 141-145.

    García Márquez speaks of his youth, ambition and philosophy of life in this interview which appeared in Triunfo of Madrid in 1977.

19.  González Bermejo, Ernesto.  "Ahora doscientos años de soledad."  In García Márquez habla de García Márquez, 33 reportajes.  Alfonso Rentería Mantilla, ed.  Bogotá:  Rentería Editores, 1979, pp. 49-64.

    Revealing and frank comments by García Márquez on the commercial success of his writings which appeared in Triunfo of Madrid in November of 1971.

20.  González Bermejo, Ernesto.  "La imaginación al poder en Macondo."  In García Márquez habla de García Márquez, 33 reportajes.  Alfonso Rentería Mantilla, ed.  Bogotá:  Rentería Editores, 1979, pp. 111-117.

During this discussion of the role of power in his later works,
García Márquez appears much affected by the coup in Chile, as
recorded in this interview published in Revista Crisis, in
Buenos Aires, in 1975.

21.  Gossaín, Juan.  "El regreso a Macondo."  In García Márquez habla
de García Márquez, 33 reportajes.  Alfonso Rentería Mantilla, ed.
Bogotá:  Rentería Editores, 1979, pp. 65-70.

Interviewed in the airport in Barranquilla, Colombia, García Márquez expresses his opinions on literature, politics, and his
travels as a Colombian reporter from El Espectador of Bogotá in
1971.

22.  Harguindey, Angel S.  "'Franco tuvo una muerte que hubiera sido
irreal en literatura':  entrevista con Gabriel García Márquez."
Madrid:  El País, Arte y Pensamiento, v. 2, no. 25, (April 2,
(April 2, 1978), pp. 1, 6-7.

García Márquez discusses his literary successes and speaks
frankly about the political situation in Latin America, especially
Cuba.

23.  Harguindey, Angel S.  "'Llegué a creer que Franco no se moriría
nunca'."  In García Márquez habla de García Márquez, 33 reportajes.
Alfonso Rentería Mantilla, ed.  Bogotá:  Rentería Editores, 1979,
pp. 169-172.

The politics of Spain, Chile, and Colombia are discussed in an
article from El País in Madrid, in 1978.

24.  Hernández, José.  "Latin American Ascendant:  The Decolonization
of a Culture."  New York, NY:  World Press Review, v. 29, no. 4,
(April, 1982), p. 61.

Originally published in El Mundo of Medellín, Colombia, (February
6, 1982).  García Márquez describes Latin American literature as
"the literature of the moment."

25.  Komisar, Lucy.  "Afraid to let Americans hear foreigners voice
'other' ideas."  Des Moines, IA:  Des Moines Register, (April 9,
1984), p. 8.

García Márquez and several other writers, actors, and political
figures have been denied entry to the United States because of
political reasons based on provisions in the MacCarran-Walter Act
of 1952.

26.  Landeros, Carlos.  "En Barcelona con Gabriel García Márquez."
México:  Siempre, (March 2, 1970), p. 18.

Stating emphatically that he detests reading about himself in the
media, García Márquez declares that the only truths for him are
Rolling Stones' songs, the Cuban Revolution, and four friends.

27. McMurray, George R. "García Márquez Interview and Legal Problems in Colombia." Appleton, WI: Hispania, v. 58, no. 3, (September, 1975), p. 153.

    Comments on an interview with García Márquez printed in the January 30, 1975 issue of Visión.

28. Mendoza, Plinio Apuleyo. "El encuentro de dos camaradas." In García Márquez habla de García Márquez, 33 reportajes. Alfonso Rentería Mantilla, ed. Bogotá: Rentería Editores, 1979, pp. 79-92.

    Reprint of two consecutive interviews of García Márquez by Mendoza which appeared originally in Revista Libre (Paris, 1972) and Revista Triunfo (Madrid, 1974).

29. Mendoza, Plinio Apuleyo. "Entretien avec Gabriel García Márquez." Paris: Silex, no. 11, (March, 1979), pp. 8-18. (Special issue: "Gabriel García Márquez - Amérique Latine."

    Personal interview with Gabriel García Márquez about his works, life, ideologies, and dreams.

30. Nepomuceno, Eric. "Gabriel García Márquez: El artesano de la palabra." In Los escritores. México: Comunicación e Información, 1981, pp. 89-101.

    An informative interview with the Colombian author on his writings, his political beliefs, and other topics, preceded by an introduction which gives new insights into the author's family life, personality and idiosyncrasies.

31. Osorio, Manuel. "Poco café y mucha política." In García Márquez habla de García Márquez, 33 reportajes. Alfonso Rentería Mantilla, ed. Bogotá: Rentería Editores, 1979, pp. 179-184.

    Cuba in Africa, President Carter and Latin American politics are discussed in an interview reported by Cuadernos para el Diálogo of Madrid, in 1978.

32. Pereira, Manuel. "'La Revolución cubana me libró de todos los honores detestables de este mundo'." In García Márquez habla de García Márquez, 33 reportajes. Alfonso Rentería Mantilla, ed. Bogotá: Rentería Editores, 1979, pp. 201-209.

    Speaking of literature, García Márquez maintains that "Literature is not learned in the University but by reading other authors with intensity." Taken from Bohemia, in La Habana, 1979. This was also published with the title "Dix mille ans de littérature: entretien avec Gabriel García Márquez." Albert Bensoussan, tr. Paris: Magazine Littéraire, no. 178, (November, 1981), pp. 20-25.

33. Preciado, Nativel. "Gabriel García Márquez en carne viva." In García Márquez habla de García Márquez, 33 reportajes. Alfonso Rentería Mantilla, ed. Bogotá: Rentería Editores, 1979, pp. 41-43.

    Commentaries on Cien años de soledad taken from the newspaper Madrid, 1969.

34. Prensa Latina. "'Es un crimen no tener participación política
    activa'." In García Márquez habla de García Márquez, 33 reportajes.
    Alfonso Rentería Mantilla, ed. Bogotá: Rentería Editores, 1979,
    pp. 133-139.

    Reflecting on the politics in his novels, García Márquez maintains
    that "a novel is a poetic transposition of reality" in this
    interview printed in Triunfo of Madrid in 1976.

35. Raillard, Alice. "Gabriel García Márquez nous parle de son dernier
    roman." Paris: La Quinzaine Littéraire, no. 362, (January 15,
    1982), pp. 6-7.

    After the publication of his latest novel, Crónica de una muerte
    anunciada, García Márquez is interviewed in Paris during which he
    speaks of his accomplishments and future plans.

36. Romero, Vicente. "Gabriel García Márquez habla sobre Cuba." In
    García Márquez habla de García Márquez, 33 reportajes. Alfonso
    Rentería Mantilla, ed. Bogotá: Rentería Editores, 1979, pp.
    147-149.

    García Márquez's position on Cuba and his defense of Fidel Castro
    is the topic of this interview for Pueblo of Madrid in 1977.

37. Saballos, Angela. "Crónica de una vida solidaria:  entrevista
    exclusiva con Gabriel García Márquez." Nicaragua: Ya Veremos,
    año 1, no. 1, (June, 1980), pp. 26-28.

    Gabriel García Márquez talks about his belief in people, his views
    on politics, his future works, and his ideals.

38. Sarret, Josep. "Estoy tan metido en la política que siento nostal-
    gia de la literatura." In García Márquez habla de García Márquez,
    33 reportajes. Alfonso Rentería Mantilla, ed. Bogotá:  Rentería
    Editores, 1979, pp. 211-218.

    Literature and politics are subjects for this interview for El Vie-
    jo Topo of Barcelona in 1979.

39. Simons, Marlise. "A Talk with Gabriel García Márquez." New York,
    NY:  The New York Times Book Review, (December 5, 1982), pp. 7, 60.

    García Márquez expresses his views on the relationship between
    literature and journalism.

40. Simons, Marlise. "Love and Age: A Talk with García Márquez."
    New York, NY:  The New York Times Book Review, v. 90, no. 14,
    (April 7, 1985), pp. 1, 18-19.

    Plans for a new book about love in youth and old age, a discussion
    of Simone de Beauvoir's book The Coming of Age, and opinions about
    the art of writing are topics within the scope of this interview.

41. Stefanovics, Tomás. "Interview with Gabriel García Márquez."
    Nancy Schena, tr. Boston:  Imagine, v. 1, no. 1, (Summer, 1984),
    pp. 24-32.

García Márquez concludes this interview with the remark, "Everyone who talks to me tries to make use of what is said for a publication." Previously published with the title of: "Entrevista
a Gabriel García Márquez." Munich: Khipu, (December, 1983), pp.
23-25.

42. Stone, Peter S. "The Art of Fiction LXIX: Gabriel García Márquez."
    Flushing, NY: Paris Review, v. 23, no. 82, (Winter, 1981), pp. 44-
    73.

    García Márquez discusses the creation of specific works, particu-
    larly One Hundred Years of Solitude, as well as fiction writing.

43. Stone, Peter S. "El descubrimiento del mundo de Gabriel García
    Márquez." Bogotá: El Tiempo, Lecturas Dominicales, (April 29,
    1979), pp. 2-5.

    Interview with García Márquez held in Mexico City in which he
    discusses his life and a book that he is writing on Cuba.

44. Stone, Peter S. "Gabriel García Márquez." In Writers at Work:
    The 'Paris Review' Interviews. 6th series. George Plimpton, ed.
    New York, NY: The Viking Press, 1984, pp. 313-339.

    This literary interview provides insights into the personality and
    narrative talent of García Márquez.

45. Suárez, Luis. "'El periodismo me dió conciencia política'." In
    García Márquez habla de García Márquez, 33 reportajes. Alfonso
    Rentería Mantilla, ed. Bogotá: Rentería Editores, 1979, pp. 195-
    200.

    Journalistic responsibility and political conscience are the topics
    of the article printed in La Calle of Madrid in 1978.

46. "Sur l'expression littéraire." Paris: La Nouvelle Revue des Deux
    Mondes, (March, 1974), pp. 630-640.

    Four Latin American novelists, including García Márquez, are
    quizzed as to their opinion of the state of contemporary Latin
    American literature.

47. Torres, Miguel. "El novelista que quiso hacer cine." In García
    Márquez habla de García Márquez, 33 reportajes. Alfonso Rentería
    Mantilla, ed. Bogotá: Rentería Editores, 1979, pp. 45-48.

    In this conversation García Márquez reveals his ambition to make
    films. This article was taken from Revista de Cine Cubano, La
    Habana, Cuba, 1969.

48. Urondo, Francisco. "La buena hora de GGM." In García Márquez
    habla de García Márquez, 33 reportajes. Alfonso Rentería Mantilla,
    ed. Bogotá: Rentería Editores, 1979, pp. 71-74.

    This article first appeared in Cuadernos Hispanoamericanos of Ma-
    drid in 1971 and reveals how fame has affected García Márquez.

49.  Vargas Llosa, Mario. "Un dictador latinoamericano: Gabriel
     García Márquez habla de su próxima novela con Mario Vargas Llosa."
     Madrid: Indice, v. 24, no. 39, (October 15, 1969), p. 39.

     García Márquez's forthcoming novel, El otoño del patriarca, is
     the subject of this interview conducted in 1969.

50.  Washburn, Yulan M.  "García Márquez está cansado de las equivoca-
     ciones de la crítica." Appleton, WI: Hispania, v. 54, no. 2,
     (May, 1971), pp. 387-390.

     Originally published in number 185 of the Revista Nacional de
     Cultura de Caracas, this article contains sections of an interview
     with Armando Durán.

51.  Zalamea, Alberto.  "GGM se confiesa a Marcel Proust." In García
     Márquez habla de García Márquez, 33 reportajes. Alfonso Rentería
     Mantilla, ed. Bogotá: Rentería Editores, 1979, pp. 155-157.

     The format of this interview with García Márquez was adapted by
     Zalamea from a questionnaire created earlier in the century by
     Proust. This article appeared originally in Hombre de Mundo of
     Mexico in 1977.

# About Gabriel García Márquez:
# the Man, the Reporter, the Writer

1. Albertocchi, Giovanni. "L'annuncio di García Márquez." Firenze,
   Italy: <u>Il Ponte-Revista Mensile di Politica e Letteratura</u>, v. 38,
   no. 10, (1982), pp. 1067-1070.

   The publication of <u>Chronicle of a Death Foretold</u> announces the
   return of García Márquez to the literary world, even though,
   annoyed with the adverse criticism of <u>The Autumn of the Patriarch</u>,
   he had maintained that he would never write another novel.

2. Alvarez García, Marcos. "Introduction." In <u>Fiction et réalité</u>:
   <u>la littérature latino-américaine</u>. Bruxelles, Belgique: Université
   Libre de Bruxelles, Institut de Sociologie. Centre d'Etude de
   l'Amerique Latine, Editions de l'Université, 1983, pp. 1-9.

   A publication honoring Latin American Literature. The introduction
   mentions García Márquez as the "Colombian who possesses a vast
   imagination."

3. Alvarez Gardeazábal, Gustavo. "The Short Story in Colombia." New
   York, NY: <u>Review</u>, no. 24, (1979), pp. 70-72.

   Attributes the rise of the short story in Colombia, a country where
   poetry has traditionally been the dominant literary form, to the
   success of Gabriel García Márquez.

4. <u>Aracataca - Estocolmo</u>. Bogotá: Instituto Colombiano de Cultura,
   1983, ₊117₊ p., unnumbered.

   Recounts the awarding of the Nobel Prize for Literature to Gabriel
   García Márquez with numerous candid, on-location photographs. First
   hand accounts of those attending the ceremony provide personalized
   documentation of the event.

5. Arenas, Reinaldo. "Gabriel García Márquez: ¿Esbirro o Burro?" Huntington Park, CA: Junta Cívico-Militar Cubana, v. 4, no. 3, (October, 1981), p. 43.

   Raises doubts about Gabriel García Márquez's integrity, who while simultaneously praising communist regimes such as Castro's, is enjoying the fruits of capitalism by maintaining a prosperous literary career in the western world.

6. Barreto, Luis León. "Confesiones de Gabriel García Márquez sobre literatura, política y periodismo." Bucaramanga, Colombia: Vanguardia Liberal, (August 19, 1973), pp. 1-9.

   García Márquez's thoughts and opinions on various subjects: Literature, politics, and journalism among others.

7. Barth, John. "The Literature of Replenishment: Postmodernist Fiction." Boston, MA: The Atlantic, v. 245, no. 1, (January, 1980), pp. 65-71.

   Establishes García Márquez as an exemplary writer in the post-modernist tradition, citing examples from One Hundred Years of Solitude.

8. Barth, John. "La littérature du renouvellement: La fiction postmoderniste." Cynthia Liebow and Jean-Benoit Puech, trs. Paris: Poétique, v. 12, no. 48, (November, 1981), pp. 395-405.

   French version of the Barth article which appeared in The Atlantic.

9. Benson, John. "Crónica de una muerte anunciada (Chronicle of an Announced Death) y Gabriel García Márquez." Pittsburgh, PA: Latin American Literary Review, v. 11, no. 21, (Fall-Winter, 1982), pp. 63-67.

   Relates the story of Gabriel García Márquez's fleeing from Colombia at the time his novel Crónica de una muerte anunciada was published with a brief summary of the novel.

10. Bernáldez Bernáldez, José M. "¿Qué fué de la narrativa latinoamericana del 'boom'?" Madrid: Cuadernos hispanoamericanos: Revista Mensual de Cultura Hispánica, no. 398, (August, 1983), pp. 385-393.

    García Márquez's role as one of the leaders of the "boom" of Latin American literature in the 1970's.

11. Beverley, John. "Gabriel García Márquez: Latin America's 'social text'." Pittsburgh, PA: Clásicos, no. 13, (1984), pp. 6-7.

    "The typical García Márquez 'fiction' parallels and supplements the vision of Latin America political economy and history provided by dependency theory in the social sciences."

12. Blasquez, Adélaide. "Gabriel García Márquez: Nobel 82." Paris: La Quinzaine Littéraire, no. 381, (November 1-15, 1982), p. 14.

García Márquez describes Cien años de soledad as the embodement of
all of his other works.

13. "Un caballo en la alcoba: cuento que Vinyes dedicó a García Márquez." Bogotá: El Espectador, (February 27, 1977), p. 7.

Ramón Vinyes, "el sabio catalán" of García Márquez's novel dedicated this story to him.

14. Cabrera Infante, Guillermo. "Nuestro prohombre en La Habana."
México: Vuelta, v. 8, no. 78, (May, 1983), pp. 51-53.

García Márquez's politics, his problems in trying to enter the
United States, and those of other authors in exile are topics
presented here.

15. Cacua Prada, Antonio. Historia del periodismo colombiano. Bogotá:
Ediciones Sua, 1984, 513 p.

In several places in this history of the Colombian press, García
Márquez is mentioned with his relationship to various newspapers.

16. Calle, Angel Luis de la. "García Márquez, guionista de una película sobre el canal de Panamá." Madrid: El País, (October 14,
1977), p. 31.

García Márquez will be the consultant for a film on the Panama
Canal.

17. Carilla, Emilio. Estudios de literatura hispanoamericana. Bogotá:
Instituto Caro y Cuervo, 1977, pp. 345-358.

García Márquez appears in the chapter which discusses the neo-
baroque phenomena in contemporary Hispanic literature.

18. Carrión, Alejandro. "La novela colombiana moderna." New York, NY:
Américas, v. 31, no. 3, (March, 1979), pp. 45-46.

The success of One Hundred Years of Solitude has influenced many
young Colombian writers.

19. Carvajalino, Guillermo. "Entre Cien años y El otoño." Calí,
Colombia: Estravagario: Revista Cultural de El Pueblo, (March 13,
1976), p. 7.

Literary world welcomes García Márque'z latest book, El otoño del
patriarca.

20. Castañeda, V. Emilio. "Latin American Literature: Historical
Perspective." University Center, MI: Alèthea, no. 13, (Spring-
Summer, 1984), pp. 47-53. (Special issue: Gabriel García Márquez:
the Man and the Magic of His Writings).

Reference is made to the four Latin American Nobelists in Literature: Gabriela Mistral, Miguel Angel Asturias, Pablo Neruda, and
Gabriel García Márquez.

21. Castañeda, V. Emilio. "Literatura hispanoamericana: perspectiva
histórica." University Center, MI: Alèthea, no. 13, (Spring-
Summer, 1984, pp. 1-8. (Special issue: Gabriel García Márquez:
the Man and the Magic of His Writings).

Spanish version of entry no. 20.

22. Cerda, Carlos. "El Descubridor." Madrid: Araucaria de Chile,
no. 21, (1983), pp. 103-105.

Elation over García Márquez's Nobel Prize and a summary of his
literary accomplishments.

23. "Chronology." Norman, OK: Books Abroad, v. 47, no. 3, (Summer,
1973), pp. 501-504.

Provides a detailed chronology of García Márquez's life up to the
completion of the first draft of The Autumn of the Patriarch.

24. Cobo Borda, Juan Gustavo. "Cuando García Márquez pensaba."
Bogotá: Eco, v. 34, no. 205, (November, 1978), p. 103.

Highlights the continuing importance of García Márquez's earlier
works, after the success of his more recent ones.

25. Coles, Robert. "García Márquez: A Personal Appreciation." Pittsburgh, PA: Latin American Literary Review, Special Issue: Gabriel
García Márquez, v. 13, no. 25, (January–June, 1985), pp. 149-150.

On a visit to Nicaragua, the author is reminded of characters in
García Márquez's writings and is convinced that "for García Márquez
the point, clearly, is to look upward with awe at 'common folk'
rather than downward in the manner of 'noblesse oblige'."

26. Comas, José. "Cohn-Bendit realiza una edición pirata y anónima de
la última novela de García Márquez." Madrid: El País, (July 3,
1981) p. 35.

A pirated edition of Crónica de una muerte anunciada with the
author G. de Aracataca is published in a German magazine.

27. "Congreso anual de la Unión de Periodistas en Benalmádena." Madrid:
El País, (April 17, 1981), p. 13.

Journalistic prize is awarded to Gabriel García Márquez by El País.

28. Conte, Rafael. "Gabriel García Márquez publica su novela, Crónica
de una muerte anunciada." Madrid: El País, (January 22, 1981),
p. 25.

Breaking a literary silence of almost eight years García Márquez
publishes his new novel and comments about the commercial problems
involved.

29. Crichton, Jennifer. "Ballatine Readies a Mass Market Coffee-table
Book." New York, NY: Publishers Weekly, v. 224, no. 25, (December 16, 1983), pp. 53 and 56.

The mass marketing of Gabriel García Márquez's Chronicle of a Death Foretold by Ballantine.

30. "Cuba pone en libertad a un antiguo dirigente cristiano, gracias a gestiones de García Márquez." Madrid: El País, (December 17, 1977), p. 4.

    García Márquez is influential in obtaining the release of a political prisoner in Cuba.

31. "Day of the Bull." Washington, DC: The Times of the Americas, (October 26, 1983), p. 24.

    As a special guest at a bullfight in Colombia, Gabriel García Márquez is called the "hero of the day," and is pictured in a photo with bullfighter Leónidas Manrique.

32. Delgado-Gal, Alvaro. "Gabriel García Márquez o el diluvio incruento." Madrid: El País, (September 13, 1981), p. 1.

    Contends that García Márquez is more of a journalist than a novelist.

33. Enciso, Luis H. "La farsa de Gabriel García Márquez." Huntington Park, CA: Junta Cívico-Militar Cubana, v. 4, no. 3, (October, 1981), p. 39.

    A Colombian government official criticizes Gabriel García Márquez's exile in México.

34. Epstein, Joseph. "How Good is Gabriel García Márquez?" New York, NY: Commentary, v. 75, (May, 1983), pp. 59-65.

    After being compared to Proust and Joyce, and known as a "classic" novelist throughout the world, Joseph Epstein questions Gabriel García Márquez's reputation as a writer.

35. Equipo de Redacción de Cromos. "Gabriel García Márquez evoca a Pablo Neruda." In García Márquez habla de García Márquez, 33 reportajes. Alfonso Rentería Mantilla, ed. Bogotá: Rentería Editores, 1979, pp. 93-96.

    García Márquez's memories of Pablo Neruda as quoted in this article taken from Cromos, Bogotá, 1973.

36. Escribano Belmonte, Antonio. "El otoño del patriarca: testamento político de García Márquez?" Bogotá: El Espectador: Magazine Dominical, (June 1, 1975), pp. 6-7.

    The political inclinations of García Márquez are said to be written in his works.

37. "El escritor García Márquez abandona Colombia por razones de seguridad personal." Madrid: El País, (March 27, 1981), p. 4.

    Because of his leftist leanings García Márquez is forced to leave Colombia.

38. "Faces, Mirrors, Masks: Twentieth Century Latin American Fiction."
    Urbana, IL:  Patterns, (June, 1984), p. 20.

    The series "Faces, Mirrors, Masks: Twentieth Century Latin American
    Fiction," from National Public Radio, will be initiated by a por-
    trait of Gabriel García Márquez - "an insight into the complexi-
    ties of his work and life."

39. "Fallo judicial a favor de Gabriel García Márquez."  Madrid:
    El País, (May 10, 1980), p. 29; (February 15, 1980), p. 24.

    The verdict in the case of Editorial Plaza and Janes vs. García
    Márquez, Carmen Balcells, and Editorial Bruguera for the publica-
    tion of a popular edition of El otoño del patriarca.

40. Franco, Jean.  "¿Qué ha pasado con el coro?:  García Márquez y el
    Premio Nobel."  New York, NY:  Areíto, v. 8, no. 32, (1983), pp.
    18-22.

    This article, which was published also, in México in Pié de página:
    Revista de Literatura, v. 3, pp. 11-14 with title: "García Márquez
    y el Nobel," contains excerpts with comments of Gabriel García
    Márquez's acceptance speech for the Nobel Prize.

41. "Gabo Finds His Place in the Sun."  London:  The Observer, no. 9973,
    (October 24, 1982), p. 7.

    Provides a profile on Gabriel García Márquez following his desig-
    nation as the 1982 winner of the Nobel Prize for Literature.

42. "Gabriel García Márquez."  Paris:  Magazine Littéraire, no. 178,
    (November, 1981), p. 14.

    Recounts Gabriel García Márquez's accomplishments as a writer,
    politician, and journalist.

43. "Gabriel García Márquez expuso a Juan Pablo, II... ."  Madrid:
    El País, (February 15, 1979), p. 26.

    In an interview with John Paul, II, Gabriel García Márquez spoke
    about HABEAS, which he sponsored to defend politicians incarcerated
    in Latin America.

44. "Gabriel García Márquez meets Ernest Hemingway."  New York, NY:
    The New York Times Book Review, v. 86, (July 26, 1981), p. 1.

    Gabriel García Márquez reveals to his readers the excitement of his
    first encounter with Ernest Hemingway, and the dramatic influence
    both Hemingway and Faulkner have had on his writing.

45. "Gabriel García Márquez ... recibió anteayer el premio de la paz
    'Jorge Dimitrov' ... ."  Madrid:  El País, (April 5, 1979), p. 30.

    The "Jorge Dimitrov" award which García Márquez received is given
    by the Republic of Bulgaria to individuals who work for the
    improvement of social justice in Latin America.

46.  García Márquez habla de García Márquez, 33 reportajes.  Alfonso
     Rentería Mantilla, ed.  Bogotá:  Rentería Editores, 1979, 218 p.

     A series of essays, articles and interviews, taken from various
     periodicals, and written during the years 1967-1979.  Each of
     these appears in this present bibliography.

47.  Gass, William H.  "Inmortal Nominations."  New York, NY:  The New
     York Times Book Review, v. 84, no. 22, (June 3, 1979), p. 13.

     Speaking of the one hundred most important books of the western
     world, Gass includes One Hundred Years of Solitude, stating that
     it is a "great book despite its popularity with the rear guard."

48.  Gavilanes Laso, J. L.  "Las coronas del laurel."  Lisbon, Portugal:
     Coloquio:  Revista de Artes e Letras, v. 71, (January, 1983),
     pp. 76-78.

     Summarizes and comments upon the literary output of three authors:
     two from Spain and one from Colombia who have received prestigious
     literary prizes in the early 80's.  The one from Colombia being
     García Márquez.

49.  "Gente:  'En pleno éxito de ventas ...'."  Madrid:  El País, (May 9,
     1981), p. 56.

     One and a half million copies of Crónica de una muerte anunciada
     are sold.

50.  Georgescu, Paul Alexandru.  "García Márquez y las metamorfosis de
     la novela."  Bogotá:  Correo de los Andes, no. 13, (January-
     February, 1982), pp. 30-32.

     From his early stories to his latest novels García Márquez's
     writings reveal his obsession with "soledad."

51.  Gilard, Jacques.  "García Márquez y el oficio de escritor:  una
     definición temprana."  Bogotá:  Eco, v. 38/3, no. 231, (January,
     1981), p. 327.

     The perfectionist technique of García Márquez's writing.

52.  Gilard, Jacques.  "El grupo de Barranquilla."  Madrid:  Revista
     Iberoamericana, no. 128-129, (July-December, 1984), pp. 905-935.

     Deals with the formative years of García Márquez, and discusses
     how the small group of intellectuals of "El Grupo de Barranquilla"
     with whom he came into contact, influenced his later writings.

53.  Gnutzmann, Rita.  "Carpentier y la herencia proustiana."  Madrid:
     Revista de Literatura, v. 44, no. 88, (July-December, 1982),
     pp. 169-180.

     Contradictory statements made by García Márquez on whether or not
     he was influenced by Faulkner are used as examples of how authors
     sometimes do not know to what point their work has been influenced
     by another's.

54. González Bermejo, Ernesto. "Gabriel García Márquez habla en Barcelona sobre El otoño del patriarca." Bogotá: El Espectador: Magazine Dominical, (November 29, 1970), pp. 3-7.

Discusses the problems in, and the reasons for writing this latest novel.

55. Gott, Richard and W. L. Webb. "Freedom Born Out of Fiction." London and Manchester: The Guardian, (October 22, 1982), p. 8.

The Nobel Prize for literature awarded to Gabriel García Márquez "will be widely seen as a political gesture to those struggling for political freedom in South and Central America."

56. Graham-Yooll, Andrew. "Back in the Bullring. García Márquez in Bogotá." London: London Magazine, New Series, v. 23, no. 12, (March, 1984), pp. 87-91.

After explaining his illness, García Márquez talks about the Falklands, Golding and the Nobel Prize, and comments on Latin American politics.

57. Greiner, Donald J. "A Tribute to Gabriel García Márquez." In Dictionary of Literary Biography Yearbook, 1982. Detroit, MI: Gale Research, 1983, p. 10.

States the reasons for which García Márquez was awarded the Nobel Prize for literature.

58. Gyllensten, Lars. "Le Lauréat du Prix Nobel de littérature 1982: Gabriel García Márquez." Göteborg, Sweden: Moderna Sprak, v. 77, no. 1, (1938), pp. 54-56.

Comments on how García Márquez's success has attributed to the present day recognition of Latin American literature as a whole.

59. Harper, Michael. "Nominees, 1983 Fiction Prize." Los Angeles Times Book Review, (November 13, 1983), p. 7.

Chronicle of a Death Foretold, an English translation of Crónica de una muerte anunciada, published by Knopf is recommended for the Fiction Prize.

60. Heise, Hans-Jürgen. "Episch mündiges Lateinamerika: Zu Büchern von Gabriel García Márquez und Mario Vargas Llosa." Frankfurt: Die Neue Rundschau, v. 85, no. 4, (1974), pp. 684-689.

The two most important modern representatives of Latin American prose -according to Heise- are Gabriel García Márquez and Mario Vargas Llosa.

61. Herrera, Roberto. "Gabriel García Márquez: El Hombre." University Center, MI: Alèthea, no. 13, (Spring-Summer, 1984), pp. 9-20. (Special issue: Gabriel García Márquez: The Man and the Magic of His Writings).

Gabriel García Márquez and his works.

62. International Who's Who, 1983-1984. London:  Europa, 1984, p. 460.

    Bio-bibliography of García Márquez.

63. Ivanov, Blagoja.  "Makondo, sved od sonistrata, svet od realnosta."
    Skopje, Macedonia, Yugoslavia:  Razgledi:  Spisanie za Literatura
    Umetmost i Kultura, v. 21, no. 6, pp. 506-517.

    This article, prompted by the publication of El coronel no tiene
    quien le escriba, gives a short biography of García Márquez and
    describes, and quotes from some of his works.

64. Ivask, Ivar.  "Allegro Barbaro, or Gabriel García Márquez."  Norman,
    OK:  Books Abroad, v. 47, no. 3, (Summer, 1973), pp. 439-440.

    A detailed description of the festivities that followed Gabriel
    García Márquez's receipt of the Books Abroad/Neustadt International
    Prize, statements by the author on his writings, and the advan-
    tages of writing in Spanish as opposed to English.

65. Jara, Umberto.  "El hijo del telegrafista."  Lima:  Debate, no. 18,
    (1982), pp. 88-90.

    Biographical account of García Márquez from his birth as the son
    of a telegraph operator to his greatness as a writer of novels.

66. Kristensen, Helge.  "Fodnoter til storpolitik."  Copenhagen,
    Denmark:  Weekendavisen, (December 24-30, 1982), p. 8.

    García Márquez's relationship with Fidel Castro.

67. Levi, Isaac A.  "Colombian Novelist Awed by His Success."  Phoenix,
    AZ:  Arizona Republic, (December 6, 1981), p. G-14.

    Provides a personal sketch of García Márquez, capturing the
    different facets of his private life as they relate to his writing.

68. Levi, Isaac A.  "Writer's Books Second Only to Bible."  Champaign,
    IL:  The News Gazette, (December 13, 1981), Section F, p. 5.

    The information in this article is the same as that in the
    preceding.

69. Lezcano, Ricardo.  "Tribuna Libre:  Puntualizaciones sobre la de-
    nuncia a través de la Prensa."  Madrid:  El País, (May 7, 1981),
    p. 54.

    García Márquez's views on freedom of the press and accuracy of
    reporting.

70. "Literature Nobel Awarded."  Champaign, IL:  The News Gazette,
    (October 21, 1982), pp. A-1, a-5.

    In an article following Gabriel García Márquez's receipt of the
    Nobel Prize, a short description and summary of his life, works,
    and political involvement is given.

71. "La llama y el hielo." Quito: Nueva, no. 109, (December, 1984), p. 60.

   Tells of the reaction of Gabriel García Márquez to the most recent book by another Colombian, Plinio Apuleyo Mendoza, highlighting the latter's criticism of García Márquez and his ideology.

72. Lohmann, Jens. "Nobelprisen skal thene latinamerikansk enhed." Copenhagen: Information, (October 26, 1982), p. 5.

   The effects of García Márquez's winning the Nobel Prize on the Latin American literary world.

73. Luchting, Wolfgang A. "Gabriel García Márquez: El negro que hizo esperar a los ángeles and Ojos de perro azul." Norman, OK: Books Abroad, v. 47, no. 3, (Summer, 1973), p. 529.

   The first book, published by Alfil of Montevideo (Uruguay), and the second by Equiseditorial of Rosario (Argentina), are pirated editions which García Márquez urged buyers to steal instead of buying.

74. Major, André. "Márquez Nobelisé." Montréal: Liberté, v. 25, no. 1, (February, 1983), pp. 107–108.

   The political reasons for García Márquez's decision to suspend his career as a novelist, which he later resumed with his creation of Crónica de una muerte anunciada.

75. Mallett, Brian J. "García Márquez, el Premio Nobel y la imagen de Colombia." Madrid: Arbor, v. 114, no. 448, (April, 1983), pp. 15–22.

   The theme of solitude, hopelessness and despair depicted in García Márquez's novels is a reflection of much of the society of Latin America.

76. Matthews, Geoffrey. "Challenging a Rubber Stamp of Disapproval." London: Times, (May 3, 1984), p. 16.

   The denial of Gabriel García Márquez's request for a five-year entry visa into the United States by the Reagan Administration is claimed to be the result of the author's ideas, and opposition to U.S. policy in Latin America.

77. McMurray, George R. "Recent Criticism of Spanish American Fiction." Albuquerque, NM: Latin American Research Review, v. 19, no. 3, (1984), pp. 184–193.

   Descriptions of recent literature on García Márquez on pp. 186–187.

78. Meinhardt, Warren L. "García Márquez: Plagiario de Balzac?" Cincinnati, OH: Hispania, v. 15, no. 1, (March, 1972), p. 42.

   Meinhardt claims that there is evidence of plagiarism from Balzac's La Comedie Humaine in García Márquez's Cien años de soledad.

79. Mellors, John. "War in Peace." London: The Listener, v. 103, no. 2654, (March 20, 1980), p. 382.

In describing the role of war during moments of peace in several literary works, John Mellors points to the end of García Márquez's In Evil Hour, where peace is later filled with violence and suffering, thus depicting war.

80. Menchacatorre, Félix. "Aspectos de García Márquez en la obra de Ramiro Pinilla." Indiana, PA: Journal of Basque Studies, v. 4, no. 2, 1983, pp. 93-99.

This report examines the influence of García Márquez on the works of the Basque writer Ramiro Pinilla, citing chiefly One Hundred Years of Solitude.

81. Mendoza, Plinio Apuleyo. "García Márquez à Paris il y a 20 ans." Paris: Silex, no. 11, (March, 1979), pp. 5-7. (Special issue: "Gabriel García Márquez - Amérique Latine.")

This article translated by Jean-Charles Gateau is an account of García Márquez's first trip to Paris and his effort to make known his works.

82. Mendoza, Plinio Apuleyo. "García Márquez e os mistérios do poder e da solidâo." Minas Gerães, Brazil: Minas Gerães, Suplemento Literário, v. 18, no. 871, (June 11, 1983), pp. 6-7.

In a conversation with a fellow Colombian journalist, Plinio Apuleyo Mendoza, Gabriel García Márquez discusses Latin America and its dictators as they directly relate to The Autumn of the Patriarch.

83. Meneses, Carlos. "Gabriel García Márquez: periodista." Xalapa, Veracruz, México: La Palabra y el Hombre, no. 44, (October-December), pp. 90-91.

García Márquez's career as a journalist complements his work as a novelist, and explains how his newspaper articles enable the reader to see his vision of the novel and of literature.

84. Meunier, Jacques. "Naar het leven." Paris: Silex, no. 11, (March, 1979), pp. 45-48. (Special issue: "Gabriel García Márquez - Amérique Latine.")

On a note dated January 26, 1976 Jacques Menier quotes the poet Nicolas Suescún as saying "Cien años de soledad is a Brueghelian novel!"

85. Meyer-Clason, Curt. "Macondo auf Deutsch: Übersetzungs-Schwierigkeiten bei Gabriel García Márquez." Nürnberg, Hispanoram, v. 29, (November, 1981), pp. 137-139.

The difficulties encountered in translating García Márquez into German.

128    Secondary Sources

86. Michener, Charles. "Latin American Laureate." New York, NY: Newsweek, v. 100, no. 18, (November 1, 1982), pp. 81-82.

García Márquez's lifestyle and his novels are described in this article written after he had been awarded the 1982 Nobel Prize for literature.

87. "El monstruo García Márquez, larga su segunda gran obra." Bogotá: El Tiempo: Lecturas Dominicales, (June 22, 1975), pp. 1, 6-7.

The phenomenal success of One Hundred Years of Solitude and García Márquez's influence in the literary world.

88. Muller, Enrique. "Se inaugura en La Habana el Congreso de Intelectuales y Escritores Latinoamericanos." Madrid: El País, (September 6, 1981), p. 27.

Fidel Castro awards García Márquez the "José Martí Literary Prize" at a conference of about two hundred and fifty intellectuals.

89. Neustadt, Walter, Jr. "Address at the Banquet Honoring the 1972 Jury of the Books Abroad/Neustadt International Priza for Literature." Norman, OK: Books Abroad, v. 47, no. 3, (Summer, 1973, 1973), pp. 441-442.

The speech given at the University of Oklahoma when Gabriel García Márquez received the Neustadt International Prize for Literature.

90. "The 1982 Nobel Prize in Literature." In Dictionary of Literary Biography Yearbook: 1982. Richard Zeigfeld, ed. Detroit, MI: Gale Research, 1983, pp. 3-6.

Short criticism of García Márquez and his works, a bibliography of the English translations of his works, and his acceptance speech on receiving the Nobel Prize.

91. "Nobel Prize Awarded to Colombian." Decatur, IL: Decatur Herald and Review, (October 22, 1982), p. B9.

Summarizes the statements made by the Swedish Academy of Letters honoring Gabriel García Márquez.

92. "The Nobel Prize in Literature Was Awarded to Gabriel García Márquez, Colombian Author of 100 Years of Solitude." New York, NY: The Wall Street Journal, (October 22, 1982), p. 1.

The Wall Street Journal announces the Nobel Prize for Literature.

93. "Nobel Prizes: Gabriel García Márquez." New York, NY: National Review, (November 12, 1982), p. 1392.

"García Márquez is a rarity among present-day authors—one who satisfies both the advocates of modernist, experimental fiction, and the devotees of Tolstoy and old-fashioned storytelling."

94. "Nobel Prizes: Magic, Matter and Money." New York, NY: Time, v. 120, no. 18, (November 1, 1982), pp. 88-89.

    Gabriel García Márquez receives the Nobel Prize in 1982. Includes an excerpt from his novel Cien años de soledad.

95, "Nobels: Chicago, Macondo." New York, NY: Nation, (November 6, 1982), v. 235, no. 15, pp. 453.

    Presentation of the Nobel Prize in 1982.

96. Norvind, Eva. "Intelectuales interrogan a GGM." In García Márquez habla de García Márquez, 33 reportajes. Alfonso Rentería Mantilla, ed. Bogotá: Rentería Editores, 1979, pp. 151-154.

    Two reporters, two novelists and an actress reveal their impressions of García Márquez in their interviews for the Revista Hombre de Mundo of México, 1977.

97. "Nueva editorial para publicar a autores latinoamericanos en España." Madrid: El País, no. 95, (March 18, 1985), p. 20.

    The new publisher, La Montaña Mágica, has been organized to emphasize Latin American literature, especially books by García Márquez and Vargas Llosa among others, to bring them to the attention of the reading public of Spain.

98. Ortega, Julio. "Latin American Literature Facing the Eighties." New Orleans, LA: New Orleans Review, v. 7, no. 3, (Fall, 1980), pp. 294-296. (Translated by Stella Clark and Julie Jones, revised by Robert Bonazzi)

    The economic and social effects of the socio-literary phenomenon known as the boom on those authors including García Márquez who precipitated it. Also published as "La literatura latinoamericana en la década del 80," in Madrid: Hiperión, (Autumn, 1980), pp. 19-26.

99. Pastor, Ricardo. "Foreword." University Center, MI: Alèthea, no. 13, (Spring-Summer, 1984), pp. i-iv. (Special issue: Gabriel García Márquez: The Man and the Magic of His Writings.)

    Pastor concludes that "to read Gabriel García Márquez is to examine the social turbulence of a constantly changing hispanic world."

100. Peña Gutiérrez, Isaías. "Entrevista con Jorge Eliecer Pardo: 'Hasta cuando Gabo, hasta siempre'." In La narrativa del frente nacional. Bogotá: Fundación Universidad Central, 1982, pp. 334-341.

    Comments on the regionalism of García Márquez's novels, characteristics of which are found in much of Latin American literature.

101. Praag-Chantraine, Jacqueline van. "Gabriel García Márquez, Prix Nobel de Littérature." Brussels: Revue Générale, no. 11, (November, 1982), pp. 29-35.

130    Secondary Sources

The Nobel Prize and biobibliographical commentary on García Márquez.

102. Prego, Omar. "García Márquez ou la mémoire inventant le réel." Paris: Amérique Latine, no. 6, (Summer, 1981), pp. 97-100.

Upon the publication of Gabriel García Márquez's latest novel, Crónica de una muerte anunciada, Prego describes its effect on three areas: literature, politics, and publishing.

103. Provencio, Pedro. "Gabriel García Márquez - Un Nobel para nuestra lengua." Madrid: Nueva Estafeta, no. 48, (1982), p. 133.

The presentation of the Nobel Prize to Gabriel García Márquez and what it means to the future of Latin American literature.

104. R. D. "Un Premio Nobel para un realista mágico." San Salvador: Estudios Centroamericanos, v. 37, no. 410, (December, 1982), pp. 1139-1141.

The implications of García Márquez's dedication of his Nobel Prize to the El Salvador guerrilla movement.

105. Rama, Angel. "Literatura y cultura en América Latina." Lima: Revista de Crítica Literaria Latinoamericana, v. 9, no. 18, (1983), pp. 7-35.

Rama discusses the role of García Márquez in inciting the insurrection of the coastal zone of Colombia (Barranquilla and Cartagena) against the cultural norms imposed by Bogotá. For support, Rama illustrates from writings of García Márquez while working for El Heraldo in the 1950's.

106. Real, Manuel de J. "Glorias e injusticias del Nobel." Quito: Vistazo, no. 413, (November 9, 1984), pp. 30-33.

A succinct history of the Nobel Prize pointing out its successes and failures in nominating the recipients and hailing the nomination of García Márquez.

107. "Rescate de textos: Cortázar y García Márquez." Bogotá: Eco, v. 33, no. 203, (September, 1978), p. 1186.

Draws attention to the importance of the Gabriel García Márquez's article, "La literatura colombiana, un fraude a la nación," citing that it aids in the understanding of his own narrative skill.

108. Reuter, M. "García Márquez Wins the Nobel Prize in Literature." New York, NY: Publishers Weekly, v. 222, no. 19, (1982), p. 16.

The tremendous success of Cien años de soledad will increase with the winning of the Nobel prize.

109.  Riding, Alan.  "For García Márquez, Revolution is a Major Theme."
      New York, NY:  The New York Times Biographical Service, v. 11,
      no. 5, (May, 1980), pp. 687-688.

      Gabriel García Márquez's political beliefs, views on revolution
      in Latin América, and criticism of the United States' involvement
      in Cuba.

110.  Riding, Alan.  "Revolution and the Intellectual in Latin America."
      New York, NY:  The New York Times Magazine, (March 13, 1983),
      pp. 28-40.

      Gabriel García Márquez's involvement in Latin American politics
      is the topic of this article about Latin American intellectuals.

111.  Riera, Carmen.  "Carmen Balcells, alquimista del libro."  Barce-
      lona:  Quimera, no. 27, (January, 1983), pp. 23-29.

      An interview with García Márquez's literary agent, Carmen Barcells.

112.  Rodríguez Jiménez, Antonio.  "Gabriel García Márquez, periodista."
      Jalapa, Veracruz, México:  La Palabra y El Hombre, no. 44, nueva
      época (October-December, 1982), pp. 90-91.

      A brief history of García Márquez's journalistic career.

113.  Rodríguez Nuñez, Víctor.  "La peregrinación de La Jirafa, García
      Márquez:  su periodismo costeño."  La Habana:  Casa de Las Améri-
      cas, (March-April), 1983), pp. 27-39.

      During his early years, García Márquez wrote a column in El He-
      raldo, (Bogotá), under the pseudonymn Séptimus.  This article
      chronicles his years as a journalist.

114.  Ruffinelli, Jorge.  "Las memorias de García Márquez."  Bogotá:
      Eco, v. 41/6, no. 252, (October, 1982), pp. 613-623.

      Remembrances of conversations with García Márquez during his
      visit to Tlacotalpan.

115.  Sánchez R., Carlos Alberto.  "El otoño del patriarca en francés."
      Bogotá:  El Espectador, Magazine Dominical, (January 30, 1977),
      p. 3.

      The publicity given to García Márquez and his works in the French
      press.

116.  Schierbeck, Ole.  "Det mest laeste er bankbogen."  Denmark:
      Politiken, (October 22, 1982), section 2, p. 1.

      The economics of producing a best-seller by a Nobel laureate.

117.  Schoo, Ernesto.  "Los viajes de Simbad García Márquez."  Buenos
      Aires:  Primera Plana, v. 5, no. 234, (June 20, 1967), pp. 23-25.

A report on García Márquez, his travels and his lifestyle,
following the publication of One Hundred Years of Solitude. This
article discusses in detail his inspirations, particularly those
from his childhood in Colombia.

118.  Shaw, Donald L. "García Márquez, Gabriel." In Makers of Modern
      Culture. New York, NY: Facts on File, 1981, p. 189.

      A brief biography of García Márquez.

119.  Sheppard, R. Z. "Where the Fiction is Fantástica:  Gabriel Gar-
      cía Márquez Spearheads Latin American Writing." New York, NY:
      Time, (March 7, 1983), pp. 78-79.

      An insightful picture of García Márquez, his place and influence
      in the Latin American literary world with succinct analyses of
      his major works.

120.  Socolov, Raymond. "Why García Márquez Won the Nobel Prize." New
      York, NY: The Wall Street Journal, (November 19, 1982), p. 25.

      An editorial page article focusing on the selection of some Nobel
      Prize winners and extolling the achievements of Gabriel García
      Márquez, the 1982 literary laureate from Colombia.

121.  "The Talk of the Town. Honors." New York, NY: The New Yorker,
      v. 56, no. 45, (December 29, 1980), pp. 27-29.

      On receiving the Commonwealth Award, García Márquez regrets not
      being able to accept personally as he needs to limit his visits
      to the United States due to the hassle he experiences on trying
      to enter the country.

122.  Teitelboim, Volodia. "García Márquez, Premio Nobel." Madrid:
      Araucaria de Chile, no. 20, (1982), pp. 15-19.

      The creative and never ending wellspring imagination of García
      Márquez won for him the Nobel Prize which was of little surprise
      among the literary world. This article was also published in
      Fiction et réalité:  la littérature latino-américaine. Brussels:
      Université Libre de Bruxelles, Editions de l'Université de
      Bruxelles, 1983, translated from the Spanish by Ch. Bonnarens,
      pp. 121-127.

123.  Ullan, José-Miguel. "Primera edición española de la novela
      Bajo el volcán, escrita por Malcolm Lowry. Presenta también
      las últimas obras de García Márquez y Rosa Chacel." Madrid:
      El País, (March 7, 1981), p. 21.

      García Márquez's Textos costeños, is introduced to the Spanish
      public.

124.  Vargas, Germán. "Cinco semblanzas." Bogotá: Golpe de Dados:
      Revista de Poesía, v. 8, no. 47, (September-October, 1980),
      pp. 81-100.

An informative series of five essays which relate the literary histories of those connected with the "Group of Barranquilla" of which García Márquez was a member. Treats separately Alvaro Cepeda Samudio, Luis Carlos López, Waldo Frank, Ramón Vinyes, and Cecilia Porras, and their connections with this group.

125. Verdevoye, Paul. "Gabriel García Márquez." In Antología de la narrativa hispanoamericana, 1940-1970. 2v. Madrid: Gredos, 1979, pp. 424-449.

A bibliography of García Márquez's works with short selections from three of them, and a short biography.

126. "Vitória de Macondo: o Prêmio Márquez's Nobel para Gabriel García Márquez consagra uma obra cujo tema é a América Latina." São Paulo: Veja, no. 738, (October 27, 1982), pp. 144-145.

An account of García Márquez's works, life, political position, and some of his opinions about literature, the Cuban Revolution, Latin America, interviews, etc.

127. Washburn, Yulan M. "García Márquez Wins Books Abroad Prize." Appleton, WI: Hispania, v. 56, no. 2, (May, 1973), pp. 497-498.

Quotes the speech made by Thor Wilhjalmsson upon placing García Márquez's name for nomination of the $10,000, Books Abroad/ Neustadt International Prize for literature which was awarded to García Márquez.

128. Who's Who in the World, 1982-1983. 6th ed. Chicago, IL: Marquis, 1983, p. 399.

Bio-bibliography of García Márquez.

129. Yañez, Mirta. "García Márquez: un tema inagotable." La Habana: Revista de la Biblioteca Nacional José Martí, v. 25, no. 1, (January-April, 1983), pp. 240-242.

A summary of García Márquez's accomplishments as portrayed in López Lemus's book Una vocación incontenible.

130. Zaid, Gabriel. "Relato donde no se escucha a un náufrago." México: Vuelta, v. 3, no. 41, (April, 1980), pp. 43-44.

Makes observations about the trip García Márquez made to Vietnam amidst the outcry over the plight of that country's "boat people."

131. Zuluaga, Conrado. "García Márquez y los amigos de Aureliano Babilonia." Bogotá: Correo de los Andes, v. 1, no. 1, (November, 1979), pp. 55-59.

Provides insight on García Márquez by portraying his closest associates.

# Miscellanea

(Grouped together in this section are miscellaneous items from various
sources which briefly mention Gabriel García Márquez and his works, but
which do not fit into the other categories of this book.)

1. Agosin, Marjorie. "Una bruja novelada: La Quintrala de Magdalena
   Petit." Provo, UT: Chasqui-Revista de Literatura Latinoamericana,
   v. 12, no. 1, (November, 1982), pp. 3-13.

   A review of Magdalena Petit's novel La Quintrala mentions Gabriel
   García Márquez among various authors as examples of Latin American
   novelists who mix fiction and history to such an extent that the
   reader has difficulty distinguishing between them.

2. Ainsa, Fernando. Los buscadores de la utopía. La significación
   novelesca del espacio latinoamericano. Caracas: Monte Avila, 1977,
   429 p.

   In examining the significance of space in the Latin American novel,
   Macondo is brought to light as a prototype of the "island villages"
   in the Colombian narrative.

3. Albertocchi, Giovanni. "Manuel Scorza, Il Quinto Cantare Peruviano:
   Verso la 'Soluzione del Mito'." Firenze, Italy: Il Ponte Revista
   di Politica e Letteratura, v. 17, (1981), pp. 446-453.

   One Hundred Years of Solitude is cited briefly in comparing it to
   Scorza's La tumba del relámpago.

4. Alvaréz Gardeazábal, Gustavo. Manual de crítica literaria. Bogotá:
   Plaza y Janes, 1980, 125 p.

   An educational text which focuses critically upon various novels,
   including those of Gabriel García Márquez and citing examples from
   his works throughout the book.

5. Anadon, José. "Carlos Fuentes on Politics, Language, and Literature." New York: Worldview, v. 23, (1980), pp. 5-7.

   In an interview with Carlos Fuentes, Anadon explores his views on politics, language, and literature, briefly referring to García Márquez.

6. Anastasyev, Nikolai. "Soviet Literature and the Artistic Experience of the 20th Century." Moscow: Soviet Literature, v. 18, no. 437, (1984), pp. 161-175.

   Includes a couple of paragraphs about the influence of Latin American literature especially that of García Márquez in particular, on World literature.

7. Aproximaciones a Gustavo Alvarez Gardeazábal. Raymond L. Williams, ed. Bogotá: Plaza y Janés, 1977, 244 p.

   A collection of studies and critiques of all the works by Alvarez Gardeazábal, a member of the "new narrative" to which Gabriel García Márquez also pertains, contains a quote within its introduction which proclaims Gabriel García Márquez as the most important author in Colombia.

8. Araújo, Helena. "Narrativa femenina latinoamericana." Gaithersburg, MD: Hispamérica-Revista de Literatura, año 11, no. 32, (August 1982), pp. 23-34.

   In discussing the development of Latin American literature and the role of woman writers, Araújo mentions that some of the recognition of these female novelists may have been robbed by authors such as Gabriel García Márquez, and others who belong to the "Boom" of Latin American Literature.

9. Bal, Mieke. "On Meanings and Descriptions." Manhattan, KS: Studies in Twentieth Century Literature, v. 6, nos. 1 and 2, (Fall, 1981 - Spring, 1982), pp. 100-115.

   Brief mention of One Hundred Years of Solitude.

10. Balladares, José Emilio. "El tiempo mítico y el tiempo del hombre en los Cantos de Cifar." Madrid: Cuadernos Hispanoamericanos, no. 355, (January 1980), pp. 51-69.

    Examining Cuadra's Cantos de Cifar, Ballardares cites One Hundred Years of Solitude as having attained a perfect synthesis of magic, of form and content through the character of Melquiades.

11. Bârna, Nicolae. "Bookish or Realistic?" Bucharest, Romania: Romanian Review, nos. 8-9, (1983), pp. 166-169.

    Makes reference to the Romanian translation of The Autumn of the Patriarch.

12. Beckermann, Thomas. "Kleiner Hinweis auf Kensaburo Oe." Berlin: Die Neue Rundschau, v. 91, (January 1980), pp. 71-75.

The themes of "who am I?" and "where am I going?" in the works of
Gabriel García Márquez, Alejo Carpentier, Kenzaburo Oe, and other
writers is brought to light in an article which cites the need for
more attention to the literature of Third World countries.

13.    Bedoya M., Luis Iván.    Ensayos sobre narrativa latinoamericana.
       Medellín, Colombia:  Ediciones Pepe, 1980, 141 p.

In this brief collection of essays about authors from Latin American
countries other than Colombia, García Márquez is mentioned for
comparison.

14.    Bell-Villade, Gene H.   "The Rise of the Latin American Novel."
       Nigeria:  Okike--An African Journal of New Writing, no. 14,
       (1978), pp. 4-24.

Bell-Villada cites the important contribution of García Márquez,
using examples from One Hundred Years of Solitude and The Autumn
of the Patriarch.

15.    Benedetti, Mario.   El recurso del supremo patriarca.   Mexico:  Nueva
       Imagen, 1981, p. 175.

A collection of critical essays centering on recurrent themes in
Latin American literature such as the supreme patriarch, the search
for peace, and the search for a lost identity.  Gabriel García
Márquez, as well as other authors' works are included.

16.    "Best Books of the 70's."   Sausalito, CA:  Black Scholar, v. 12,
       no. 2, (March-April 1981), pp. 80-90.

One Hundred Years of Solitude appears on several "best books" list
citing works of the 1970's.

17.    Beverley, John.   "Literatura e ideología:  En torno a un libro de
       Hernán Vidal."  Pittsburgh, PA:  Revista Iberoamericana, v. 33, nos.
       102-103, (January-June, 1978), pp. 77-88.

Classifies Gabriel García Márquez as part of the vanguard of the
"boom" in this article about Marxist literary criticism.

18.    Blanchard, Marc Eli.  "Paul Valéry, Walter Benjamin, André Malraux:
       la littérature et le discours de crise."  Louisianna State Univer-
       sity.  Baton Rouge, LA:  L'Esprit Créateur, v. 23, no. 4 (Winter
       1983), pp. 38-50.

In a study of European Literature written between the two world wars
Gabriel García Márquez is considered to be a proponent of the belief
that Latin America and the rest of the Third World "are proof of a
new critical imagination in their relations with the European and
North American cultures."

19.    "The Books That Made Writers."  New York:  The New York Times Book
       Review, v. 84, no. 47, (November 25, 1979), pp. 7, 80, 82, 84.

Commenting on how Franz Kafka's The Metamorphosis influenced him to
become a writer, García Márquez states, "it was the revelation that
through literature it was possible to explore this other reality
that was hidden behind immediate reality."

20. Bougnoux, Daniel. "Fernando Botero: l'arrondissement." Paris:
    Silex, no. 11, (March, 1979), pp. 132-138. (Special issue: "Gabriel
    Márquez - Amerique Latine")

    In this article on the artwork of Fernando Botero, Bougnoux speaks
    of Gabriel García Márquez and three characters from his novel,
    Antonio, Isabel, and Remedios.

21. Bougnoux, Daniel et Michéle Crozet. "Ivan Theimer." Paris: Silex,
    no. 11, (March, 1979), pp. 52-59.

    Analyzes the art works of Ivan Theimer, and comments on José
    Arcadio Buendía, Ursula, Petra Cotes, and Colonel Aureliano Buendía,
    characters from García Márquez's Cien años de soledad.

22. Camacho Guizado, Eduardo. "Novela colombiana, panorama contemporá-
    neo." Bogotá: Letras Nacionales, v. 2, no. 9 (July-August, 1966),
    pp. 18-37.

    In this history of the Latin American novel, the author includes
    the earlier works of Gabriel García Márquez.

23. Carew, Jan. "Lo scrittore caraibico e l'esilio." Firenze, Italy:
    Il Ponte: Revista Mensile di Politica e Letteratura, v. 38, no. 3,
    (1982), pp. 241-264.

    Devotes a paragraph on page 259 to García Márquez and the massacre
    of the laborers in Cien años de soledad.

24. Cartano, Tony. "Domaine étranger." Paris: La Quinzaine
    Litteraire, no. 300, (April, 16/30, 1979), p. 14.

    Reviews the list of foreign novels which La Quinzaine has recogniz-
    ed, criticized, and shown concern for their accurate translations.
    Among them, he mentions Gabriel García Márquez's Cien años de
    soledad.

25. Castellanos, Jorge and Miguel A. Martínez. "El dictador hispano-
    americano como personaje literario." Austin, TX: Latin American
    Research Review, v. 16, no. 2, (1981), pp. 79-105.

    The Hispanic American dictator is studied as a character in many
    Latin American novels, as it is in Gabriel García Márquez's El otoño
    del patriarca.

26. Castillo, Rafael C. "Recommended: Gabriel García Márquez." Tempe,
    AZ: English Journal, v. 73, no. 6, (October, 1984), pp. 77-78.

    Short reviews of some of the translations of García Márquez's novels
    recommended for reading by high school students.

138    Secondary Sources

27. Christ, Ronald. "An Interview with José Donoso." Boston, MA:
    Partisan Review, v. 39, no. 1, (1982), pp. 23-44.

    José Donoso's views on Latin American fiction especially mentions
    Gabriel García Márquez's Cien años de soledad.

28. Clark, John R. and Anna Lydia Motto. "The Progress of Cannibalism
    in Satire." Pittsburg, KS:   Midwest Quarterly, v. 25, no. 2,
    (Winter, 1984), pp. 174-186.

    Fiction has offered many societies a method of encountering canni-
    balism with fascination although it is considered taboo in the real
    world.  Gabriel García Márquez's example is studied among several
    other authors and their works.

29. Clementelli, Elena y Minardi, Vittorio, eds.  La letteratura latino-
    americana e la sua problematica europea.  Rome:  Istituto italo
    latino americano, 1978, 547 p.

    A collection of critiques of Latin American literature written by
    several Italian, French, and Spanish critics compares the Latin
    American literature, themes, and ideology to those of their own
    countries.  Gabriel García Márquez is mentioned several times
    throughout the publication.

30. Conte, Rafael. "La novela española en 1981." Lincoln, NE: Anales
    de la Literatura Española Contemporánea, v. 8, (1983), pp. 127-142.

    This review of the Spanish novel in 1981 describes the quality and
    quantity of the selection, and includes an appendix of Latin
    American publications in which Gabriel García Márquez is mentioned
    for his novel, El otoño del patriarca.

31. Cuadra, José de la. Los Sangurimas. Quito, Ecuador:  Editorial El
    Conejo, 1984, 116 p.

    The "Estudio introductorio" to this novel carries a criticism of
    the author and his book, and includes articles on Humberto E.
    Robles, and more importantly one by Jacques Gilard comparing Los
    Sangurimas to Cien años de soledad on pages 17-32.

32. Cullhed, Anders. "Myt och fiktion:  Om nyöversatt litteratur fran
    Latinamerika."  Stockholm:  BLM-Bonniers Litterara Magasin, v. 53,
    no. 1, (February, 1984), pp. 54-56.

    The history of Latin American literature from Popul Vuh to García
    Márquez is the topic of this critical essay.

33. Cypess, Sandra. "Latin Americans in the Theater and TOLA." New
    Haven, CT:  Theater, v. 12, no. 1, (1980), pp. 38-45.

    The roles TOLA, and the Latin American Theater Review and others
    have played in the production of Latin American drama.  Gabriel
    García Márquez is cited as a contemporary Latin American novelist,
    whose works are often produced on stage.

34. Eco, 1960-1975: ensayistas colombianos. Recopilación e índice de Alvaro Rodríguez. Bogotá, Colombia: Instituto Colombiano de Cultura, 1976, 478 p.

    Quotes García Márquez on page 257, when treating the subject of the Colombian novel in the 1960's, more specifically, the poor quality of that genre.

35. "Etching her home in exile." London and Manchester: The Guardian, (August 28, 1982), p. 11.

    An exhibition of the works of Victoria Ortiz gains much of its inspiration from the works of Gabriel García Márquez and, in particular, the wealth of female characters.

36. "Editors' Choice 1979." The New York Times Book Review, v. 84, no. 52, (December 30, 1979), pp. 1, 10.

    In the 1979, New York Times "Editor's Choice" of books from the 70's, Gabriel García Márquez's One Hundred Years of Solitude was chosen as the "one title from the 70's most likely to succeed 100 years from its birth."

37. Feijoó. María del Carmen and Sarah Hirschman. Gente y cuentos: educación popular y literatura. Buenos Aires, Argentina: Centro de Estudios de Estado y Sociedad, 1984, 72 p.

    This book explains the purpose and results of an adult education program in literature. Among others were included two stories of García Márquez, i.e. "Los funerales de la Mamá Grande," and "La siesta del martes."

38. Fell, Claude. "Mito y novela en la literatura latinoamericana." Santiago de Chile: Pontificia Universidad Católica de Chile, Revista Universitaria, no. 15, 2o. trimestre, (1985), pp. 11-16.

    The reanimation and exploitation of the great myths in Latin American literature with a mention of their use in Cien años de soledad and La hojarasca.

39. America Latina en su literatura. César Fernando Moreno, coordinator. Mexico, D.F.: Siglo Veintiuno Editores, 1972, 494 p.

    Contains scattered notations in various chapters on García Márquez.

40. Fernández Muñoz, María Teresa. "El lenguaje profanado." Madrid: Cuadernos Hispanoamericanos, no. 359, (May, 1980), pp. 419-428.

    In a review of Carlos Fuentes' works, María Teresa Fernández Muñoz mentions Gabriel García Márquez's Cien años de soledad, and compares the 37 natural sons of Aureliano Buendía in the novel, to the young men of Fuentes' novel Terra Nostra.

41. Field, Howard. "Knopf Disputes Stories on Imports of Death Foretold." New York: Publishers Weekly, v. 223, no. 6, pp. 16-18.

Knopf threatens legal action against bookstores importing foreign versions of <u>Chronicle of A Death Foretold</u> for sale before its release by Knopf.

42. Foster, David William. "<u>El beso de la mujer araña</u>, by Manuel Puig." Pittsburgh: <u>Latin American Literary Review</u>, v. 7, no. 14, (Spring-Summer, 1979), pp. 73–74.

Manuel Puig claims that his novel reviewed by Foster "is perhaps the first since Gabriel García Márquez's <u>Cien años de soledad</u> that lends itself so readily to both a 'readerly' and a 'writerly' reading."

43. "400 escritores de los cinco continentes explican las razones que les hacen escribir." Madrid: <u>El País</u>, no. 97, (Monday, April 1, 1985), p. 23.

In one sentence each writer tells his reason for writing. Gabriel García Márquez in his sentence states that he is searching for more friends.

44. Franco, Jean. "Narrador, autor, superestrella: La narrativa latino-americana en la época de cultura de masas." Puerto Rico: <u>Revista Iberoamericana</u>, v. 47, nos. 114–115, (January–June, 1981), pp. 129–148.

Jean Franco analyzes the Latinamerican literature of the "boom" era and discusses the relationships betwen the authors, the narrators in the works, and the prominent characters of the stories. Among various authors of this era, Franco mentions Gabriel García Márquez and his novel <u>Cien años de soledad</u>.

45. Franco, Jean. "Trends and priorities for research in Latin American literature." Minneapolis, MN: <u>Ideologies and Literature: a Journal of Hispanic and Luso-Brazilian Studies</u>, v. 4, no. 16, (1983), pp. 107–120.

Cites Josefina Ludmer's study of <u>One Hundred Years of Solitude</u> as an example of practical criticism helping in the understanding of ideology.

46. Franklin, Wayne. "Speaking and Touching: The Problem of Inexpressibility in American Travel Books." In <u>America: Exploration and Travel</u>. Steven E. Kagle, ed. Bowling Green: Bowling Green State University Popular Press, 1979, pp. 18–38.

A comparative description of the narrative style of American writers and the earliest explorers of the New World, showing how the narrative techniques of these adventurers influenced contemporary writers such as García Márquez in <u>One Hundred Years of Solitude</u>. (Originally published in <u>Exploration</u>, v. 4, no. 1, (December, 1976), pp. 1–12).

47. Frumkin, Gene. "Surrealism and Psyche." New York: <u>Chelsea</u>, no. 41, (1982), pp. 136–151.

Illustrates the surreal-psyche connection in modern literature including <u>One Hundred Years of Solitude</u>.

48.  García Mendez, Javier.  "Pour une écoute bakhtinienne du romain
     latinoaméricain."  Montréal:  Etudes Françaises, v. 20, no. 1,
     (Spring, 1984), pp. 101-136.

     The Russian Bakhtine ideology and its influence in Latin American
     literature is studied giving examples from several works including
     Gabriel García Márquez's El otoño del patriarca.

49.  Gnutzmann, Rita.  "La novela hispanoamericana en segunda persona."
     Tübingen:  Iberoromania, no. 17 (1983), pp. 100-120.

     On page 100 of this article the author refers in a note to the use
     of the second person, i.e. the reader as a contributor to the
     dialogue in El otoño del patriarca.

50.  González, Patricia.  "Colombia:  El IV Festival del Nuevo Teatro."
     Lawrence, KS:  Latin American Theatre Review, v. 14, no. 1, (Fall,
     1980), pp. 79-90.

     Reports on the IV National Festival of New Colombian Theatre, at
     which texts from García Márquez were adopted for dramatization.

51.  Gonzáles-Berry, Erlinda.  "Caras viejas y vino nuevo:  Journey
     Through A Disintegrating Barrio."  Pittsburgh, PA:  Latin American
     Literary Review, v. 7, no. 14, (Spring-Summer, 1979), pp. 62-72.

     Refers to The Autumn of the Patriarch in an end-note which explains
     the technique of omitting explicit introductory verbs.

52.  González-del-Valle, Luis and Bradley A. Shaw.  "The New Spanish
     American Narrative."  Hamilton, New Zealand:  Pacific Quarterly, v.
     3, no. 1, (1978), pp. 86-96.

     These two authors analyze the New Spanish American narrative by
     comparing it to other Spanish American works.

53.  Graham, Allison.  "History, Nostalgia, and the Criminality of
     Popular Culture."  Athens, GA:  The Georgia Review, v. 38, no. 2,
     (Summer, 1984), pp. 348-364.

     Draws an analogy between the insomnia plague and loss of memory in
     Macondo to American culture after the mid-1970's, and cites the
     American film industry for examples.

54.  Gyurko, Lanin A.  "Artist and Critic as Self and Double in Cortázar's
     'Los pasos en las huellas.'"  Stanford, California:  Hispania , v.
     65, no. 3, (September, 1982), pp. 352-364.

     Traces the role of critics in Latin American novels.  Gabriel García
     Márquez is quoted several times on his opinion of the critics of his
     works.

55.  Halperin Donghi, Tulio.  "Nueva narrativa y ciencias sociales
     hispanoamericanas en la década del sesenta."  Gaithersburg, MD:
     Hispamérica:  Revista de Literatura, año 9, no. 27, (December, 1980),
     pp. 3-18.

Donghi discusses the Latin American literature of the 70's, and mentions Gabriel García Márquez's use of history and memory in his works Cien años de soledad, and El otoño del patriarca.

56. Head, Bessie. "Social and Political Pressures that Shape Literature in Southern Africa." Arlington, TX: WLWE-World Literature Written in English, v. 18, no. 1, (April, 1979), pp. 20-26.

A quote from Gabriel García Márquez's One Hundred Years of Solitude which describes ancient Southern Africa as a peaceful nation.

57. Hollinghurst, Alan. "Post War." London: New Statesman, v. 99, no. 2552, (February 15, 1982), pp. 252-   .

Several readings are essential to understand In Evil Hour for "Márquez's feat is to eliminate characterization and to give us a picture of society that remains vividly real while shading into myth."

58. Herrera, Earle. El reportaje, el ensayo: De un género a otro. Caracas: Editorial Equinoccio, 1983, 162 p.

The works of García Márquez along with those of other authors, are cited in Herrera's study of journalistic reports and literary essays as distinct but not distant genres.

59. Jitrik, Noé. "Entre el corte y la continuidad. Hacia una escritura crítica." Pittsburgh, PA: Revista Iberoamericana, v. 33, nos. 102-103, (January-June, 1978), pp. 99-109.

A reference to the influence of García Márquez on other writers.

60. Kakutani, M. "Mysteries Join the Mainstream." New York: The New Times Book Review, (January 15, 1984), p. 1.

In discussing the increasing publications of mystery stories by famous authors, Gabriel García Márquez is mentioned briefly for his Chronicle of a Death Foretold and his use of "conventions of mystery to make philosophical points about the nature of storytelling itself."

61. Kuehl, Linda. "Joan Didion: The Art of Fiction LXXI." Paris: Paris Review, v. 20, no. 74, (Summer, 1978), pp. 142-163.

Joan Didion mentions Gabriel García Márquez's The Autumn of the Patriarch during an interview saying that she has always desired to write an entire novel that could be read in one sitting, and that perhaps Gabriel García Márquez with this novel, has accomplished that desire.

62. "Last minute list." London and Manchester: The Guardian, (December 23, 1982), p. 8.

In a best-of-the-year listing, Gabriel García Márquez is cited as a meritorious author.

63. Lastra, Pedro. "Sobre Juan Rodríquez Freyle (Notas de lectura)."
Bogotá: Eco, v. 41/6, no. 252 (October, 1982), pp. 624-637.

In discussing El carnero, illustrations from various works are
introduced including García Márquez's Cien años de soledad.

64. Levine, Suzanne Jill. "El espejo de agua." Mexico: Revista de la
Universidad de Mexico, v. 39, no. 26, (June, 1983), pp. 36-39.

The mirror symbolism om various works, mentioning briefly those of
García Márquez.

65. Lewis, Robert E. "Los naufragios de Alvar Núñez: historia y
ficción." Pittsburgh, PA: Revista Iberamericana, v. 38, nos. 120-
121, (July-December, 1982), pp. 681-694.

"There are no writers less believable and at the same time more
attached to reality than the writers of the Indies, because the
problem which they fought was the creation of a reality that never
left the imagination."

66. Luby, Barry and Wayne Finke. "Contemporary Latin American Literature." Madison, NJ: Literary Review, v. 23, no. 2, (Winter, 1980),
pp. 165-175.

Political philosophy and social justice seem to be the prevalent
themes among Latin American contemporary writers.

67. MacAdam, Alfred and Charles Ruas. "The Art of Fiction LXVIII:
Carlos Fuentes." Flushing, NY: Paris Review, v. 23, no. 82,
(Winter, 1981), pp. 141-175.

During an extensive interview about his life, talents, and literary
works, Carlos Fuentes mentions García Márquez, Faulkner, Derek
Walcott, Aimé Césaire, and Carpentier, as authors included in "a
trilingual culture in and around the whirlpool of the Baroque."

68. Madrid Malo, Nestor. "Estado actual de la novela en Colombia."
Washington, D.C.: Revista Interamericana de Bibliografía, v. 17,
(1967), pp. 68-82.

The present-day state of the Colombian novel, is the topic of
Madrid's article in which he credits García Márquez with having
originated the "nouvelle vague", a new direction characterized by
the novel's orientation towards the techniques and style of the
American novelists, and away from the tradition of European
influence.

69. Martin, Fred. "De liedjeszanger als massamedium. Straatzangers in
de achttience en negentiende eeuw." Leiden: Tidjdschrift voor
Geschiedenis, v. 97, no. 3, (1984), pp. 422-446.

In this article on traveling ballad singers, the author mentions
Francisco, the balladeer in One Hundred Years of Solitude.

70. Martínez, Zulma Nelly. "José Donoso." Takoma Park, MD: <u>Hispamérica-Revista de Literatura</u>, año 7, no. 21, (December, 1978), pp. 53-74.

In an interview with Martínez, José Donoso mentions that he feels that Manuel Puig is the most original Latin American writer of today. He claims that Puig does not receive the credit he deserves because of today's emphasis on the works of Gabriel García Márquez, and Vargas Liosa.

71. Martinière, Guy. "Racines romanesques et temporalité historique dans l'oeuvre de García Márquez." Paris: <u>Silex</u>, no. 11, (March, 1979), pp. 100-105.

Martinière focuses on Gabriel García Márquez's change in career from a novelist to a political journalist.

72. Maturo, Graciela. "Fantasía y realismo en la literatura." Rosario, Argentina: <u>La Capital</u>, (Sunday, April 6, 1980), p. 16.

Highlights some nuances of Spanish American surrealism not found in European works, citing Gabriel García Márquez as one of the most important writers in this genre.

73. Maturo, Graciela. <u>La literatura hispanoamericana: De la utopía al paraíso</u>. Buenos Aires: Fernando Garcia Cambeiro, 1983, 213 p.

The creation and development of fantasy and myth within the literature of Latin America is analyzed; includes citations and examples from Gabriel García Márquez's works and that of other Hispanic authors.

74. Maturo, Graciela. "La moderna novela latinoamericana: de la utopía al paraíso." Buenos Aires: <u>Megafón</u>, v. 1, no. 2, (December, 1975), pp. 87-104.

This discussion of the contemporary Latin American novel mentions quite briefly Gabriel García Márquez.

75. McDowell, Edwin. "Publishing: Harper's-García Márquez Rift." New York: <u>The New York Times</u>, (Friday, June 3, 1982), p. 22.

Harper and Row publishers lose the rights to publish Gabriel García Márquez's <u>Chronicle of a Death Foretold</u> to Ballantine Books after refusing to accept a license of only 10 years for the book, as opposed to one of no time limitations.

76. McDowell, Edwin. "U.S. is Discovering Latin America's Literature." New York: <u>The New York Times</u>, (February 16, 1982), p. 22.

"A growing number of book publishers in the United States, . . . are issuing transalations of more books by more Latin American writers than ever before."

77. McMurray, George R. (Review of <u>Casa de Campo</u> by José Donoso.) Provo, UT: <u>Chasqui-Revista de Literatura Latinoamericana</u>, v. 9, nos. 2-3, (1981), pp. 85-88.

The scene from José Donoso's novel Casa de campo which depicts the
cannibalistic killing of Mignor is "reminiscent of that in Gabriel
García Márquez's El otoño del patriarca."

78. Mejía Duque, Jaime.  "El 'Boom' de la narrativa latinoamericana."
In his Literatura y realidad.  Medellín, Colombia:  Editorial La
Oveja Negra, 1976, pp. 227-248.

Credits the Cuban revolution for the "boom" in the Latin American
narrative and cites Gabriel García Márquez among the writers of the
"boom."

79. Mena, Lucila Inés.  "La función de los prólogos en El día señalado
de Manuel Mejía Vallejos."  Gaithersburg, MD:  Hispamérica:  Revista
de Literatura, año 9, nos. 25-26, (April-August, 1980), pp. 137-146.

In this essay on the depiction of violence in Mejía Vallejos' work
El día señalado, several paragraphs are devoted to the use of
violence in García Márquez's novels.

80. Menton, Seymour.  Magic realism rediscovered, 1918-1981.  Philadelphia, PA:  The Art Alliance Press; London:  Associated University
Presses, 1983, 119 p.

A thorough study of Magic Realism, which gives examples of the trend
from Gabriel García Márquez's works.

81. Montero, Janina.  "Historia y novela en Hispanoamérica:  El lenguaje
de la ironía."  Philadelphia:  Hispanic Review, (Autumn, 1979), v.
47, no. 4, pp. 505-519.

The satirical argumentation found in the historical anecdotes of One
Hundred Years of Solitude is touched upon in this treatment of
history in the Latin American novel.

82. Montero, Janina.  "Observations on the Hispanic American novel and
its public."  Pittsburgh, PA:  Carnegie-Mellon University, Latin
American Literary Review, v. 6, no. 11, (Fall-Winter, 1977), pp. 1-
12.

Latin American fiction in the works of contemporary novelists is
finally taking its place in the international scene.  Cien años de
soledad is chief among these.

83. "Neglected Books of the Twentieth Century (Part Five)."  New York:
Antaeus, no. 35, (Autumn, 1979), pp. 107-114.

One Hundred Years of Solitude, by Gabriel García Márquez, appears on
this reading list of twentieth century books that are neglected.
This list was compiled in 1979, before García Márquez's novel had
reached the status of a best seller.

84. Oates, Joyce Carol.  "'At Last I Have Made a Woman of Her':  Images
of Women in Twentieth Century Literature."  Athens, GA:  The Georgia
Review, v. 37, no. 1, (Spring, 1983), pp. 7-30.

Makes reference in a footnote to the "magic realism" in Gabriel
García Márquez's portrayal of Remedios in One Hundred Years of
Solitude.

85.  "Paperbacks:  New and Noteworthy."  The New York Times Book Review,
     v. 85, no. 1, (January 6, 1980), p. 31.

     The English publication of a collection of short stories including
     Innocent Eréndira is announced.

86.  Peña Gutiérrez, Isaías.  "Génesis y contratiempos de una narrativa:
     Colombia, 1960-1977," Bogotá:  Ediciones el Huaco, (1979), pp. 5-33,
     in Estudios de literatura.

     Concludes that the political unrest, military rule, revolutions,
     violence, and exile were the seeds for the "Boom" in Latin American
     literature.

87.  Plavius, H.  "Man and the World.  The Seventies.  A Dialogue."  New
     York:  Soviet Studies in Literature, v. 14, no. 4, (Fall, 1978),
     pp. 27-64.

     In a long interview between German critic Heinz Plavius, and Soviet
     writer, Chingiz Aitmatov, Gabriel García Márquez's One Hundred Years
     of Solitude is mentioned in passing while discussing the literary
     technique of presenting history in a present form.

88.  Pope, Robert.  "Beginnings."  Athens, GA:  Georgia Review, v. 36,
     no. 4, (Winter, 1982), pp. 733-751.

     In this study of the opening passages of narratives, García Márquez's
     One Hundred Years of Solitude is selected among others to give
     emphasis to the idea that the beginnings of narratives affect the
     readers.  (pp. 750-751).

89.  Quintana, Juan.  "El 'tiempo' en la actual novelística hispano-
     americana."  Madrid:  Cuadernos Hispanoamericanos, no. 363 (September
     (September, 1980), pp. 630-   .

     The concept of time is analyzed in several modern Latin American
     novels.  Gabriel García Márquez's Cien años de soledad, is briefly
     mentioned and is said to be such a complex novel that merely a short
     analysis of the time concept within the work would not do justice to
     a literary interpretation.

90.  Rabassa, Gregory.  "A Comparative Look at the Literatures of Spanish
     America and Brazil:  The Dangers of Deception."  In Ibero-American
     Letters in a Comparative Perspective, edited by Wolodymyr T. Zyla
     and Wendell M. Aycock.  Proceedings of the Comparative Literature
     Symposium, vol. 10.  Comparative Literature Symposium on Ibero-
     American Letters in a Comparative Perspective, Texas Tech University,
     Lubbock, Texas, January 26-28, 1978.  Lubbock:  Texas Tech Press,
     1978, pp. 119-132.

     García Márquez is very briefly mentioned in this article.

91.  Rabassa, Clementine.  "The Creative Function of Black Characters in
     Alejo Carpentier's Reasons of State."  Pittsburgh, PA:  Latin
     American Literary Review, v. 6, no. 12, (Spring-Summer, 1978), pp.
     26-37.

     Makes reference to Gabriel García Márquez's The Autumn of the
     Patriarch when mentioning how contemporary Latin American authors
     have captured the essence of the autocratic governments which pre-
     vail in the region.

92.  "Recent Latin American Novels."  Washington, D.C.:  The New Republic,
     v. 183, no. 17, issue 3433, (October 25, 1980), p. 34.

     Two of Gabriel García Márquez's works i.e., One Hundred Years of
     Solitude and The Autumn of the Patriarch are included in this list
     of English translations of recent works by Latin American novelists.

93.  Reed, J. D.  "Canal Caper."  (Review of Getting to Know the General
     by Graham Greene.)  New York:  Time, v. 123, no. 17, (October 22,
     1984), pp. 103-104.

     Graham Greene's traveling companion in Panamá is compared to a
     García Márquez character.

94.  Remnick, David.  "Interview with Philip Levine."  Ann Arbor,
     Michigan:  The Michigan Quarterly Review, v. 19, no. 3, (Summer,
     1980), pp. 282-298.

     During this interview, Levine cites One Hundred Years of Solitude
     to be among his significant literary experiences.

95.  Rincón, Carlos.  "Sobre la transformación del campo, de la crítica
     y la didáctica: la llamada subliterature."  In his El cambio en la
     noción de literatura.  Bogotá:  Biblioteca Colombiano de Cultura,
     pp. 163-193.

     García Márquez's influence in producing the type of literature that
     appeals to the public is introduced on pages 163-170.

96.  Roca Martínez, José Luís.  "Contribución a la bibliografía literaria
     del dictador Juan Manuel Rosas."  Madrid:  Revista de Indias, v. 41,
     nos. 163-164, (January-June, 1981), pp. 203-262.

     The Latin American dictator as a theme in Gabriel García Márquez's
     El otoño del patriarca, and other Latin American works.

97.  Rodríguez-Luis, Julio.  La literatura hispanoamericana, entre
     compromiso y experimento.  Madrid:  Fundamentos, 1984, 297 p.

     An analysis of the Latin American literary movement from Sor Juana
     Inés up to and including Gabriel García Márquez.

98.  Rodríguez Monegal, Emir.  "The New Latin American Novel."  In Dimíc,
     Milan V., and Juan Ferraté, eds.  Actes du VII$^e$ Congrès de l'Associa-
     tion Internationale de Littérature Association.  Stuttgart:  Kunst
     und Wissen, Erich Bieber, 1979, pp. 433-434.

Monegal analyzes the impact of the Latin American novel on contemporary North American and European writers.

99.  Rojas-Mix, Miguel. "El dictador sí tiene quien le escriba." Lima: Revista de Crítica Literaria Latinoamericana, v. 6, no. 11, (First Semester of 1980), pp. 123-126.

Changing the title El coronel no tiene quien le escriba from negative to affirmative, the author states that the tendency to view all Latin American writers as having leftist sympathies is erroneous, citing examples of writers with conservative political philosophies to prove this point.

100. Romero, Armando. "Nota preliminar." Madrid: Revista Iberoamericana, nos. 128-129, (July-December, 1984), pp. 629-630.

A summary of the preparation of this special issue honoring Colombian literature, emphasizing the contribution of García Márquez.

101. Ruffinelli, Jorge. El lugar de Rulfo y otros ensayos. Mexico: Universidad Veracruzana, 1980, 217 p.

In a chapter on Asturias' El Señor Presidente, the author points out the influence this book has had on other Latin American novels, including those by García Márquez.

102. Sainz de Medrano, Luis. "El lenguaje como preocupación en la novela hispanoamericana actual." Madrid: Anales de Literatura Hispanoamericana, v. 3, no. 9, (1980), pp. 235-254.

In listing all the important Latin American writers from the "clásicos" through the "boom" Gabriel García Márquez's literary style is cited in El otoño del patriarca.

103. Samper Pizano, Daniel, ed. Antología. Alvaro Cepeda Samudio. Bogotá: Colcultura, 1977, 482 p.

Alvaro Cepeda Samudio's patriotism is compared to that of Gabriel García Márquez.

104. San Juan, E., Jr. "Literature and revolution in the Third World." Amsterdam: Social Praxis, v. 6, nos. 1-2, (1979), pp. 19-34.

In this commentary on Third World literature Cien años de soledad is cited briefly.

105. Santamaría, Germán. "Prólogo." In Vitola by Germán Uribe. Bogotá: 1980, pp. 13-26.

Credits the works of García Márquez with saving Spanish-language literature.

106. Santos Moray, Mercedes. "El otoño en Cuba." Bogotá: El Espectador: Magazine Dominical, (September 3, 1978), pp. 5, 10.

This is a reprint of a prologue to the Cuban edition of El otoño del patriarca published in Havana by Editorial Arte y Literatura in 1978, in which Santos Moray discusses the dictator theme of Yo el supremo, El recurso del método and El otoño del patriarca.

107. Schulte, Rainer.  "Latin America:  a New Perspective in Narration." New Orleans, LA:  Loyola University, New Orleans Review, v. 7, no. 3, (Fall, 1980), pp. 213-215.

With the publication of Latin American novels in translation, including those of García Márquez there has been an influence of these authors on contemporary writers.

108. Schwarz, Joachim Von.  "Nach Auschwitz leben – Aspekte einer moralischen Geschichtsschreibung."  Gütersloh, West Germany: Cütersloher Verlagshaus G. Mohn.  Zeitschrift für evangelische Ethik, v. 28, no. 2, (1984), pp. 187-204.

The uprising of laborers protesting living conditions at the banana plantations and the way they've been disposed of amidst the silence of the people in One Hundred Years of Solitude is compared to what happened in the concentration camps during World War II.

109. Scott, Nina M.  "Inter-American Literature:  An Antidote to the Arrogance of Culture."  Bloomington, IN:  College English, v. 41, no. 6, (February, 1980), pp. 635-64 –

This essay describes a course on North/South American literature given by Nina M. Scott.  For her, Faulkner was a strong and inspirational influence on García Márquez and other Latin American writers.

110. Segre, Cesare.  "Se una notte d'inverno uno scrittore sognasse un aleph di dieci colori."  Torino, Italy:  Strumenti Critici, 1979, nos. 39-40, (October, 1979), pp. 177-214.

In this in-depth discussion of the state of contemporary literature, Segre quotes from One Hundred Years of Solitude on page 207.

111. Siebenmann, Gustav.  "Técnica narrativa y éxito literario:  su correlación a la luz de algunas novelas latinoamericanas."  Tübingen, Germany:  Iberoromania, v. 7, (1978), pp. 50-66.

Treats of the "boom" in contemporary Latin American literature with Gabriel García Márquez in the vanguard.

112. Sosnowski, Saul.  "Entrevista a Carlos Fuentes."  Gaithersburg, MD: Hispamerica-Revista de Literature, año 9, no. 27, (December, 1980), pp. 69-97.

In an interview with Sosnowski, Carlos Fuentes discusses his life and works.  He also analyzes contemporary Latin American literature and mentions Gabriel García Márquez and Vargas Llosa as authors who in their works treat reality as a complex phenomenon.

113. Terterian, I. "Sharing an Esthetic Goal: The Latin American Novel and the Development of an Art Form." New York: Soviet Studies in Literature, v. 17, no. 2, (Spring, 1981), pp. 31-36.

     In this study of the Latin American novel as a "community of artistic goals", García Márquez is quoted as saying, "I think that we need to search in the realm of language and narrative forms if we want all the fantastic reality of Latin America to be part of our books. . ." (Originally published in Russian in Moscow: Voprosy Literaty, no. 11, (1979), pp. 116-149).

114. Tritten, Susan. "Reviews of Latin American Literature in the United States' Magazines: Aid or Impediment to Understanding." Norman, OK: World Literature Today , v. 58, no. 1, (Winter, 1984), pp. 36-39.

     Evaluates the treatment which Gabriel García Márquez and his fellow Latin American writers receive in North American magazines, showing how the reviewers reveal North American attitudes and perspectives in the process.

115. Valdivieso, Jaime. Realidad y ficción en Latinoamérica. Mexico: J. Mortiz, 1975, 149 p.

     A study of reality and fiction in Latin American literature which analyzes several works by various authors. Gabriel García Márquez is quoted briefly.

116. Wagner, William F. "Gabriel García Márquez." Cottonwood, MN: The Wagner Latin American Newsletter, v. 9, no. 5, (February 25, 1981), p. 8.

     Announces the publication of Crónica de una muerte anunciada bringing to an end García Márquez's "literary strike."

117. Whitfield, Stephen J. "Strange Fruit - The Career of Samuel Zemurray." Waltham, MA: American Jewish History, v. 73, no. 3, (March, 1984), pp. 307-323.

     A discussion of the banana industry, especially its presence in One Hundred Years of Solitude.

118. Williams, Raymond L. "Structure and Transformation of Reality in Alvarez Gardeazábal: El bazar de los idiotas." Lexington: Kentucky Romance Quarterly, v. 27, no. 2, (1980), pp. 245-261.

     The use of cycles in Alvarez Gardeazábal's novel El bazar de los idiotas , is compared to García Márquez's writing style.

119. Willis, Susan. "Eruptions of Funk: Historicizing Toni Morrison." Terre Haute, IN: Black American Literature Forum, v. 16, no. 1, (Spring, 1982), pp. 34-42.

     End-note compares a character from Morrison's Tar Baby to Remedios in One Hundred Years of Solitude because both show imperfect assimilation into the bourgeois culture.

120. Yurkievich, Saúl. "Tradizione e innovazione nella lettura latinoamericana." Genova: L'Immagine Riflessa, v. 4, (1980), pp. 165-
190.

Stresses the unique style of the Latin American contemporary literature whose themes blend history with myth, and politics with
narratives.

121. Zuluaga Ospina, Alberto. "La función del diminutivo en español."
Bogotá: Thesaurus, Boletín del Instituto Caro y Cuervo, v. 25,
(1970), pp. 23-48.

This study of the use of the diminutive in Spanish, mentions
textual passages in Cien años de soledad, where it has been used
to convery different meanings.

122. Zweig, Paul. "Ominous People Doing Odd Things." (Review of We
Love Glenda So Much by Julio Cortázar, 145 p. New York, NY:
Alfred A. Knopf.). New York: NY: The New York Times Book Review,
(March 27, 1983), pp. 1, 37-38.

"His opposite (Cortázar's) is probably García Márquez, whose fables
tell of a mysterious home woven out of folklore, market smells
and the common folk sleepwalking in myth."

# Reviews of
# Gabriel García Márquez's
# Books and Stories

Cien años de soledad

1. Audejean, Christian. "One Hundred Years of Solitude by Gabriel García Márquez." New York: Center for Inter-American Relations, 70 Review, (1971), pp. 166-168, (translated from the French).

   "The reader who immediately allows himself to be carried away by the first sentence of this immense lyrical tale will not stop before having read the last ..."

2. Avant, John Alfred. "One Hundred Years of Solitude by Gabriel García Márquez." Gregory Rabassa, tr. New York: The Library Journal, v. 95, (February 15, 1970), p. 683.

   In this review One Hundred Years of Solitude is referred to, mistakenly, as an Argentinean novel. García Márquez is a Colombian author.

3. Dicksteih, Morris. "La pornografía del poder." Bogotá: El Tiempo; Lecturas Dominicales, (April 10, 1977), p. 11.

   This article which appeared originally in Seven Days Magazine contains a summary and a review of One Hundred Years of Solitude and The Autumn of the Patriarch.

4. "Gabriel García Márquez. One Hundred Years of Solitude." Gregory Rabassa, tr. Middletown, CT: Choice, v. 7, (September, 1970), p. 846.

   A brief review of "a phenomenon in the Spanish American novel."

5.  Gass, William H.  "A Fiesta for the Form."  Washington, D.C.:
    The New Republic, v. 183, no. 17, issue 3433, (October 25, 1980),
    pp. 33-34, 36-39.

    Gass reviews several contemporary Latin American novels, and lists
    Gabriel García Márquez's One Hundred Years of Solitude and The
    Autumn of the Patriarch among them.

6.  Gilles, Serge.  "One Hundred Years of Solitude by Gabriel García
    Márquez."  New York:  Center for Inter-American Relations, 70
    Review, (1971), pp. 168-171, (translated from the French).

    Raises the question of how French readers will receive a novel
    about a world so foreign to their own.

7.  Gray, Paul Edward.  "New Fiction in Review."  New Haven, CT:  The
    Yale Review, v. 60, no. 1, (October, 1970), pp. 101-102.

    One Hundred Years of Solitude, "the fusion of the mundane and the
    magical, the real and the surreal" is reviewed together with
    several contemporary works.

8.  Hahnl, Hans Heinz.  "One Hundred Years of Solitude by Gabriel Gar-
    cía Márquez."  New York:  Center for Inter-American Relations, 70
    Review, (1971), p. 183, (translated from the German).

    "It is novel and fairy tale, epic and saga; it is realism and
    surrealism, romanticism and involvement."

9.  Korkin, Vladimir.  "To Find One's Own Fate ..."  Moscow:  Soviet
    Literature, v. 12, no. 369, (1978), pp. 151-156.

    In this conversation between Aitmatov and Korkin, Aitmatov ex-
    presses his impressions while reading One Hundred Years of Soli-
    tude.

10. Lorenz, Gunther W.  "One Hundred Years of Solitude by Gabriel Gar-
    cía Márquez."  New York:  Center for Inter-American Relations, 70
    Review, (1971), pp. 183-186, (translated from the German).

    Characterizes One Hundred Years of Solitude as possibly the most
    unusual novel of our time; examines theme and structure to
    support this premise.

11. Orchids and Bloodlines."  New York:  Time, v. 95, (March 16, 1970),
    p. 96.

    In this summary of One Hundred Years of Solitude, the reviewer
    sees the key to the entire work as a manipulation of the time
    element.

12. Peerman, Dean.  "García Márquez: Beyond Chaos."  Chicago, IL:  The
    Christian Century, v. 99, no. 36, (November 17, 1982) pp. 1159-
    1160.

    Cien años de soledad in the light of the author's political views.

13. Praag-Chantraine, Jacqueline van. "Gabriel García Márquez, Prix Nobel de Littérature 1982." Paris: Revue Générale, v. 11, (November, 1982), pp. 29-35.

Prompted by Gabriel García Márquez acceptance of the Nobel Prize in 1982, Praag-Chantraine reviews Cien años de soledad, and gives a summary of García Márquez's life.

14. Puccini, Dario. "One Hundred Years of Solitude by Gabriel García Márquez." New York: Center for Inter-American Relations, 70 Review, (1971), pp. 190-191, (translated from the Italian).

Downplays slightly the influence of Faulkner on Gabriel García Márquez, while reiterating the important lesson of Borges for him.

15. "Review Essay: Latin American Novels." Bowling Green, OH: Journal of Popular Culture, v. 13, no. 1 (Summer, 1979), pp. 181-185.

One Hundred Years of Solitude and The Autumn of the Patriarch are recommended to the novice reader.

16. "One Hundred Years of Solitude." Yellow Springs, OH: The Antioch Review, v. 30, no. 1, (1970), p. 129.

"The book (One Hundred Years of Solitude) is an imperative; its quality is that of restoring health-to-dreams-in-life, to the language, to the reader." A reprint of this review was found in Contemporary Literary Criticism, v. 8, edited by Dedria Bryfonski and Phyllis Carmel Mendelson, Detroit: Gale Research Company, 1978, p. 230.

17. Sant'Anna, Sérgio. "One Hundred Years of Solitude by Gabriel García Márquez." New York: Center for Inter-American Relations, 70 Review, (1971), pp. 178-182, (translated from the Portuguese).

Stresses that in One Hundred Years of Solitude, Gabriel García Márquez is searching for an understanding of reality, as opposed, only, to demonstrating truth.

18. Schmitt, Hans-Jürgen. "One Hundred Years of Solitude by Gabriel García Márquez." New York: Center for Inter-American Relations, 70 Review, (1971), pp. 186-189, (translated from the German).

Mentions the difficulty middle-European readers have in understanding subjects and themes so far removed from their reality, such as those of One Hundred Years of Solitude.

19. Sosnowski, Saul. "One Hundred Years of Solitude, by Gabriel García Márquez." Scranton, PA: Best Sellers, v. 30, no. 4, (May 15, 1970), p. 68.

Summarizes and briefly reviews the English version of Cien años de soledad.

20.  "Stranger in Paradise." London:  The Times Literary Supplement,
     no. 3428, (November 9, 1967), p. 1054.

     Review of One Hundred Years of Solitude, with a summary of the
     novel.

21.  West, Paul.  "One Hundred Years of Solitude."  New York:  Center
     for Inter-American Relations, 70 Review, (1971), pp. 158-160,
     (originally published in Book World, February 22, 1970).

     "... this extraordinary novel obliterates the family tree in a
     prose jungle of overwhelming magnificence, even to the extent of
     only infrequently letting the people talk in their own right."

22.  Wolff, Geoffrey.  "Fable Made Flesh."  New York:  Newsweek, v. 75,
     no. 9, (March 2, 1970), pp. 88-89.

     In his review of One Hundred Years of Solitude, Wolff refers to the
     novel as a "political fable" and a "comic masterpiece."

23.  Wood, Michael.  "One Hundred Years of Solitude by Gabriel García
     Márquez."  New York:  Center for Inter-American Relations, 70
     Review, (1971), pp. 160-165.

     "For the first time, I think, a writer has caught not only the
     color and shape of Latin American despair but also its tone ..."


Collected Stories of Gabriel García Márquez

 1.  Champlin, Charles.  "Collected Stories by Gabriel García Márquez."
     New York, NY: Harper and Row.  Los Angeles, CA:  Los Angeles Times,
     (December 16, 1984), pp. 1, 12.

     "Like all the best stories anytime, these dark lyrics ... demand
     to be read aloud."

 2.  Gray, Paul.  "Fragments of a Fabulous World."  Chicago, IL:  Time,
     December 31, 1984), p. 68.

     A review of Collected Stories by Gabriel García Márquez, trans-
     lated by Gregory Rabassa and S. J. Bernstein.  This collection of
     26 stories contains nothing new since all of them have been pub-
     lished before 1972.  Prominent among them are: "The Third Resig-
     nation," (1974), "Eva is Inside Her Cat," (1948), "The Woman Who
     Came at Six O'clock," (1950), "Nabo," (1951), "There Are No Thieves
     in This Town," (1962), "Balthazar's Marvelous Afternoon," (1962),
     and "Big Mama's Funeral," (1962).

 3.  Hassett, J. J.  "García Márquez, Gabriel.  Collected Stories."
     Gregory Rabassa and J. S. Bernstein, trs.  New York: Harper and
     Row, 1984, 311 p.

     Hassett, briefly reviews Collected Stories which contains twenty-
     six tales written between 1946 and 1972, translated from the
     Spanish and which is highly recommended to the English speaking
     public.

4.  "The Magical Realism of García Márquez." Review of <u>Collected
    Stories</u> by Gabriel García Márquez and translated from the Spanish
    by Gregory Rabassa and S. J. Bernstein. New York: <u>Book World</u> v.
    14, no. 47 (November 18, 1984), p. 3.

    The reviewer regrets the omission of two of García Márquez's works;
    <u>No One Writes to the Colonel</u> and <u>Leaf Storm</u> from this collection of
    26 stories.

5.  Patrakis, Harry Mark. "García Márquez Stories a Magical Mystery
    Tour." Chicago, IL: <u>Bookworld</u>, <u>The Chicago Tribune</u>, (November 18,
    1984), Section 13, pp. 27, 29.

    Review of <u>Collected Stories</u>, by Gabriel García Márquez, translated
    by Gregory Rabassa, and published by Harper and Row. Comments on
    the collection of twenty-six stories concentrating on "Eréndira" and
    "The Handsomest Drowned Man in the World."

6.  Simon, John. "Incontinent Imagination." New York: <u>The New
    Republic</u>, v. 192, no. 5, (February 4, 1985), pp. 32-34.

    A review of <u>Collected Stories</u>, by Gabriel García Márquez, published
    by Harper and Row. A departure from the usual with a negative and
    denigrating criticism of García Márquez's works.

7.  Stuewe, Paul. "Imports." Toronto, Canada: <u>Quill and Quire</u>, v. 51,
    no. 1, (January, 1985), p. 29.

    The reviewer of <u>Collected Stories</u>, by Gabriel García Márquez, Gregory
    Rabassa and S. J. Bernstein, tr., published by Fitzhenry and
    Whiteside, 1984, regrets the omission of certain stories from the
    collection.

8.  Updike, John. "Living Death." New York: <u>The New Yorker</u>, (May 20,
    1985), pp. 118-126.

    Updike gives a critical appraisal together with a little of the
    historical background of the twenty-six stories contained in the
    book, <u>Collected Stories</u>, issued by Harper and Row and translated by
    Gregory Rabassa and S. J. Bernstein.

<u>El coronel no tiene quien le escriba</u>

1.  Adams, Phoebe. "<u>No One Writes to the Colonel and Other Stories</u>,
    Gabriel García Márquez." New York: <u>Atlantic</u>, v. 222, no. 4,
    (October, 1968), p. 150.

    The stories in this anthology taken together "form a communal por-
    trait of great social complications and psychological interest."

2.  Badger, Mildred K. "<u>No One Writes to the Colonel and Other Stories</u>
    by Gabriel García Márquez," J. S. Bernstein, tr. New York: <u>Library
    Journal</u>, v. 93, no. 10, (May 15, 1968), pp. 2021-2022.

The reviewer states that this English translation of a novel and
eight short stories "is not for the reader looking for escape."

3. Dooley, Eugene A. "No One Writes to the Colonel by Gabriel García
Márquez." Scranton, PA: Best Sellers, v. 28, no. 14, (October 15,
1968), p. 284.

According to this reviewer, the overall impression portrayed by this
work is one of "sadness and depression."

4. Labanyi, Jo. "Gabriel García Márquez, El coronel no tiene quien le
escriba." Liverpool, England: Bulletin of Hispanic Studies, v. 61,
(1983), p. 266.

Recommends this edition for students with questions on character and
situation, while pointing out some of its shortcomings.

5. Williamson, Edwin. "El coronel no tiene quien le escriba, by Gabriel
García Márquez." Cambridge, England: The Modern Language Review,
v. 79, pt. 2, (April, 1984), pp. 480-481.

Edited by Giovanni Pontiero, this book in an edition for university
students, presents the original Spanish text with footnotes,
commentaries, and end notes which provide explanations of the style,
characterizations and plot.


Crónica de una muerte anunciada

1. Adams, Phoebe-Lou. "Review of Chronicle of a Death Foretold by
Gabriel García Márquez." New York: The Atlantic, v. 251, no. 5,
(May, 1983), p. 103.

States that the scandal in Chronicle of a Death Foretold may be
considered exotic to the North American readers.

2. Adams, Robert M. "Chronicle of a Death Foretold by Gabriel García
Márquez." New York Review of Books, v. 30, (April 14, 1983), pp. 3-
4.

The solitude which is present in all García Márquez's characters is
more prevalent in this chronicle.

3. Baumgaertner, Jill. "Triangulation: Review Essay." Valparaiso,
IN: The Cresset, Valparaiso University, v. 47, no. 3, (January,
1984), pp. 17-19.

In her review of Chronicle of a Death Foretold, the author states,
"Márquez's novel forces legend to unravel itself until we are left
with pure physical gore."

4. Benson, John. "Review of Crónica de una muerte anunciada (Chronicle
of an Announced Death) by Gabriel García Márquez." Pittsburgh, PA:
Latin American Literary Review, v. 11, no. 21, (Fall-Winter, 1982),
pp. 63-67.

"It is not surprising that while posing as a real-life reporter within a work of fiction (Crónica de una muerte anunciada) Gabriel García Márquez has fictionalized a real life event to the point that it is astoundingly real."

5.  Bensoussan, Albert.  "Les yeux du mage."  Paris:  Magazine Littéraire, no. 178, (November, 1981), pp. 32-33.

    In reviewing Gabriel García Márquez's Crónica de una muerte anunciada, Albert Bensoussan comments that one can describe the novel as a detective story.

6.  Berger, John.  "The Secretary of Death Reads It Back."  London: New Society, v. 61, no. 1033, (September 2, 1982), pp. 386-387.

    Chronicle of a Death Foretold, Berger claims, is a preservation of mystery and not a detective story in that the novel never solves the mystery, but the truth is left for the reader to investigate.

7.  Buford, Bill.  "Haughty Falconry and Collective Guilt."  London: Times Literary Supplement, no. 4145, (September 10, 1982), p. 965.

    Examines how Gabriel García Márquez uses journalistic techniques to create fiction with a "magical" element, that is truly reflective of the tropical Colombian world and all its strangeness in Chronicle of a Death Foretold.

8.  Burgess, Anthony.  "Macho in a Minor Key."  Farmingdale, NY:  New Republic, v. 188, no. 17, (May 2, 1983), p. 36.

    Referring to Chronicle of a Death Foretold, Burgess states that it "is an honest record, cunningly contrived, but it seems to abet a complacent debasement of morality rather than to open up larger vistas."

9.  Caillaux Zazzall, Jorge.  "Crónica de una muerte anunciada." Lima, Peru:  Debate, no. 9, (July, 1981), pp. 93-94.

    The themes of fate and morality comprise the subject of Gabriel García Márquez's novel Crónica de una muerte anunciada.

10. Carrillo, Germán D.  "Crónica de una muerte anunciada por Gabriel García Márquez."  Pittsburgh, PA:  Revista Iberoamericana, v. 49, nos. 123-124, (April-September, 1983), pp. 647-648.

    Reveals the journalist and the novelist in this work.

11. Carter, Angela.  "Victims of Machismo."  London:  The Guardian, (Thursday, September 2, 1982), p. 8.

    Rigid sex roles for males and females contribute to a death foretold for which society's unstated rules bear a collective responsibility.

12. Cornejo Polar, Antonio.  "García Márquez, Gabriel.  Crónica de una muerte anunciada."  Lima, Peru:  Revista de Crítica Literaria Latinoamericana, v. 7, no. 13, (First Semester of 1981), pp. 140-142.

Provides a valuable insight into the novel Chronicle of a Death Foretold. The author pays particular attention to García Márquez's use of characterization to support the themes of tragic destiny and fate.

13. DeFeo, Ronald. "Chronicle of a Death Foretold by Gabriel García Márquez." New York: Nation, v. 236, (May, 14, 1983), p. 609.

   Establishes that Chronicle of a Death Foretold may not be what readers expect after the previous novel - The Autumn of the Patriarch - but goes on to highlight the newer novel's own merits.

14. EFE. La Habana. "Crónica de una muerte anunciada, última obra de García Márquez." Madrid: El País, (Thursday, March 20, 1980), p. 25.

   A short review which quotes García Márquez comparing the novel to a marriage.

15. Fowles, John. "The Falklands and a Death Foretold." London and Manchester: The Guardian, (Saturday, August 14, 1982), p. 7.

   Parallels the ancient psyche still present which caused the murder in Chronicle of a Death Foretold with those same tribal instincts which led to the war in the Falkland Islands.

16. Gass, William H. "More Deaths Than One: Chronicle of a Death Foretold." New York: New York Magazine, v. 16, no. 15, (April 11, 1983), pp. 83-84.

   "Chronicle of a Death Foretold, like Faulkner's Sanctuary, is about the impotent revenges of the impotent; it is about misdirected rage . . . ".

17. Gilard, Jacques. "Un immenso discours sur la mort." Paris: Magazine Littéraire, no. 178, (November, 1981), pp. 15-19.

   After briefly commenting on García Márquez's writing career, Gilard analyzes the treatment of death, time and reality in Crónica de una muerte anunciada.

18. Greenwall, Bill. "Review of Chronicle of a Death Foretold by Gabriel García Márquez." London: New Statesman , v. 104, (September 3, 1982), p. 22.

   This novel demonstrates the author's "almost desultory artistry with which he extends an incident into an event."

19. Grier, Peter. "Nobel Winner's Novella-Vivid, Fatalistic." Boston, MA: The Christian Science Monitor, v. 75, no. 156, (Wednesday, July 6, 1983), p. 9.

   Characterizes Chronicle of a Death Foretold as "an examination of the nature of complicity and fate, and of how a searing event can alter many lives over time."

20. Grossman, Edith. "Truth is Stranger Than Fact." (Review of García
    Márquez, Gabriel, Chronicle of an Announced Death. New York:
    Review, no. 30, (September-December, 1981), pp. 271-272.

    Examines how García Márquez ". . . has reshaped the reality of
    historical events and people and altered them with his uniquely
    comic and mythic touch."

21. Hughes, David. "Murder." London: The Spectator, v. 249, no. 8044,
    p. 24.

    In reviewing Chronicle of a Death Foretold, Hughes refers to it as
    "One hundred pages of quality. . . a fiction that reverberates far
    beyond its modest length."

22. Hutchison, Paul E. "Chronicle of a Death Foretold by Gabriel García
    Márquez." Chicago, IL: Library Journal, v. 108, (April 1, 1983),
    p. 758.

    Recommends Chronicle of a Death Foretold as an introduction to the
    works of Gabriel García Márquez.

23. Lozano Simonelli, Fabio. "Crónica de una muerte anunciada."
    Bogotá: Correo de los Andes, v. 3, no. 9, (May-June, 1981), pp.
    27-28.

    In a review of Crónica de una muerte anunciada, Lozano Simonelli
    claims that in the works of Gabriel García Márquez one finds the
    history, the anti-history and the lack of history of Colombia.

24. Mano, D. Keith. "A Death Foretold." New York: National Review,
    v, 35, (June 10, 1983), p. 699.

    Suggests that García Márquez's account of Latin American life may
    be perceived as "exotic."

25. Michaels, Leonard. "Murder Most Foul and Comic." (Review of
    Chronicle of a Death Foretold by Gabriel García Márquez, trans. by
    Gregory Rabassa, 120 p. New York: Alfred A. Knopf.) N.Y.: The
    New York Times Book Review, (March 27, 1983), p. 1, 36-37.

    Comments particularly on the humor and the grotesque in Chronicle of
    a Death Foretold.

26. Morazán, Julio. "Exile's Return." New York: Village Voice.
    Literary Supplement, v. 20, (October, 1981), pp. 20-21.

    In reviewing Crónica de una muerte anunciada, particular attention
    is devoted to the role women play in the novel.

27. Moreno, Fernando. "Crónica de una muerte anunciada, Gabriel García
    Márquez." Madrid, Spain: Araucaria de Chile, no. 15, (1981), pp.
    209-211.

    By juxtaposition in this novel the author reveals the brevity of
    life punctuated by the certainty of death.

28.  "Le nouveau livre de García Márquez."  Paris:  <u>Livraisons</u>, no. 1,
     (October, 1981), p. 42.

     <u>Crónica de una muerte anunciada</u> breaks García Márquez's literary
     silence and sets a record for the number of Latin American novels
     sold in France.

29.  Oviedo, José Miguel.  "A la (mala) hora señalada."  México, DF:
     <u>Revista de la Universidad de Mexico</u>, v. 36, no. 7, (November, 1981),
     pp. 38-42.

     Gabriel García Márquez's short novel <u>Crónica de una muerte anunciada</u>,
     is compared to his other works.

30.  "Paperback Choice."  London:  <u>The Observer</u>, no. 10026, (Sunday,
     November 6, 1983), p. 31.

     A brief review which refers to <u>Chronicle of a Death Foretold</u> as a
     "leisurely short novel with a single knot of intrigue."

31.  Prescott, Peter S.  "Murder and Machismo."  New York, NY:  <u>Newsweek</u>,
     v. 100, no. 18, (November 1, 1982), p. 82.

     The author provides background information on previous works by
     García Márquez in his review of <u>Chronicle of a Death Foretold</u>.

32.  Rabassa, Gregory.  "García Márquez's New Book:  Literature or
     Journalism?"  Norman, OK:  <u>World Literature Today</u>, v. 56, no. 1,
     (Winter, 1982), pp. 48-51.

     Journalism and fiction combine in <u>Chronicle of a Death Foretold</u>.

33.  Rodman, Selden.  "Triumph of the Artist."  New York, NY:  <u>The New
     Leader</u>, v. 66, no. 10, (May 16, 1983), pp. 16-17.

     Reviewing <u>Chronicle of a Death Foretold</u>, Rodman searches for a
     connection between the public man and the artist and concludes that
     García Márquez as an "artist triumphs over the public man, over the
     sociologist."

34.  Rushdie, Salman.  "Angel Gabriel."  London Review of Books,
     (September 16-October 6, 1982), pp. 3-4.

     Commenting on <u>Chronicle of a Death Foretold</u>, Rushdie states "Where
     all his previous books exude an air of absolute authority over the
     material, this one reeks of doubt.  And the triumph of the book is
     that this new hesitancy. . . is turned to excellent account and
     becomes a source of strength. '

35.  Scott, Nina M.  "Destiny and Causality."  Washington, D.C.:  <u>Américas</u>,
     v. 34, no. 1, (January-February, 1982), pp. 60-61.

     The novel, <u>Crónica de una muerte anunciada</u> (<u>Chronicle of a Death
     Foretold</u>), used destiny and causality to describe a murder which
     could have been prevented by any number of people, and the effect
     this crime had on an entire town.

36. Tregebov, Michael. "Review of Chronicle of a Death Foretold by Gabriel García Márquez." Toronto: Canadian Forum, v. 63, no. 729, (June, 1933), p. 32.

    A review of Gabriel García Márquez's Chronicle of a Death Foretold claims that the novel demonstrates how "a novelist can be literary and popular at the same time. . .," and that "García Márquez is literary because he's popular."

37. Valverde, Umberto. "Nace una nueva novela de García Márquez." Bogotá: Correo de los Andes, v. 3, no. 7, (January–February, 1981), pp. 56-53.

    Anticipates the release of Chronicle of a Death Foretold and its impact on Latin America as well as the world.

38. Vargas, Germán. "Crónica de una muerte anunciada." Bogotá: Correo de los Andes, v. 3, no. 8, (March–April, 1981), p. 28.

    Germán Vargas, a close friend of Gabriel García Márquez, writes about Crónica de una muerte anunciada, the novel which broke the six year silence of his literary production, and compares it to El coronel no tiene quién le escriba.

39. Welborn, Elizabeth. "Suspense, South American Style." New York: McCall's, v. 110, no. 7, (April, 1983), p. 52.

    A succint review of Chronicle of a Death Foretold.

40. Yardley, Jonathan. "García Márquez and the Broken Mirror of Memory." (Review of Chronicle of a Death Foretold). New York: Book World, v. 13, no. 13, (March 27, 1983), p. 3.

    Yardley considers Chronicle of a Death Foretold "to be a deliberate tribute to Faulkner."


## La hojarasca

1. Cobo Borda, Juan Gustavo. "Rescate de textos." Bogotá, Colombia: Eco, v. 34, no. 209, (March, 1979), pp. 485-487.

    Comments on La mujer que llegaba a las seis and La hojarasca and similarities to works by other writers.

2. De Feo, Ronald. "Portents, Prodigies, Miracles." New York: Nation, (May 15, 1972), pp. 632-634.

    In Leaf Storm and Other Stories, "the wit is in evidence that made One Hundred Years of Solitude such a delight."

3. "La vorágine de los fantasmas" (sobre La hojarasca y El coronel no tiene quien le escriba). Santiago de Chile: Ercilla, no. 1617, (June 1, 1966), p. 34.

    Briefly treats of the hyperbole of two of García Márquez's novels.

La increíble y triste historia de la cándida Eréndira y de su abuela
desalmada

1.  Bell-Villada, Gene H.  "Precious and Semi-Precious Gems" (Review of
    Innocent Eréndira and Other Stories by Gabriel García Márquez,
    translated by Gregory Rabassa).  New York:  Review, no. 24, (1979),
    pp. 97-100.

    Bell-Villada describes the title work of "Eréndira..." as a "gem"
    and provides the reader with a sampler of his writings from the in-
    experienced 19 year old to the mature author at 45.

2.  Boyd, William.  "Metaphysical Fairy Stories."  London:  Books and
    Bookmen, v. 24, no. 12, (September, 1979), pp. 36-37.

    In a discussion of philosophy and the use of the metaphysical in
    various literary works of fiction, Gabriel García Márquez's style in
    Innocent Eréndira, is one that the "Europeans would expect from Latin
    America:  earthy, sprawling, often ludicrously hyperbolic."

3.  Graham-Yooll, Andrew.  "Surrealist Historian." London Magazine, v.
    19, no. 8, (November, 1979), pp. 91-93.

    In his review of Innocent Eréndira and Other Stories by Gabriel García
    Márquez and translated by Gregory Rabassa, Graham-Yooll states that
    García Márquez writes not as a surrealist but as a chronicler of
    surrealist subjects.

4.  "García Márquez.  Innocent Eréndira and Other Stories."  Chicago, IL:
    Christian Century, v. 95, (October 25, 1978), p. 1020.

    A brief review commending the publication of this book when there was
    a scarcity of English translations of García Márquez's works.

5.  "Innocent Eréndira and Other Stories."  New York:  Time, v. 112, no.
    2, (July 10, 1976), p. 81.

    The early stories of García Márquez do not predict the future master
    of the Latin American novel.

6.  Luchting, Wolfgang A.  "Review of Gabriel García Márquez:  La
    increíble y triste historia de la cándida Eréndira y de su abuela
    desalmada."  Norman, OK:  Books Abroad, v. 47, no. 1, (Winter, 1973),
    p. 115.

    ". . . these stories exude a degree of maturity (although I find that
    'Eréndira' suffers from occasional ruptures and a tendency to meander)
    characteristic of the end of something.  A splendid collection."

7.  Morrison, Blake.  "872,315 pesos."  London:  New Statesman, v. 97,
    no. 2513, (May 18, 1979), p. 727.

    The title of this article refers to the cost of replacing her grand-
    mother's house which Eréndira has accidently burned down.  In this
    review of Innocent Eréndira and Other Stories, Morrison dwells on the
    excessive hyperbole in the writings of García Márquez.

8.  Sturrock, John. "Review of Innocent Eréndira by Gabriel García Márquez." (excerpts). In Contemporary Literary Criticism, v. 10, edited by Dedria Bryfonski. Detroit: Gale Research Company, 1979, pp. 217-218.

    A novel about "exploitation and what makes exploitation so distressingly easy--the subhuman resignation that has much to answer for in García Márquez's unhappy world."

9.  Troiano, James J. "Review of García Márquez, Gabriel." Innocent Eréndira and Other Stories. New York, NY: Library Journal, v. 103, no. 12, (June 15, 1978), p. 1289.

    Brief review of Gregory Rabassa's translation of these stories written between 1949 and 1972.


La mala hora

1.  Coover, Robert. "The Gossip on the Wall." New York, NY: The New York Times Book Review, v. 84, no. 45, (November 11, 1979), pp. 3, 30.

    In Evil Hour, contains "unit, perception, imaginative richness, and easy accessibility."

2.  Coover, Robert. "Paperbacks: New and Noteworthy." New York, NY: The New York Times Book Review, v. 85, no. 46, (November 16, 1980), p. 47.

    In a short review of Gabriel García Márquez's In Evil Hour, Robert Coover states that the novel is "marked" by "wit, perception, imaginative richness and accessibility."

3.  Davis, Mary E. "García Márquez, Gabriel. In Evil Hour." New York, NY: Review. Center for Inter-American Relations, no. 30, (September-December 1981), pp. 78-79.

    Considers an earlier García Márquez novel from the perspective of his later works, focusing on what distinguishes In Evil Hour from his other novels.

4.  Dougherty, Ruth. "Review of García Márquez, Gabriel. In Evil Hour." New York, NY: Library Journal, v. 104, no. 18, (October 15, 1979), p. 2235.

    Comments on the "uniformly excellent translation" of La Mala hora, by Gregory Rabassa.

5.  Hoffman, Roy B. "Speedy Márquez." New York, NY: The Village Voice, v. 25, no. 6, (February 11, 1980), p. 40.

    "In Evil Hour represents a movement in the direction of what Gabriel García Márquez has termed the "total novel" which "sets up a self-sufficient world which may reveal the creator's own.

6.  Hollinghurst, Alan.  "In Evil Hour."  London:  New Statesman,
    v. 99, no. 2552, (February 15, 1982), pp. 251-252.

    In the column entitled, "Post War" the reviewer refers to In Evil
    Hour as a work of "extraordinary concentration."

7.  Larson, Charles R.  "In Evil Hour by Gabriel García Márquez."
    Washington, D.C.:  New Republic, v. 181, no. 17, (October 27, 1979),
    pp. 39-40.

    "In Evil Hour stands on its own as a more limited exploration of at
    least one of García Márquez's concerns, the question of leadership."

8.  Logan, William.  "The Writings on the Wall."  Review of In Evil Hour.
    Washington, D.C.:  The Washington Post Book World, (November 25,
    1979), pp. 5-6.

    "In Evil Hour. . . displays García Márquez's incipient control of a
    broad range of characters and a complex narrative. . .".

9.  "Recent Arrival."  Chicago, IL:  The Christian Century, v. 97, no.
    1, (January 2-9, 1980), p. 28.

    Cites Gregory Rabassa's translation of In Evil Hour by Gabriel
    García Márquez as a "perfect introduction" to the Colombian author's
    works."

10. Sage, Lorna.  "A Handful of Dust."  London:  The Observer, no. 9832,
    (Sunday, February 3, 1980), p. 39.

    In reviewing In Evil Hour, Sage refers to this story as a product
    of García Márquez's reveling in an "immense verbal energy. . .
    trapped in an atmosphere of changeless decay."

11. "Short List."  London:  Punch, v. 278, no. 7269, (February 13, 1980),
    p. 284.

    A brief description of Gabriel García Márquez's In Evil Hour, which
    was recently translated into English.

12. Silverman, Jay.  "Review of Gabriel García Márquez's In Evil Hour,
    Innocent Eréndira and Other Stories, The Autumn of the Patriarch,
    One Hundred Years of Solitude."  Baton Rouge, LA:  National Forum,
    v. 60, no. 3, (Summer, 1980), pp. 45-46.

    "He (García Márquez) portrays the painful realities of poverty,
    oppression, and violence in an unadorned, precisely detailed style,
    yet this same style reveals the fantasy and comedy that flourish
    even amidst suffering."

13. Sturrock, John.  "Under the Weather."  "Review of In Evil Hour by
    Gabriel García Márquez."  London:  Times Literary Supplement, no.
    4010, (February 2, 1980), p. 108.

    In Evil Hour, the English translation of La mala hora is considered
    by the reviewer to be "a pessimistic little book," which he
    summarizes succinctly.

14.  Swan, Annlyn. "A Prelude to A Masterpiece." New York, NY:
     Newsweek, v. 94, (December, 1979), pp. 128-130.

     Characterizes In Evil Hour as a "celebration of life" which "flows
     with earthly detail and mordant wit."

15.  Walters, Ray. "Preview of Fall Books." New York, NY: The New York
     Times Book Review, vol. 84, no. 36, (September 9, 1979), pp. 7, 39-
     41.

     In Evil Hour is mentioned briefly, as recently published in English.

16.  Wood, Michael. "Claims of Mischief." New York, NY: The New York
     Review of Books, v. 26, nos. 21-22, (January 24, 1980), pp. 43-47.

     In Evil Hour, "belongs to the period of García Márquez's idolatry
     of the cinema. . . . One of the attractive aspects of the book is
     that it does not try to hide its awkwardness."


El olor de la guayaba

1.  Gazzolo, Ana M. "El olor de la guayaba." Madrid: Cuadernos
    Hispanoamericanos, no. 394, (April, 1983), pp. 202-204.

    There are underlying and deeper implications revealed in this book
    which details the conversations of García Márquez with Mendoza.

2.  Millet, Richard. "Le réalisme magique de García Márquez." Paris:
    La Quinzaine Litteraire, no. 382, (November 17-30, 1982). p. 7.

    Millet describes the author as a secret man, and a rare master of
    literature, in his review of El olor de la guayaba.

3.  Saldivar, Dasso. "Una larga conversación." (Review of El olor de
    la guayaba by Gabriel García Márquez). Madrid: Nueva Estafeta,
    no. 47, (1982), pp. 93-94.

    In this review of Gabriel García Márquez's El olor de la guayaba,
    political themes are examined as well as Gabriel García Márquez's
    personal views on politics.

4.  Wilson, S. R. "Review of Gabriel García Márquez, El olor de la
    guayaba: Conversaciones con Plinio Apuleyo Mendoza by Plinio
    Apuleyo Mendoza." Pittsburgh, PA: Latin American Literary Review,
    v. 21, no. 22, (Spring-Summer, 1983), pp. 108-110.

    "The major reason to read Olor de la guayaba is to watch a superb
    story teller mend and patch together, with brilliant colors and
    fascinatingly adroit reweavings, the structure and form of his own
    life."

El otoño del patriarca

1. Alvarado, María Christina. "El otoño del patriarca: poema o
   esperpento?" Medellín: Síntesis Universitaria, v. 12, no. 1, 2a.
   época, (October, 1975), pp. 10-11.

   Interviews with José Manuel Arango, Hernán Botero and Augusto
   Escobar, about El otoño del patriarca.

2. Amat, Nuria. "Al margen de El otoño de patriarca." Bogotá, Colombia:
   El Espectador, Magazine Dominical, (January 2, 1977), p. 4.

   Amat considers El otoño de patriarca to be an exciting elixir, to be
   taken, only in small doses.

3. Bedoya M., Luis Iván. "El otoño del patriarca: reseña y
   commentario." Medellín: Acopel; Temas de Linguística y Literature,
   no. 5, (November-December, 1975), pp. 74-76.

   In this novel of extended metaphors we view the exterior and interior
   of the general in a narration which is a continuation of the regionalism of former works.

4. Dicksteih, Morris. "La pornografía del poder." Bogotá: El Tiempo:
   Lecturas Dominicales, (April 10, 1977), p. 11.

   In this article which appeared originally in Seven Days Magazine, the
   reviewer of El otoño del patriarca sees this novel as an illustration
   of "tyranny as its own victim."

5. Kennedy, William. "El sorprendente retrate de un monstruo tirano del
   Caribe." Bogotá, Colombia: El Espectador: Magazine Dominical,
   (November 14, 1976), p. 1, 3. (Translated from the article in the
   New York Times.)

   El otoño del patriarca is seen by the reviewer as an attack on any
   society which approves of a dictatorship.

6. Langhorne, Elizabeth. "Of Time and the Patriarch." University, VA:
   Virginia Quarterly Review, v. 53, (Spring, 1977), pp. 366-370.

   Preceded by a succinct biographical account, this resume of García
   Márquez's work, Autumn of the Patriarch, refers to the novel as a
   "bourgeois novel of manners and character."

7. McElroy, Wendy. "The Autumn of the Patriarch by Gabriel García
   Márquez (excerpts)." In Contemporary Literary Criticism, v. 10,
   edited by Dedria Bryfonski. Detroit: Gale Research Company, 1979,
   p. 217.

   According to McElroy, "Even the imagery, which is quite striking
   'tiptoing like an evil thought, soft boiled dreams, a postcard heart',
   is overdone. The result of all this resembles a cluttered closet."
   Her original review appeared in World Research INK, San Diego,
   California, September, 1977.

8.  Mújica, Elisa. "El otoño del patriarca." Bogotá:  El Tiempo:
    Lecturas Domincales, (June 1, 1975), p. 3.

    Summary review of El otoño del patriarca.

9.  Omegna, Nelson. "García Márquez, O outono do patriarca." Rio de
    Janeiro:  Revista do Instituto Histórico e Geográfico Brasileiro,
    (January-March, 1979), v. 322, pp. 302-303.

    This review describes The Autumn of the Patriarch as a very politi-
    cal, yet very human novel, and recommends it, particularly for the
    Latin American reader, whose own political experience makes this
    novel about power without limits, particularly relevant.

10. Ramírez Mercado, Sergio. "El otoño del patriarca: el derecho de
    aburrirse." Buenos Aires, Argentina:  Repertorio Latino Americano,
    v. 9, no. 54, (April-May-June, 1983), pp. 5-6.

    This reviewer finds El otoño del patriarca, with its repetition,
    imitation, hyperbole and endless paragraphs, rather boring.

11. Saldívar, Dasso. "El otoño no se escribe en un otoño." Bogotá:
    El Espectador, Magazine Dominical, (August 18, 1974), p. 8.

    Political solitude in The Autumn of the Patriarch is reviewed,
    singling out several experiences where García Márquez revealed
    personal knowledge of dictators.

12. Samper Nieto, Nohra. "La novela del dictador." Bogotá:  Temas,
    Universidad Jorge Tadeo Lozano, Facultad de Ciencias de la
    Comunicación, (October, 1975), pp. 12-13.

    Brief review of El otoño del patriarca.

13. Sánchez Arango, Amparo. "El poema del patriarca." Bogotá:  El
    Espectador:  Magazine Dominical, (October 10, 1976), p. 4.

    The patriarch is presented as a character who is a villain the
    reader learns to love.

14. Sheppard, R. Z. "Un poco más de Kafka." Bogotá:  El Tiempo;
    Lecturas Dominicales, (December 5, 1976), p. 4.

    The greater portion of this brief review of El otoño del patriarca
    is a Spanish translation of an earlier review entitled, "Número uno
    . . . ", Time, November 1, 1976, p. 48.

15. Téllez B., Hernando. "Un lector escudriña El otoño del patriarca."
    Bogotá:  El Tiempo; Lecturas Dominicales, (September 12, 1976), p. 5.

    The structure, theme and style of El otoño del patriarca are
    analyzed in this review.

16. Trigo, Pedro. "El otoño del patriarca." México:  Rumbo, no. 44,
    (June-July, 1975), p. 13.

    Evaluates the novel of dictatorship in this brief review.

17. Troiano, J. J. "García Márquez, Gabriel. The Autumn of the
    Patriarch." New York, NY: Library Journal, v. 101, no. 20,
    (November 15, 1976), p. 2394.

    Comments on the difficulty of reading the English translation of
    El otoño del patriarca because of its long sentences and inter-
    minable paragraphs.

18. Vargas, Roberto. "Notas sobre El otoño del patriarca." Barranquilla,
    Colombia: La Palabra: Revista de la Facultad de Educacion de la
    Universidad del Atlántico, v. 1, no. 2, (October-November, 1977),
    pp. 16-20.

    More difficult for the common reader than other novels by García
    Márquez, is this one, replete with ambiguities and hyperboles.

19. Wagener, Françoise. "La soledad del patriarca." Bogotá: El Tiempo;
    Lecturas Dominicales, (February 6, 1977), pp. 6-7.

    El otoño del patriarca puts one in mind of the writings of Balzac,
    Rabelais, Proust and Malraux.

20. Wood, Michael. "Unhappy Dictators." New York, NY: New York Review
    of Books, v. 23, (December 9, 1976), pp. 57-58.

    In this comparative review of García Márquez's Autumn of the
    Patriarch and Alejo Carpentier's Reasons of State, it is evident
    that "the similarities in these two works are predictably the result
    of the hisorical events surrounding the protagonists."

21. Yardley, Jonathan. "Una obra maestra." Bogotá: El Tiempo; Lecturas
    Dominicales, (December 5, 1976), pp. 4-5.

    Comments briefly on El otoño del patriarca.

22. Zlobina, M. "Osen Patriarkha - Gabriel García Márquez." Moscow:
    Novyi Mir, no. 1, (1980), pp. 272-276.

    A recent translation of Autumn of the Patriarch into Russian, is the
    topic of this review. Attention is focused on the use of myth to
    develop thematic unity in the piece.


El relato de un náufrago

1. Gamarra, Pierre. "Terra Nostra." Paris: Europe-Revue Litteraire
   Mensuelle, v. 58, no. 609, (1980), pp. 191-198.

   In reviewing several new books, Gamarra comments on Gabriel García
   Márquez's Récit d'un naufragé and discusses the main theme of the
   book.

# Reviews of Books about
# Gabriel García Márquez

1. Aaron, M. Audrey. "Melquíades, Alchemy and Narrative Theory: The Quest for Gold in 'Cien años de soledad,' by Chester S. Halka." University, MS: Hispania, v. 65, no. 4, (December, 1982), pp. 664-665.

   A review of a published dissertation.

2. Benson, John. "Gabriel García Márquez by George R. McMurray." Pittsburgh, PA: Latin American Literary Review, v. 8, no. 15 (Fall-Winter, 1979), pp. 39-42.

   In reviewing this book, Benson recommends it as a "compact introduction" to the works of Gabriel García Márquez, citing that it is extremely difficult to treat the literary works of this writer in one short volume.

3. Benson, John. "Obra periodística, vol. 1: Textos costeños; Journalistic Writing, vol. 1: Coastal texts) by Gabriel García Márquez." Pittsburgh, PA: Latin American Literary Review, v. 21, no. 22, (Spring-Summer, 1983), pp. 103-105.

   Cites the importance of the collection of texts from García Márquez's early journalistic career stating that this brings together "many missing links in the chain of his writings."

4. Brand, Wolfgang. "Lectura de García Márquez: Doce Estudios." Dirección e introducción: M. Corrales Pascual. Centro de Publicaciones de la Pontificia Universidad Católica del Ecuador, Quito, 1975, VI/290 S., Germanisch-Romanische Monatsschrift, v. 29, (1979), pp. 370-372.

   A negative review of Lectura de García Márquez which is a collection of twelve original essays on Gabriel García Márquez, written by various authors. For Brand, the reviewer, it is disappointing because it is not a scholarly work but rather a collection of

generalities without substance. Brand also discusses Gabriel García
Márquez and the enormous flow of criticism written about him since
the publication of One Hundred Years of Solitude.

5.  Carrillo, Germán D.  "A propósito de García Márquez, historia de un
    deicidio." Washington, DC: Revista Interamericana de Bibliografía,
    v. 23, no. 2, (April-June, 1973), pp. 184-191.

    Critical evaluation of Mario Vargas Llosa's book, García Márquez,
    historia de un deicidio, in which the author systematically presents
    the forces which drove García Márquez to write, and portrays for us
    the ways in which García Márquez struggles to find his identity.

6.  Carrillo, Germán D.  "Gabriel García Márquez by Peter G. Earle."
    Pittsburgh, PA: Hispanic Review, v. 52, no. 3, (Summer, 1984),
    pp. 422-424.

    Carrillo summarizes and reviews a book consisting of essays dealing
    with García Márquez's life and works.

7.  Forgues, Roland.  "Gabriel García Márquez y América Latina."  In
    Silex, no. 11, April 1979.  Gaithersburg, MD: Hispamérica, v. 9,
    no. 27, (December, 1980), pp. 116-118.

    Comments on various works of Gabriel García Márquez.

8.  Gilard, Jacques.  "Invito alla lettura di García Márquez by Roberto
    Paoli." Toulouse, France:  Caravelle, no. 37, (1981), pp. 227-228.

    Jacques Gilard reviews Roberto Paoli's study of Gabriel García
    Márquez's works and bibliography Invito alla lettura di García
    Márquez, saying that at times Paoli is too brief in description,
    lacks emphasis on chronology, and completely overlooks Gabriel
    García Márquez's many writings as a reporter from the years 1948
    to 1980.

9.  Gilard, Jacques.  "The Presence of Faulkner in the Writings of
    García Márquez, by Harley D. Oberhelman." Toulouse: Caravelle,
    no. 37, (1981), pp. 228-229.

    A critical review of Oberhelman's work.

10.  González Vigil, Ricardo.  "Gabriel García Márquez, edited by Pier
     Luigi Crovetto." Lima, Peru: Lexis, Revista de Lingüística y
     Literatura, v. 4, no. 1, (July, 1980), pp. 107-109.

     The nine articles in this volume present a "vision ... of the
     narrative universe of Gabriel García Márquez as an expression of
     of Hispanic American reality."

11.  Matamoro, Blas.  "Melquíades, Alchemy and Narrative Theory: the
     Quest for Gold in 'Cien años de soledad,' by Chester S. Halka."
     Madrid:  Cuadernos Hispanoamericanos, no. 383, (May, 1982),
     p. 463.

     Brief comments on Halka's book which treats of the gold-related
     themes in Cien años de soledad.

12. McMurray, George R. "Creación mítica en la obra de García Márquez, by Katalin Kulin." Norman, OK: World Literary Today, (formerly Books Abroad), v. 55, no. 4, (Autumn, 1981), p. 647.

   A brief review of Katalin Kulin's study Creación mítica en la obra de García Márquez. McMurray recommends her book as a piece of well documented criticism for a non-specialist seeking an overall view of García Márquez's writing.

13. Menton, Seymour. "La función de la historia en 'Cien años de soledad,' by Lucila-Inés Mena." Gaithersburg, MD: Hispamérica, v. 9, (December, 1980), pp. 114-115.

   In this review, Menton recommends this book on the function of history in One Hundred Years of Solitude for its analysis of the novel's historical structure and its insight into several important characters.

14. Miguez, José Antonio. "Gabriel García Márquez: La línea, el círculo y las metamórfosis del mito, by Michael Palencia-Roth." Madrid: ARBOR: Ciencia, Pensamiento y Cultura, v. 110, nos. 465-466, (September-October, 1984), pp. 136-138.

   A Critical review and exploration of Palencia-Roth's book.

15. Oberhelman, Harley D. "Gabriel García Márquez, edited by Pier Luigi Crovetto." Manhattan, KS: University of Kansas: Journal of Spanish Studies: Twentieth Century, v. 8, no. 3, (Winter, 1980), pp. 313-314.
   Evaluates a first complete volume of critical material on Gabriel García Márquez in Italian.

16. Ruíz, Hugo. "Nueve asedios a García Márquez." Bogotá: Boletín Cultural y Bibliográfico, v. 12, no. 11, (1969), pp. 17-24

   Review of the book, Nueve asedios a García Márquez which contains nine essays by prominent literary persons.

17. Salas, Horacio. "Creación mítica en la obra de García Márquez, by Katalin Kulin." Madrid: Cuadernos Hispanoamericanos, no. 372, (January, 1981), pp. 719-720.

   In this short review of Katalin Kulin's Creación mítica en la obra de García Márquez, a critical analysis of the use of myth by Gabriel García Márquez in his works, Horacio Salas states that the study presents itself as a "test of the interest in, and the universality of one of the most read authors of today."

18. Schwartz, Kessel. "Gabriel García Márquez, by George R. McMurray." University, MS: Hispania, v. 61, no. 1, (March, 1978), pp. 183-184.

   George R. McMurray's carefully researched book of analyses of García Márquez's works comes under the scrutiny of Kessel Schwartz.

19. Shaw, Bradley A. "Recent Bibliographies on Latin American Literature." Austin, TX: Latin American Research Review, v. 19, no. 1, pp. 190-197.

Shaw reviews and critiques Margaret Eustella Fau's Gabriel García Márquez: An Annotated Bibliography, 1947-1979.

20. Siemens, William L. "The Evolution of Myth in Gabriel García Márquez from 'La hojarasca' to 'Cien años de soledad,' by Robert Lewis Sims." University, MS: Hispania, v. 67, no. 2, (May, 1984), p. 311.

Siemens gives a brief summary of Robert Lewis Sims' book.

21. Tirado, Manlio. "La revolución nicaragüense: historia y primeros análisis." (Review of La batalla de Nicaragua by Gabriel García Márquez et al). México: Plural, v. 9, 2a. época, no. 106, (July, 1980), pp. 74-78.

In La batalla de Nicaragua by García Márquez, Selzer, and Wakeman, the critic claims that Gabriel García Márquez's contribution was very small, and that his signature merely represented an effort to make the book a best seller.

22. Yáñez, Mirta. "García Márquez: un tema inagotable." La Habana: Revista de la Biblioteca Nacional José Martí, v. 25, no. 1, (January-April, 1983), pp. 240-242.

Comments on Virgilio López Lemus' book García Márquez: una vocación incontenible, which is the study of García Márquez's writings.

23. Zuluaga Osorio, Conrado. "Una jirafa extraviada." Bogotá: Correo de los Andes, no. 17, (September-October, 1982), p. 49.

Review of Textos costeños, volume one, about the early journalistic career of García Márquez.

# Index of Names

The numbers in this index refer to page numbers and not entry numbers.

## ABOUT THE COMPILERS

MARGARET EUSTELLA FAU is Professor of Library Administration, Spanish Language Subject Specialist, and Modern Language Library Assistant at the University of Illinois at Urbana-Champaign. She compiled *Gabriel García Márquez: An Annotated Bibliography, 1947-1979* (Greenwood Press, 1980), which was named a *Choice* Outstanding Academic Book in 1980.

NELLY SFEIR DE GONZALEZ is Latin American Bibliographer and Associate Professor of Library Administration at the University of Illinois at Urbana-Champaign. She also compiled *Doctoral Dissertations on Latin America and the Caribbean: An Analysis and Bibliography of Dissertations Accepted at American and Canadian Universities, 1966-1970.*